**Author**
Wing Shing Ma

**Translator**
Andrew Allen

**Editors**
Shawn Sanders
Duncan Cameron
Angel Cheng

**Production Artist**
Hung-Ya Lin

**US Cover Design**
Calvin Choi

**Production Manager**
Janice Chang

**Art Director**
Yuki Chung

**Marketing**
Nicole Curry

**VP Operations**
Thomas Kuo

**Storm Riders Volume Eleven 1989. First Printing. Published by Jonesky Limited. Storm Riders, its logo and its symbol are registered trademarks of Jonesky Limited. All other related characters are TM and @1989. All rights reserved. Any similarities to persons living or dead are purely coincidental. With the exception of artwork used for review purposes, none of the contents of this publication may be reprinted without the permission of Jonesky Limited.**

*www.comicsworld.com*

**English translation by
ComicsOne Corporation 2002**

**Publisher**
**ComicsOne Corp.**
**48531 Warm Springs Blvd., Suite 408**
**Fremont, CA 94539**
**www.ComicsOne.com**

**First Edition: March 2003**
**ISBN 1-58899-161-X**

*The "chess form" head figure is mark of and used under licence from Magnum Consultants Limited.*

# STORM RIDERS 風雲

## Relationship Chart

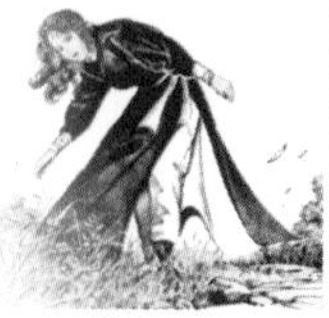

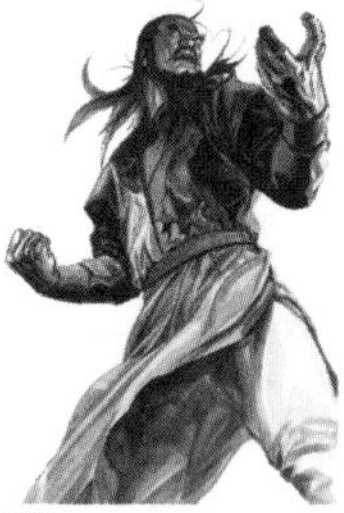

**Yoruo**: This is the beloved daughter of World Fighting Association leader-Conquer. Her relationship with Wind is meaningful, yet still much is to be revealed. She graciously assists Duan-Lang in his escape - in honor of her friendship with Wind.
**Technique**: Deity of Wind Kick

**Conquer**: Exceptionally powerful martial artist with plans of controlling the World Fighting Association. He takes on Wind and Cloud as his disciples in order to fulfill his destiny.
**Technique**: Chi of Triplication Returns to One, Triplication Fingers

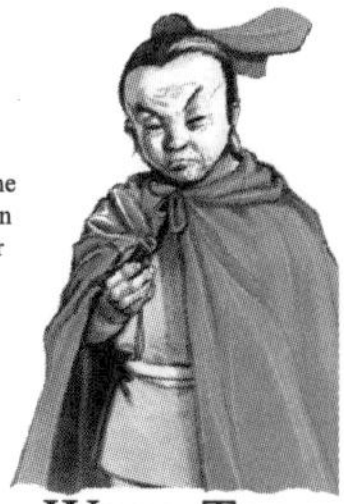

**Wong Tong:** For over a decade Wong Tong lead a faction of 108 merciless assassins collectively known as the Heavenly Pool. However, the people of the country called on the mighty Sword Saint to confront the guild. He smashed the Heavenly Pool after a vicious battle, reducing their number to a mere 12. These "Deadly Twelve" joined Conquer and helped him establish his Conquer Clan. Once the clan was in place they retired to "Highest Chamber", and planned to stay for the rest of their days. But the chamber is destroyed…
**Technique:** The mysterious youth scroll

Yoruo — Daughter of Conquer — **Conquer** — Ally of Conquer — Wong Tong

Three Disciples of Conquer

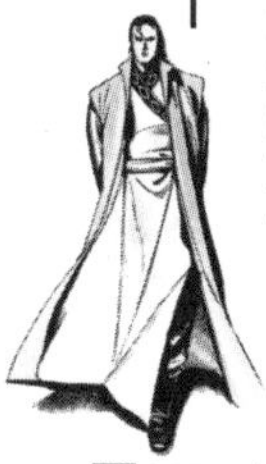

**Frost**: Long-time disciple of Conquer. Married to Conquer's adopted daughter Kong-Chi. Leader of the Frost Corps: an elite fighting unit which is a part of the World Fighting Association.
**Technique**: Sky Frost Fist

## Frost

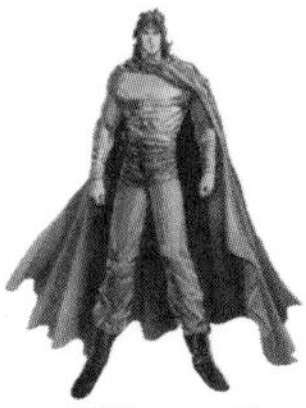

**Cloud**: Son of Master Ho and disciple of Conquer. Leader of the Cloud Corps: an elite fighting unit which is part of the World Fighting Association.
**Technique**: Repelling Palm
**Weapon**: Ultimate Sword (briefly, Unrivaled Sword)

## Cloud
(Bu-Jing-Yun)

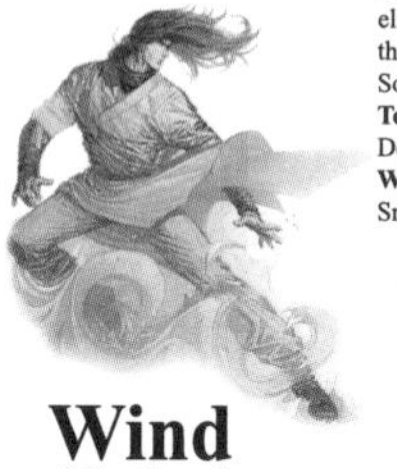

**Wind**: Disciple of Conquer and leader of the Wind Corps: an elite fighting unit which is part of the World Fighting Association. Son of Master Nie.
**Techniques**: Ice Heart Knack, Deity of Wind Kick
**Weapon**: Inherits the Snowy Saber

## Wind
(Nie-Fong)

Cloud — Good Friends — Bushi; (Will become) Disciple of Nameless — Nameless; Rival — Sword Needy

Wind — Enemy of Wind — DuGu Ming; Friends; Former Friends — Duan-Lang

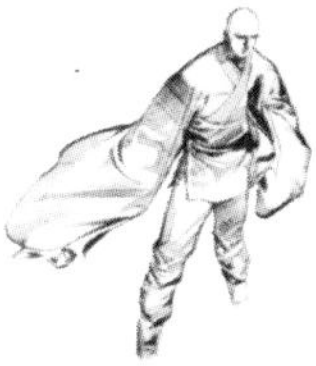

## Bushi

**Bushi:** Friend of Nameless and Buddhist Master. Because of Bushi's mastery of inner peace, Nameless intended for Bushi to be young Cloud's master.
**Technique:** Transformation Knack, Transformation Defense

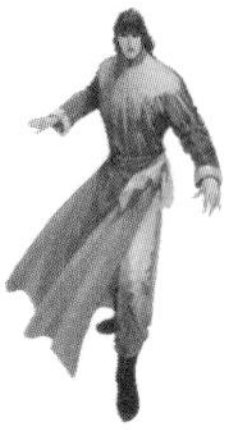

## Nameless

**Nameless**: Nameless was once the undisputed master of the Kung Fu world, having defeated Sword Saint in a secret battle, driving him into exile. Nameless was said to have died of grief at age 23, after his enemies poisoned his wife. However, Sword Saint, Nameless's old rival, believes that he is still alive and seeks him out before his epic duel with Conquer.
**Technique:** Nameless Sword Skill
**Weapon**: Hero Sword

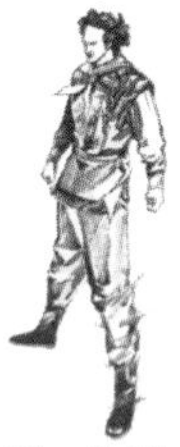

## DuGu Ming

**DuGu Ming:** Son of the master of Peerless Castle, DuGu Yifang. He is the only survivor of Conquer's assault on Peerless Castle. He seeks revenge on Conquer for killing his father.
**Technique:** Dragon Kick

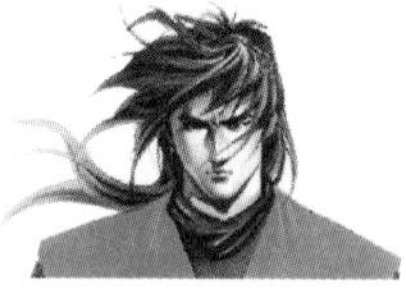

## Duan-Lang

**Duan-Lang**: The Son of Master Duan has come a long way since his exile from the World Fighting Association. He has recently reclaimed his family heirloom - the Flame Kylin Sword! Upon finding it, he also discovers its dark secret and the three-way connection between his ancestors, the sword and the Flame Kylin itself!
**Technique:** Duan Technique
**Weapon**: Inherits the Flame Kylin Sword

Nameless — Disciple of Conquer — Jien-Chen

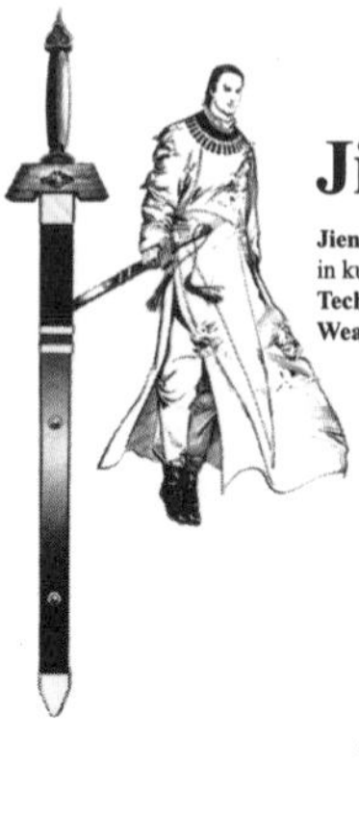

## Jien-Chen

**Jien-Chen:** This is the only pupil of Nameless. His skill in kung fu is even more than the late Sword Saint could handle!
**Technique:** Nameless Sword Skill
**Weapon:** Inherits the Hero Sword

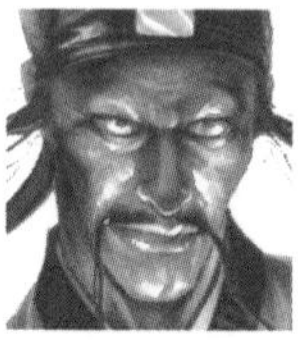

## Sword Needy

Much about this lean hyperactive individual is still shrouded in mystery. However, we know he is a master of several techniques from so many different premium sword styles that it has left him with a muddled and impure kung fu form. His real Name is "Sword Greedy." Yet he is a master swordsman in constant pursuit of the perfect blade so "Greedy" became "Needy!"
**Technique:** Sword Vision

# CHAPTER 40

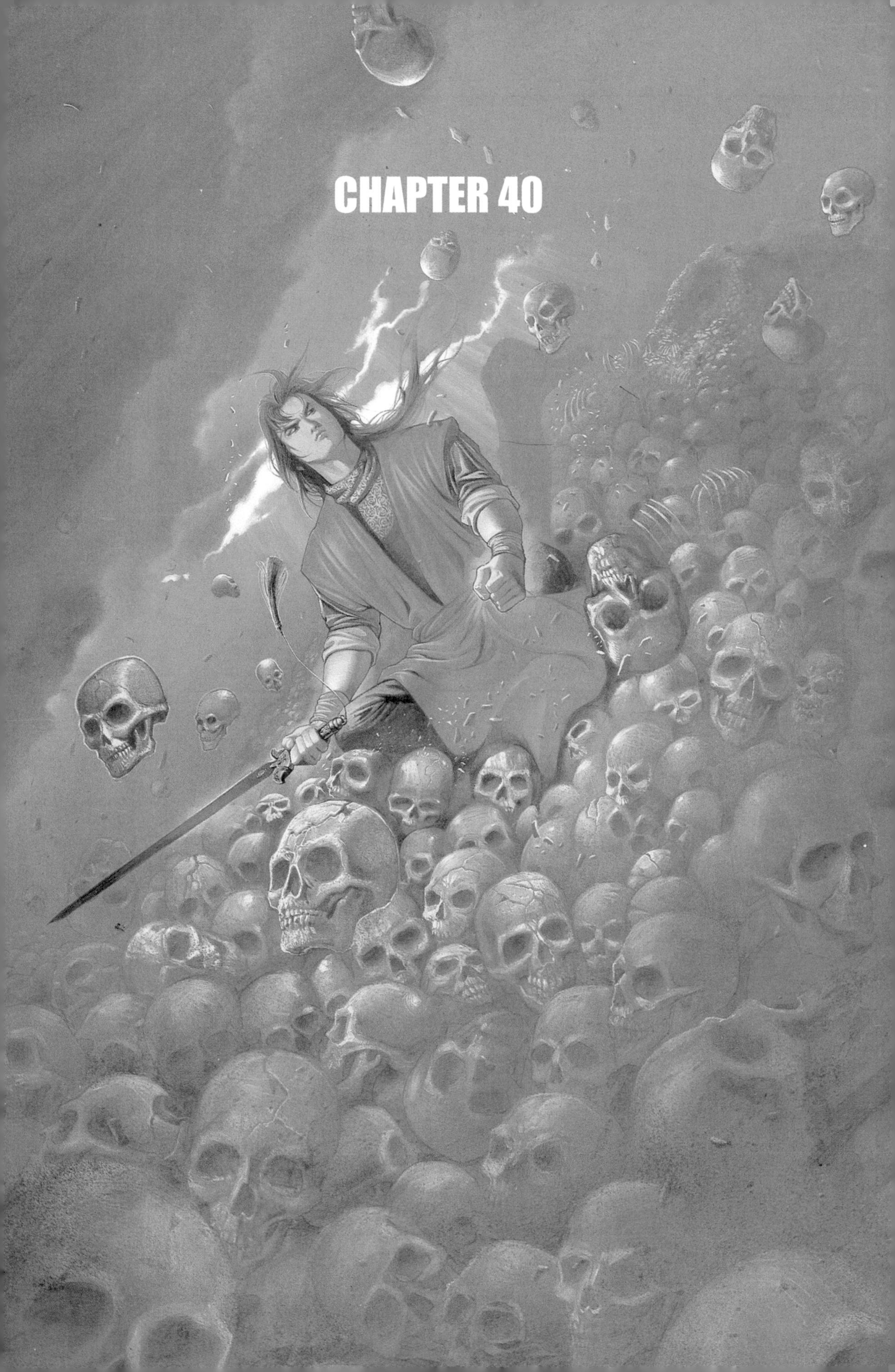

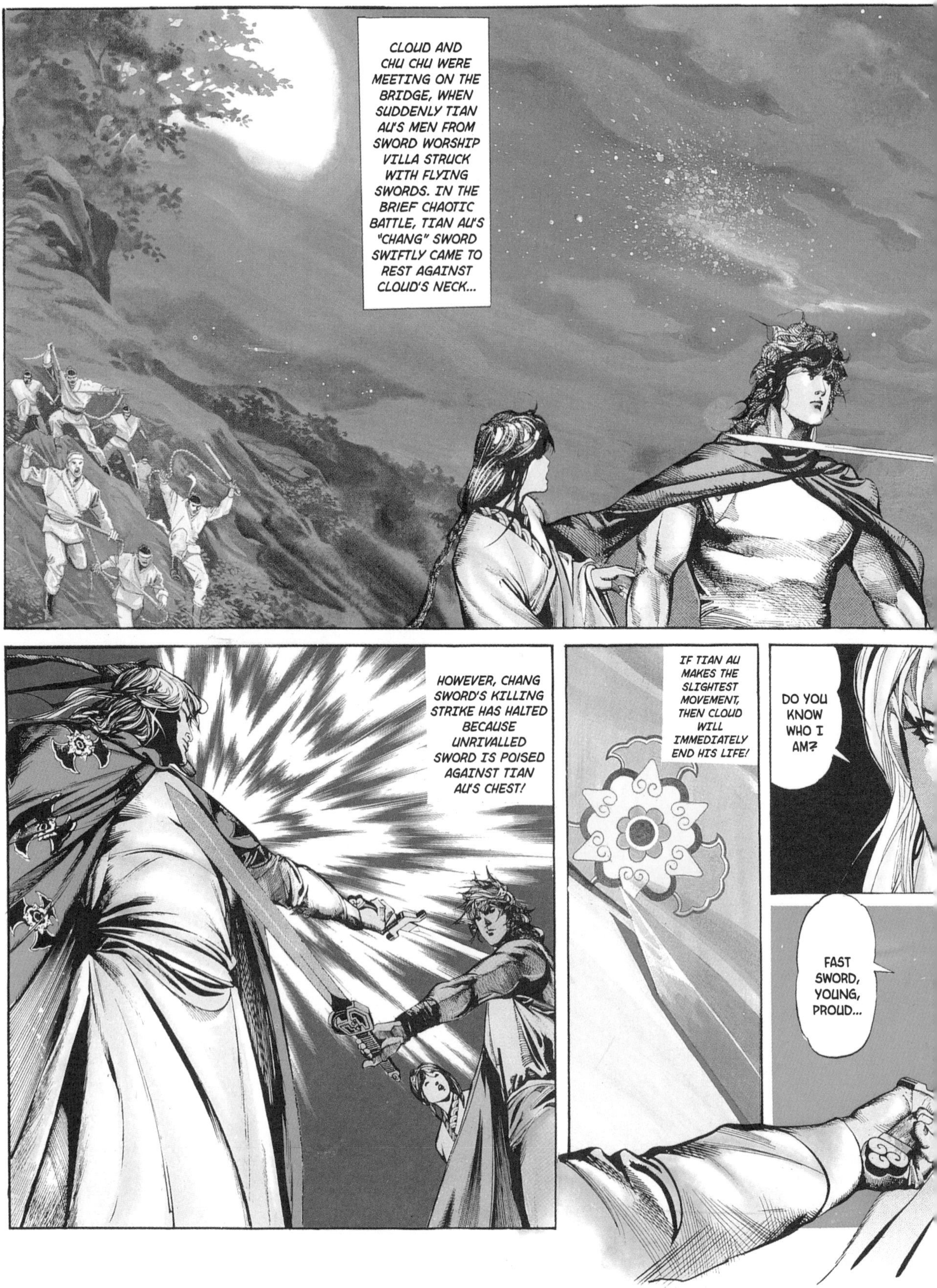
CLOUD AND CHU CHU WERE MEETING ON THE BRIDGE, WHEN SUDDENLY TIAN AU'S MEN FROM SWORD WORSHIP VILLA STRUCK WITH FLYING SWORDS. IN THE BRIEF CHAOTIC BATTLE, TIAN AU'S "CHANG" SWORD SWIFTLY CAME TO REST AGAINST CLOUD'S NECK...
HOWEVER, CHANG SWORD'S KILLING STRIKE HAS HALTED BECAUSE UNRIVALLED SWORD IS POISED AGAINST TIAN AU'S CHEST!
IF TIAN AU MAKES THE SLIGHTEST MOVEMENT, THEN CLOUD WILL IMMEDIATELY END HIS LIFE!
DO YOU KNOW WHO I AM?
FAST SWORD, YOUNG, PROUD...

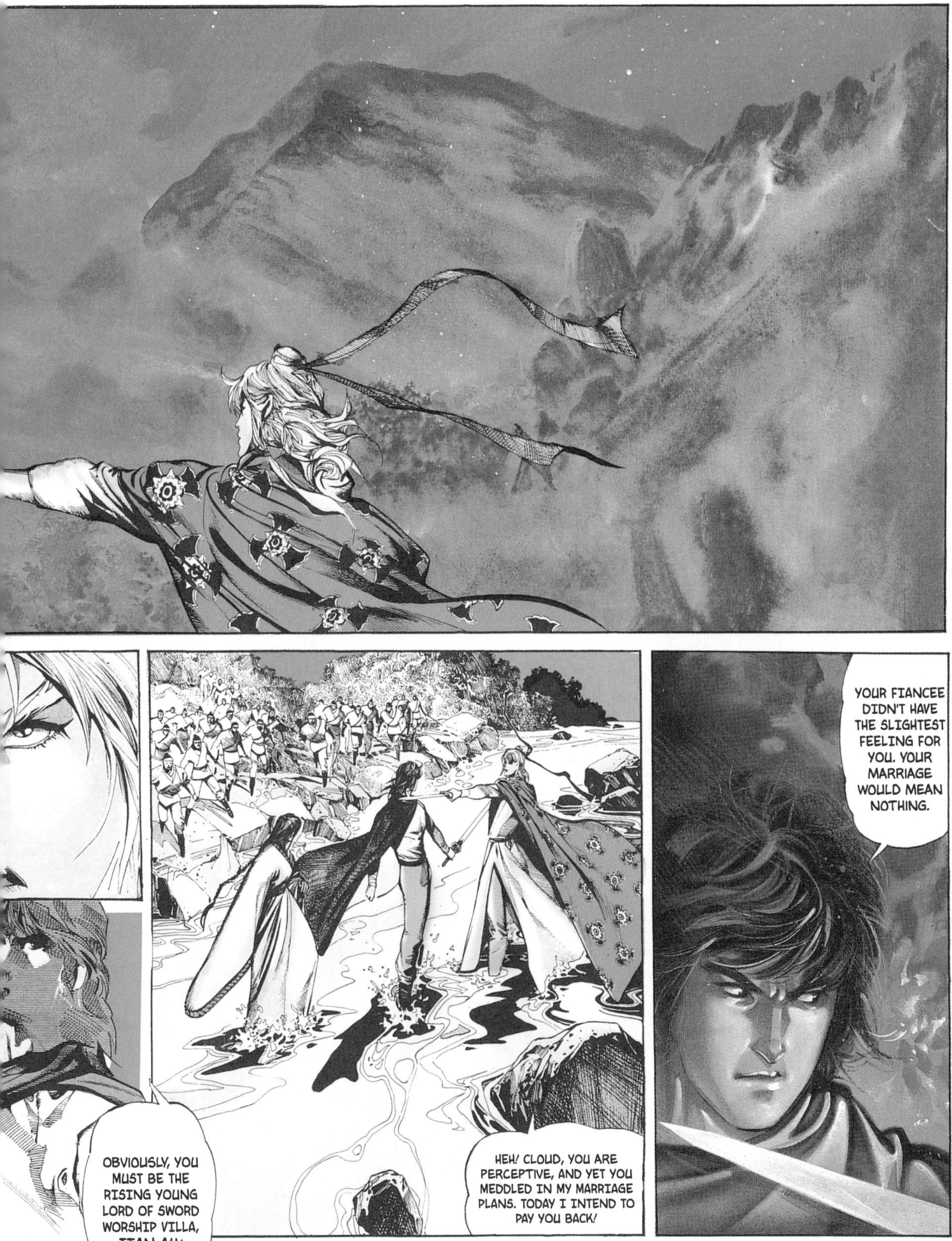

OBVIOUSLY, YOU MUST BE THE RISING YOUNG LORD OF SWORD WORSHIP VILLA, TIAN AU!
HEH! CLOUD, YOU ARE PERCEPTIVE, AND YET YOU MEDDLED IN MY MARRIAGE PLANS. TODAY I INTEND TO PAY YOU BACK!
YOUR FIANCEE DIDN'T HAVE THE SLIGHTEST FEELING FOR YOU. YOUR MARRIAGE WOULD MEAN NOTHING.

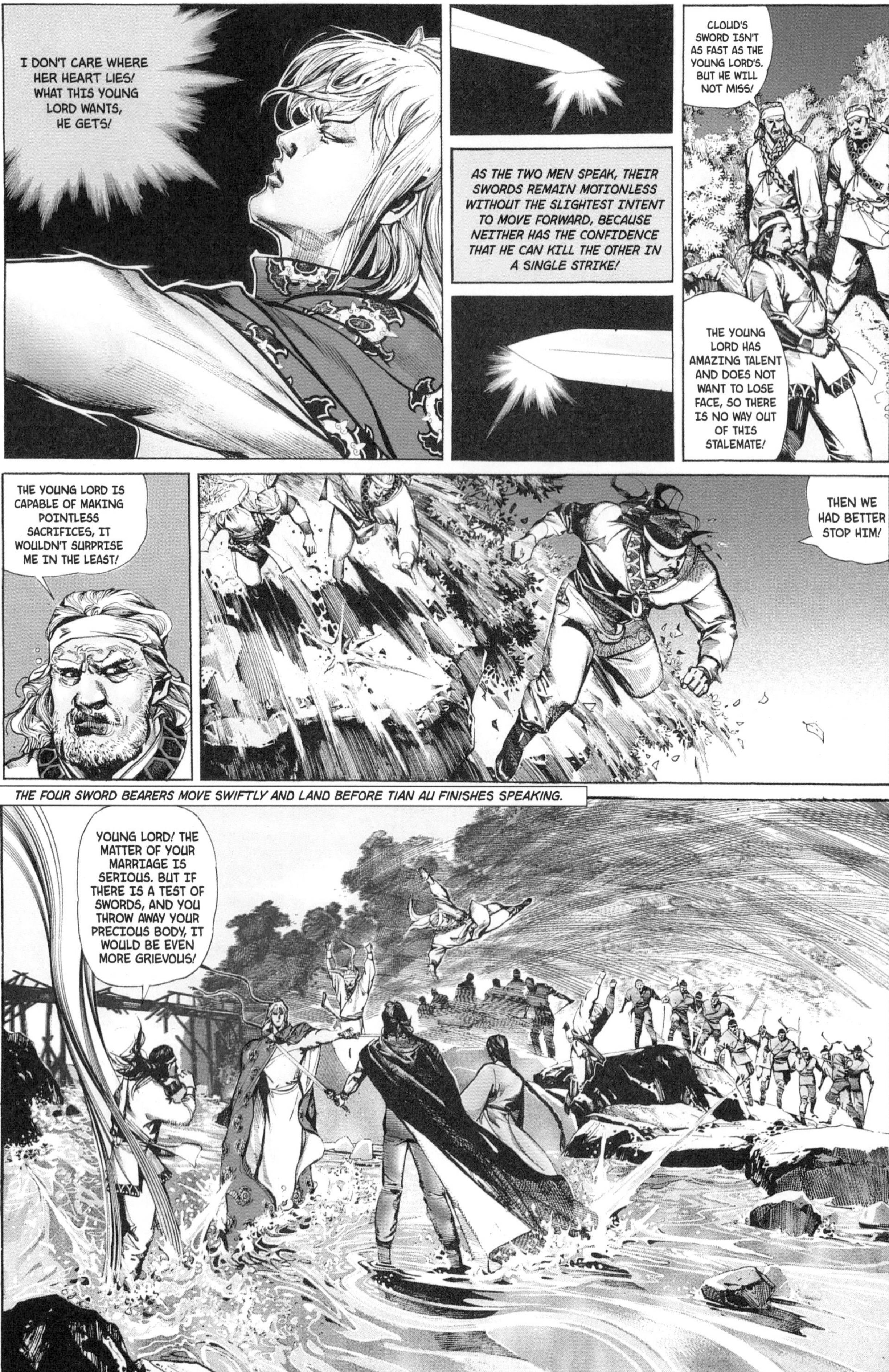
I DON'T CARE WHERE HER HEART LIES! WHAT THIS YOUNG LORD WANTS, HE GETS!
AS THE TWO MEN SPEAK, THEIR SWORDS REMAIN MOTIONLESS WITHOUT THE SLIGHTEST INTENT TO MOVE FORWARD, BECAUSE NEITHER HAS THE CONFIDENCE THAT HE CAN KILL THE OTHER IN A SINGLE STRIKE!
CLOUD'S SWORD ISN'T AS FAST AS THE YOUNG LORD'S. BUT HE WILL NOT MISS!
THE YOUNG LORD HAS AMAZING TALENT AND DOES NOT WANT TO LOSE FACE, SO THERE IS NO WAY OUT OF THIS STALEMATE!
THE YOUNG LORD IS CAPABLE OF MAKING POINTLESS SACRIFICES, IT WOULDN'T SURPRISE ME IN THE LEAST!
THEN WE HAD BETTER STOP HIM!
THE FOUR SWORD BEARERS MOVE SWIFTLY AND LAND BEFORE TIAN AU FINISHES SPEAKING.
YOUNG LORD! THE MATTER OF YOUR MARRIAGE IS SERIOUS. BUT IF THERE IS A TEST OF SWORDS, AND YOU THROW AWAY YOUR PRECIOUS BODY, IT WOULD BE EVEN MORE GRIEVOUS!

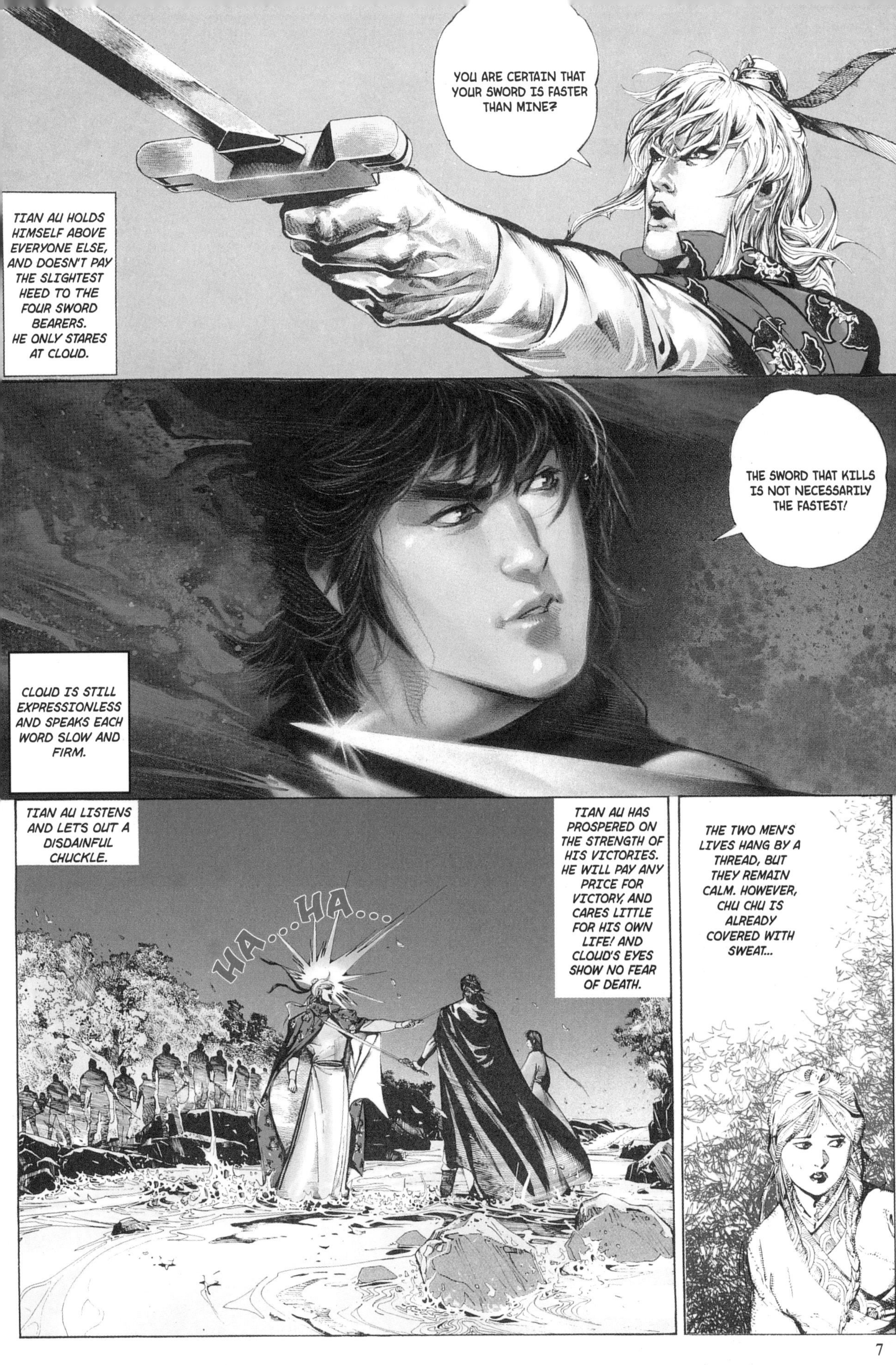

TIAN AU HOLDS HIMSELF ABOVE EVERYONE ELSE, AND DOESN'T PAY THE SLIGHTEST HEED TO THE FOUR SWORD BEARERS. HE ONLY STARES AT CLOUD.
YOU ARE CERTAIN THAT YOUR SWORD IS FASTER THAN MINE?
THE SWORD THAT KILLS IS NOT NECESSARILY THE FASTEST!
CLOUD IS STILL EXPRESSIONLESS AND SPEAKS EACH WORD SLOW AND FIRM.
TIAN AU LISTENS AND LETS OUT A DISDAINFUL CHUCKLE.
HA...HA...
TIAN AU HAS PROSPERED ON THE STRENGTH OF HIS VICTORIES. HE WILL PAY ANY PRICE FOR VICTORY, AND CARES LITTLE FOR HIS OWN LIFE! AND CLOUD'S EYES SHOW NO FEAR OF DEATH.
THE TWO MEN'S LIVES HANG BY A THREAD, BUT THEY REMAIN CALM. HOWEVER, CHU CHU IS ALREADY COVERED WITH SWEAT...

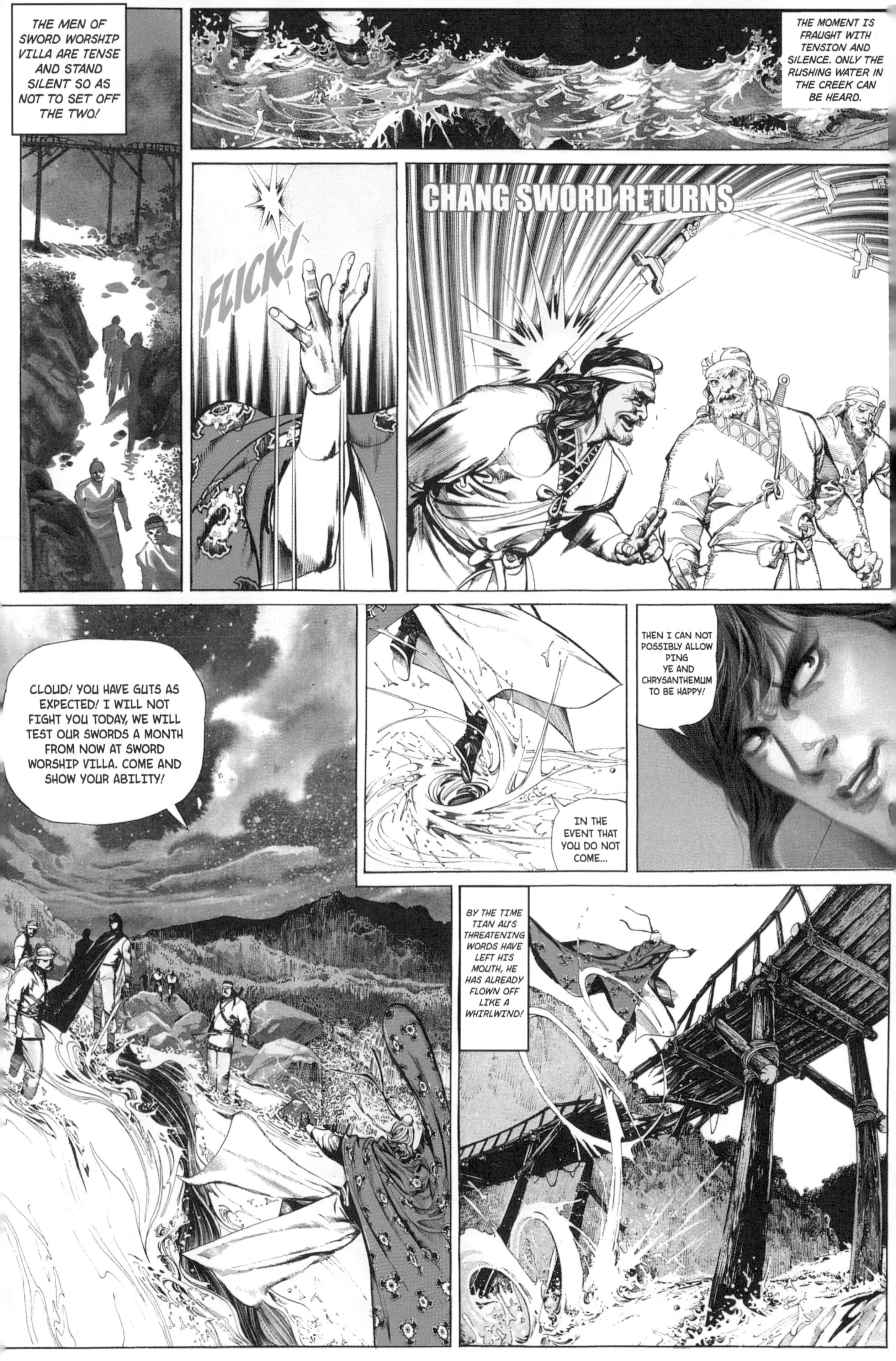
THE MEN OF SWORD WORSHIP VILLA ARE TENSE AND STAND SILENT SO AS NOT TO SET OFF THE TWO!
THE MOMENT IS FRAUGHT WITH TENSION AND SILENCE. ONLY THE RUSHING WATER IN THE CREEK CAN BE HEARD.
FLICK!
CHANG SWORD RETURNS
CLOUD! YOU HAVE GUTS AS EXPECTED! I WILL NOT FIGHT YOU TODAY, WE WILL TEST OUR SWORDS A MONTH FROM NOW AT SWORD WORSHIP VILLA. COME AND SHOW YOUR ABILITY!
IN THE EVENT THAT YOU DO NOT COME...
THEN I CAN NOT POSSIBLY ALLOW PING YE AND CHRYSANTHEMUM TO BE HAPPY!
BY THE TIME TIAN AU'S THREATENING WORDS HAVE LEFT HIS MOUTH, HE HAS ALREADY FLOWN OFF LIKE A WHIRLWIND!

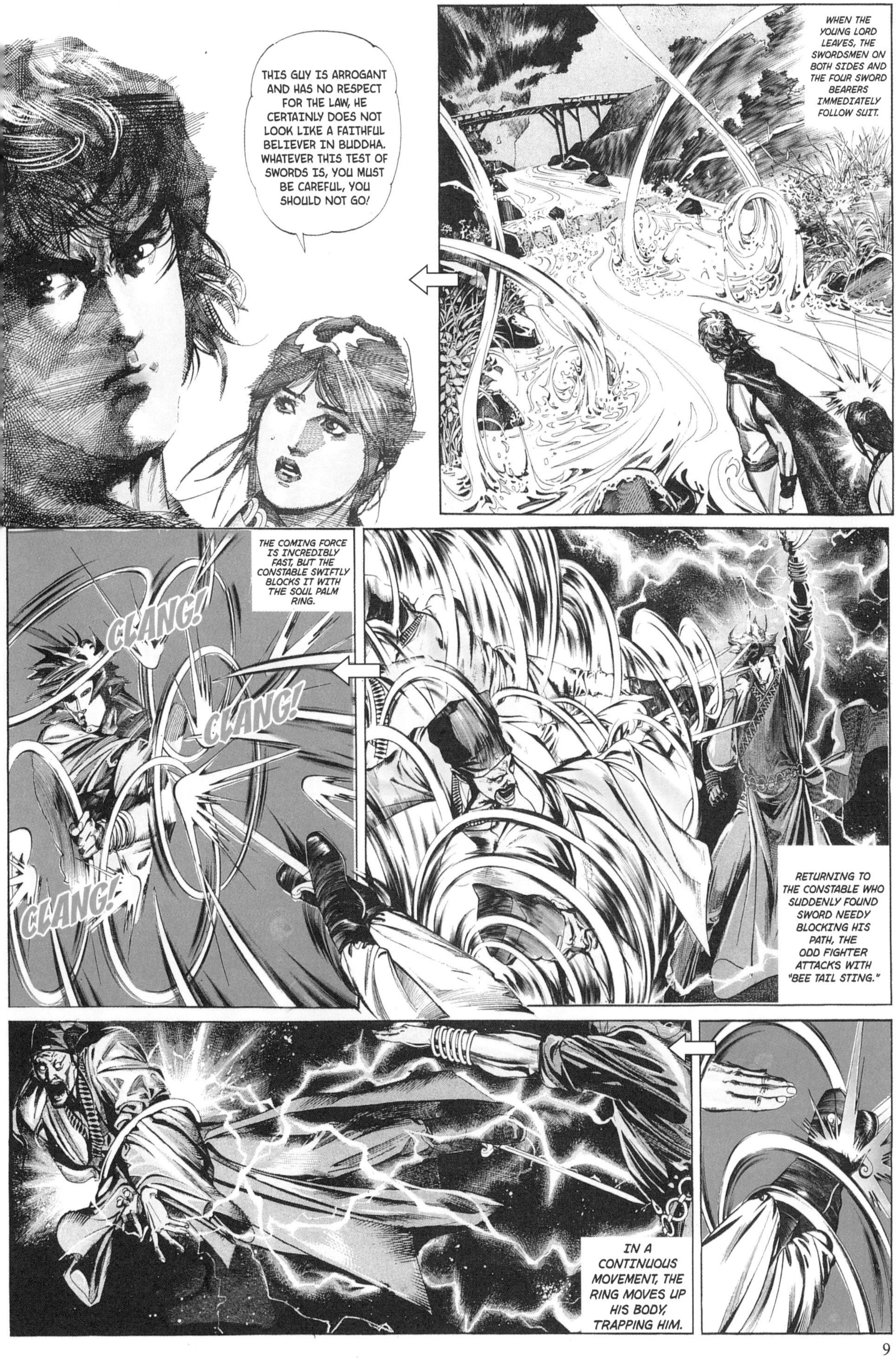
THIS GUY IS ARROGANT AND HAS NO RESPECT FOR THE LAW, HE CERTAINLY DOES NOT LOOK LIKE A FAITHFUL BELIEVER IN BUDDHA. WHATEVER THIS TEST OF SWORDS IS, YOU MUST BE CAREFUL, YOU SHOULD NOT GO!
WHEN THE YOUNG LORD LEAVES, THE SWORDSMEN ON BOTH SIDES AND THE FOUR SWORD BEARERS IMMEDIATELY FOLLOW SUIT.
RETURNING TO THE CONSTABLE WHO SUDDENLY FOUND SWORD NEEDY BLOCKING HIS PATH, THE ODD FIGHTER ATTACKS WITH "BEE TAIL STING."
THE COMING FORCE IS INCREDIBLY FAST, BUT THE CONSTABLE SWIFTLY BLOCKS IT WITH THE SOUL PALM RING.
CLANG!
CLANG!
CLANG!
IN A CONTINUOUS MOVEMENT, THE RING MOVES UP HIS BODY, TRAPPING HIM.

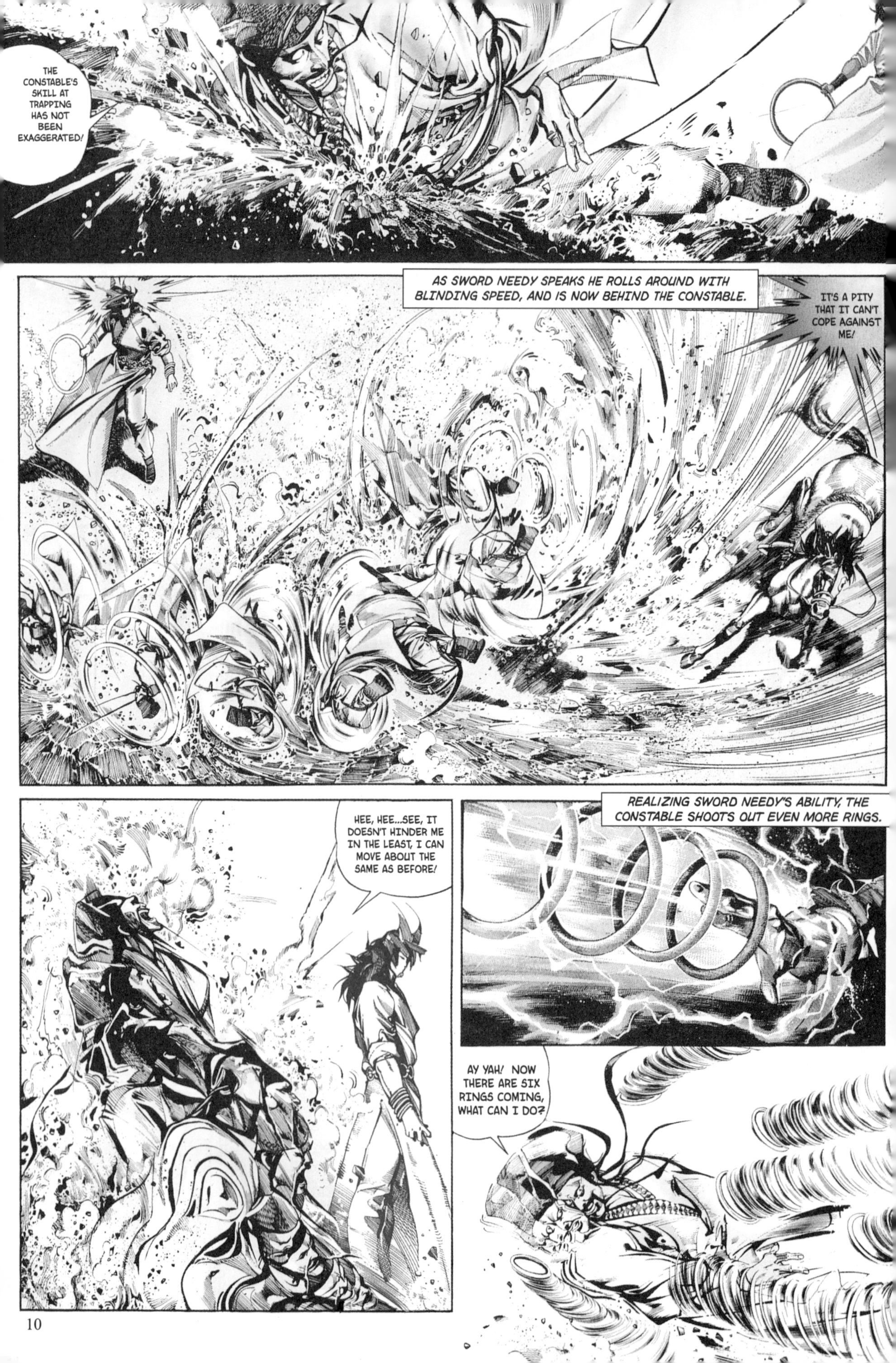
THE CONSTABLE'S SKILL AT TRAPPING HAS NOT BEEN EXAGGERATED!
AS SWORD NEEDY SPEAKS HE ROLLS AROUND WITH BLINDING SPEED, AND IS NOW BEHIND THE CONSTABLE.
IT'S A PITY THAT IT CAN'T COPE AGAINST ME!
HEE, HEE...SEE, IT DOESN'T HINDER ME IN THE LEAST, I CAN MOVE ABOUT THE SAME AS BEFORE!
REALIZING SWORD NEEDY'S ABILITY, THE CONSTABLE SHOOTS OUT EVEN MORE RINGS.
AY YAH! NOW THERE ARE SIX RINGS COMING, WHAT CAN I DO?

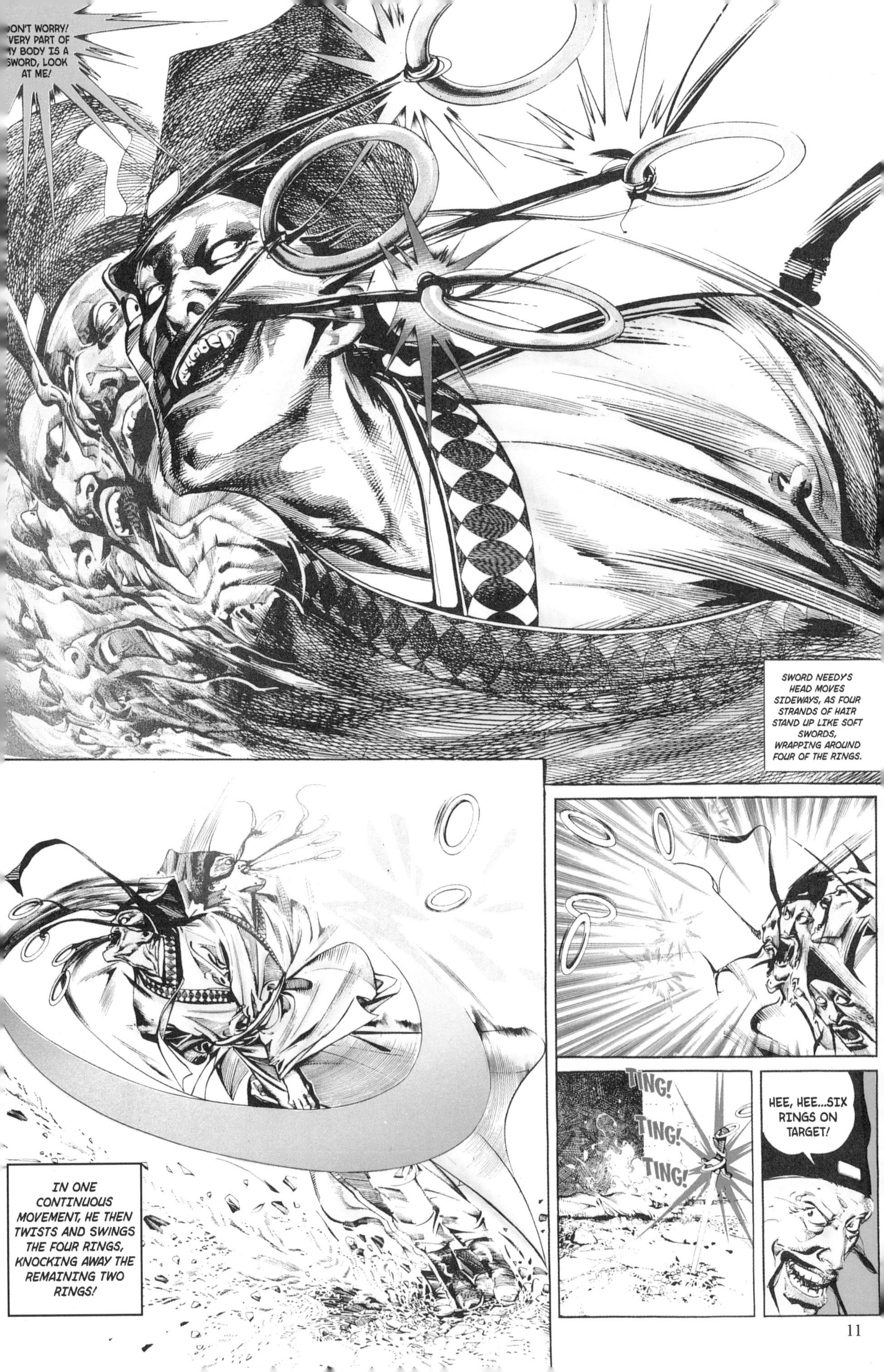
DON'T WORRY! EVERY PART OF MY BODY IS A SWORD, LOOK AT ME!
SWORD NEEDY'S HEAD MOVES SIDEWAYS, AS FOUR STRANDS OF HAIR STAND UP LIKE SOFT SWORDS, WRAPPING AROUND FOUR OF THE RINGS.
IN ONE CONTINUOUS MOVEMENT, HE THEN TWISTS AND SWINGS THE FOUR RINGS, KNOCKING AWAY THE REMAINING TWO RINGS!
TING!
TING!
TING!
HEE, HEE...SIX RINGS ON TARGET!

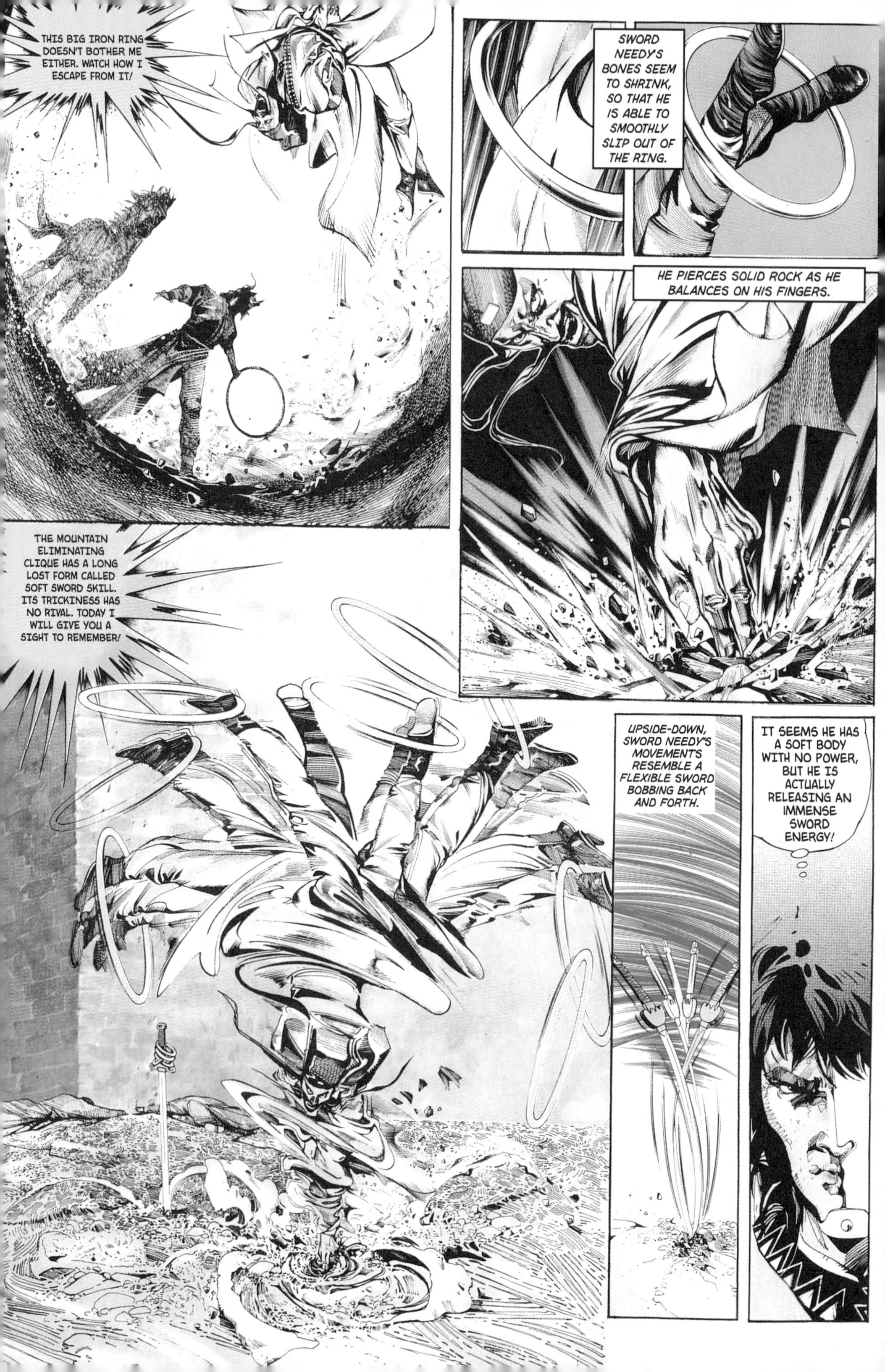
THIS BIG IRON RING DOESN'T BOTHER ME EITHER. WATCH HOW I ESCAPE FROM IT!
SWORD NEEDY'S BONES SEEM TO SHRINK, SO THAT HE IS ABLE TO SMOOTHLY SLIP OUT OF THE RING.
HE PIERCES SOLID ROCK AS HE BALANCES ON HIS FINGERS.
THE MOUNTAIN ELIMINATING CLIQUE HAS A LONG LOST FORM CALLED SOFT SWORD SKILL. ITS TRICKINESS HAS NO RIVAL. TODAY I WILL GIVE YOU A SIGHT TO REMEMBER!
UPSIDE-DOWN, SWORD NEEDY'S MOVEMENTS RESEMBLE A FLEXIBLE SWORD BOBBING BACK AND FORTH.
IT SEEMS HE HAS A SOFT BODY WITH NO POWER, BUT HE IS ACTUALLY RELEASING AN IMMENSE SWORD ENERGY!

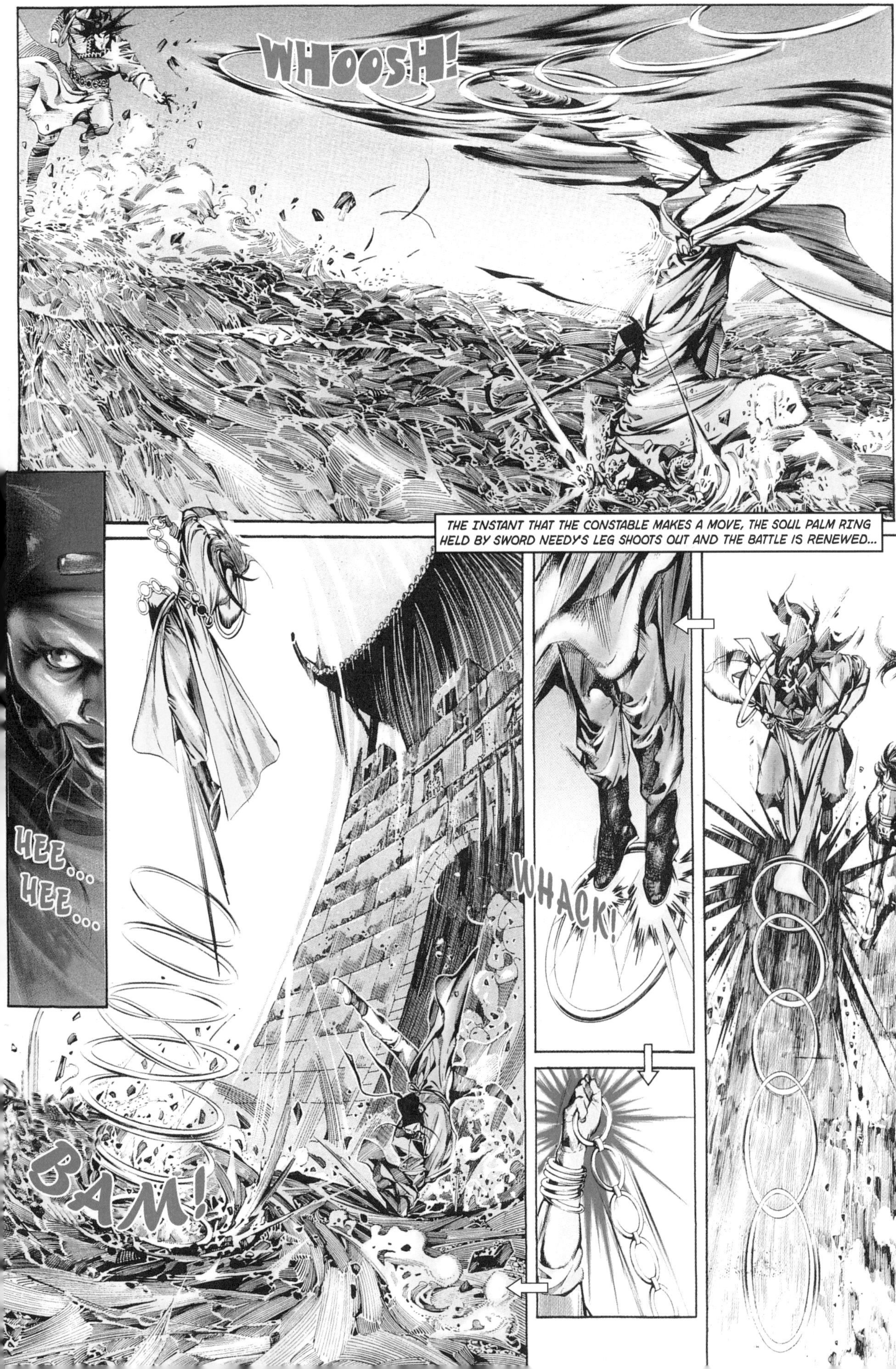
WHOOSH!
THE INSTANT THAT THE CONSTABLE MAKES A MOVE, THE SOUL PALM RING HELD BY SWORD NEEDY'S LEG SHOOTS OUT AND THE BATTLE IS RENEWED...
HEE... HEE...
WHACK!
BAM!

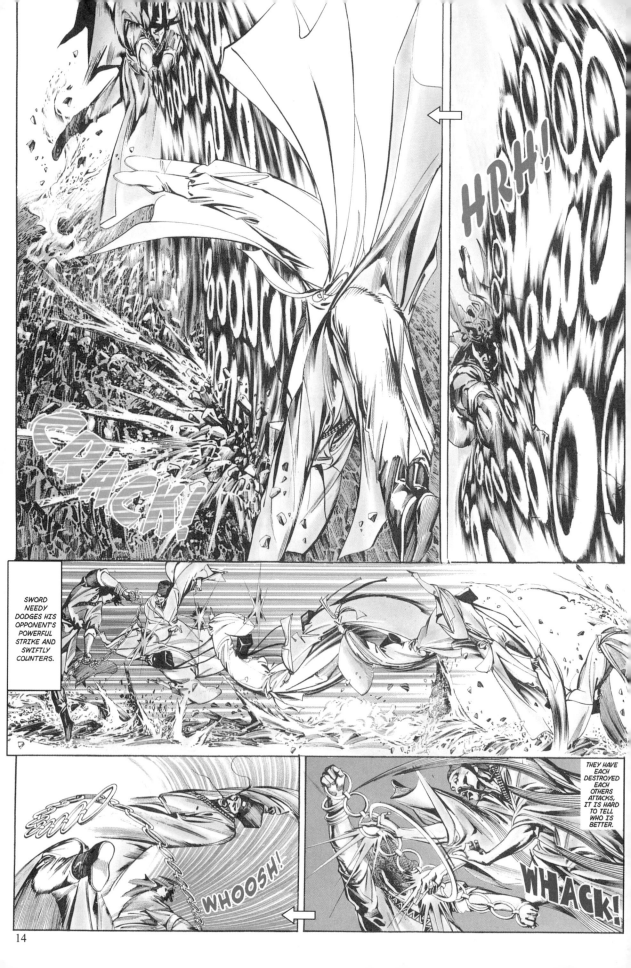

HRH!!

CRACK!

SWORD NEEDY DODGES HIS OPPONENT'S POWERFUL STRIKE AND SWIFTLY COUNTERS.

THEY HAVE EACH DESTROYED EACH OTHERS ATTACKS, IT IS HARD TO TELL WHO IS BETTER.

WHOOSH!!

WHACK!

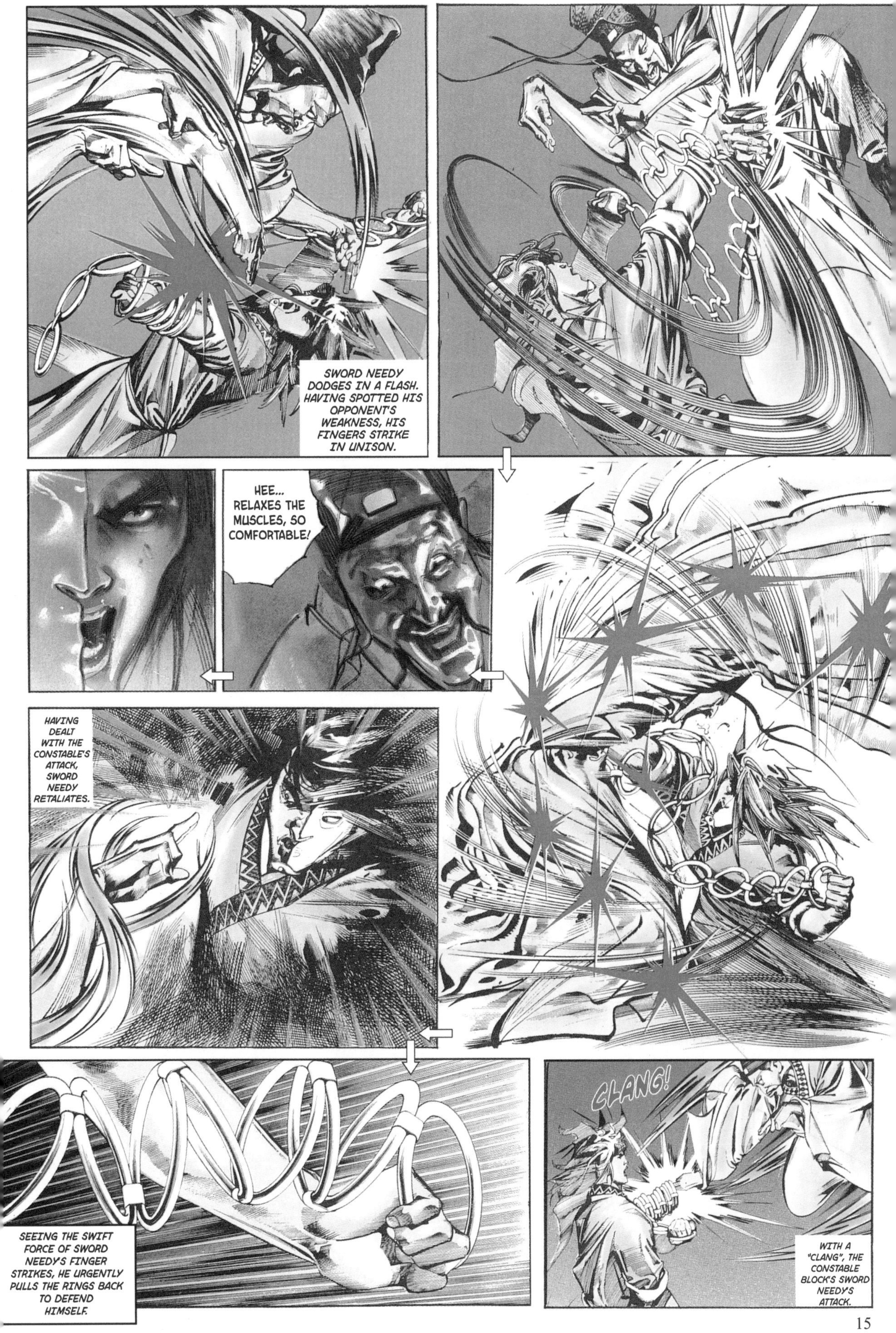
SWORD NEEDY DODGES IN A FLASH. HAVING SPOTTED HIS OPPONENT'S WEAKNESS, HIS FINGERS STRIKE IN UNISON.
HEE... RELAXES THE MUSCLES, SO COMFORTABLE!
HAVING DEALT WITH THE CONSTABLE'S ATTACK, SWORD NEEDY RETALIATES.
SEEING THE SWIFT FORCE OF SWORD NEEDY'S FINGER STRIKES, HE URGENTLY PULLS THE RINGS BACK TO DEFEND HIMSELF.
CLANG!
WITH A "CLANG", THE CONSTABLE BLOCK'S SWORD NEEDY'S ATTACK.

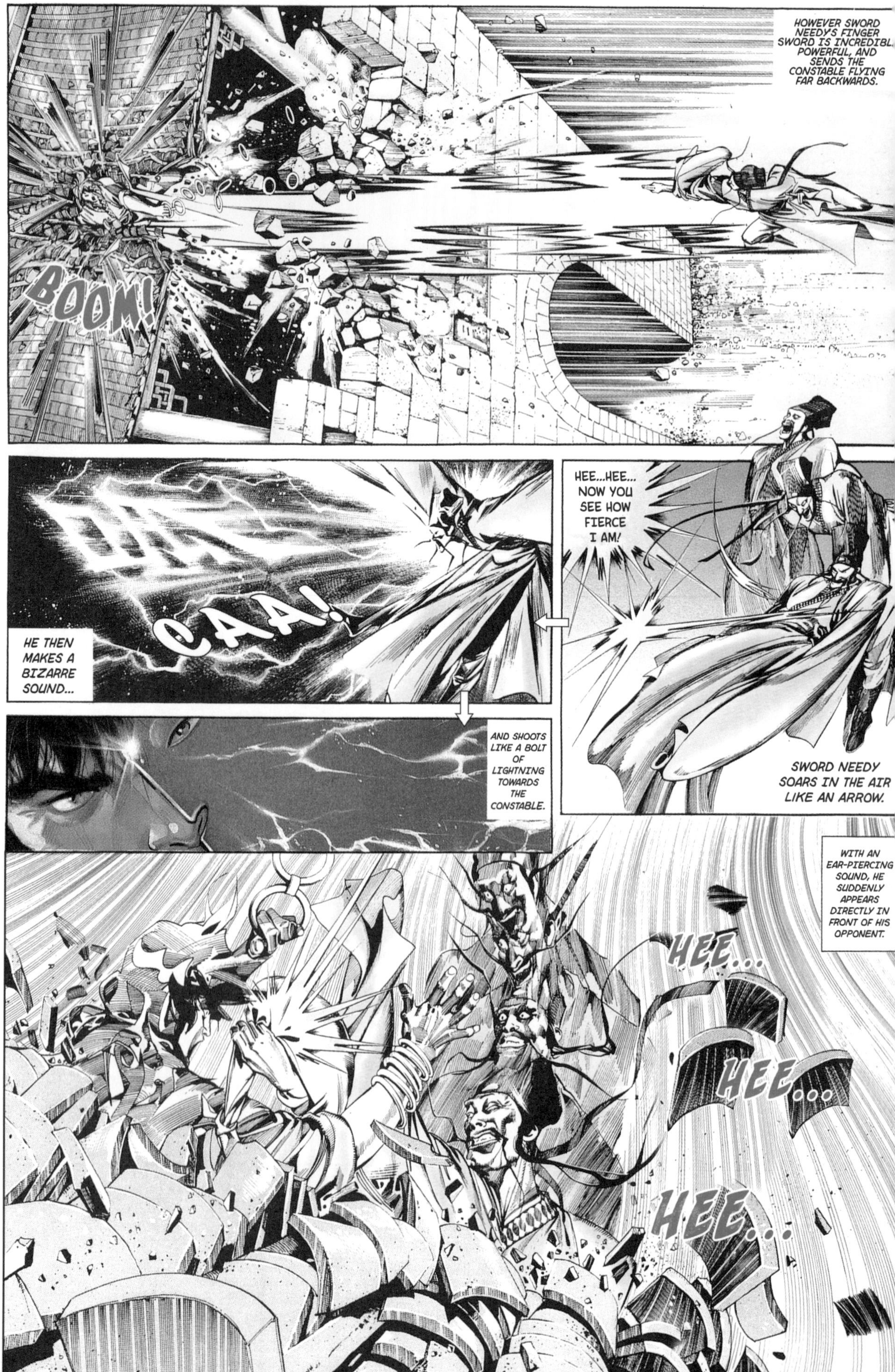
HOWEVER SWORD NEEDY'S FINGER SWORD IS INCREDIBL. POWERFUL, AND SENDS THE CONSTABLE FLYING FAR BACKWARDS.
BOOM!
HEE...HEE... NOW YOU SEE HOW FIERCE I AM!
CAA!
HE THEN MAKES A BIZARRE SOUND...
AND SHOOTS LIKE A BOLT OF LIGHTNING TOWARDS THE CONSTABLE.
SWORD NEEDY SOARS IN THE AIR LIKE AN ARROW.
WITH AN EAR-PIERCING SOUND, HE SUDDENLY APPEARS DIRECTLY IN FRONT OF HIS OPPONENT.
HEE...
HEE...
HEE...

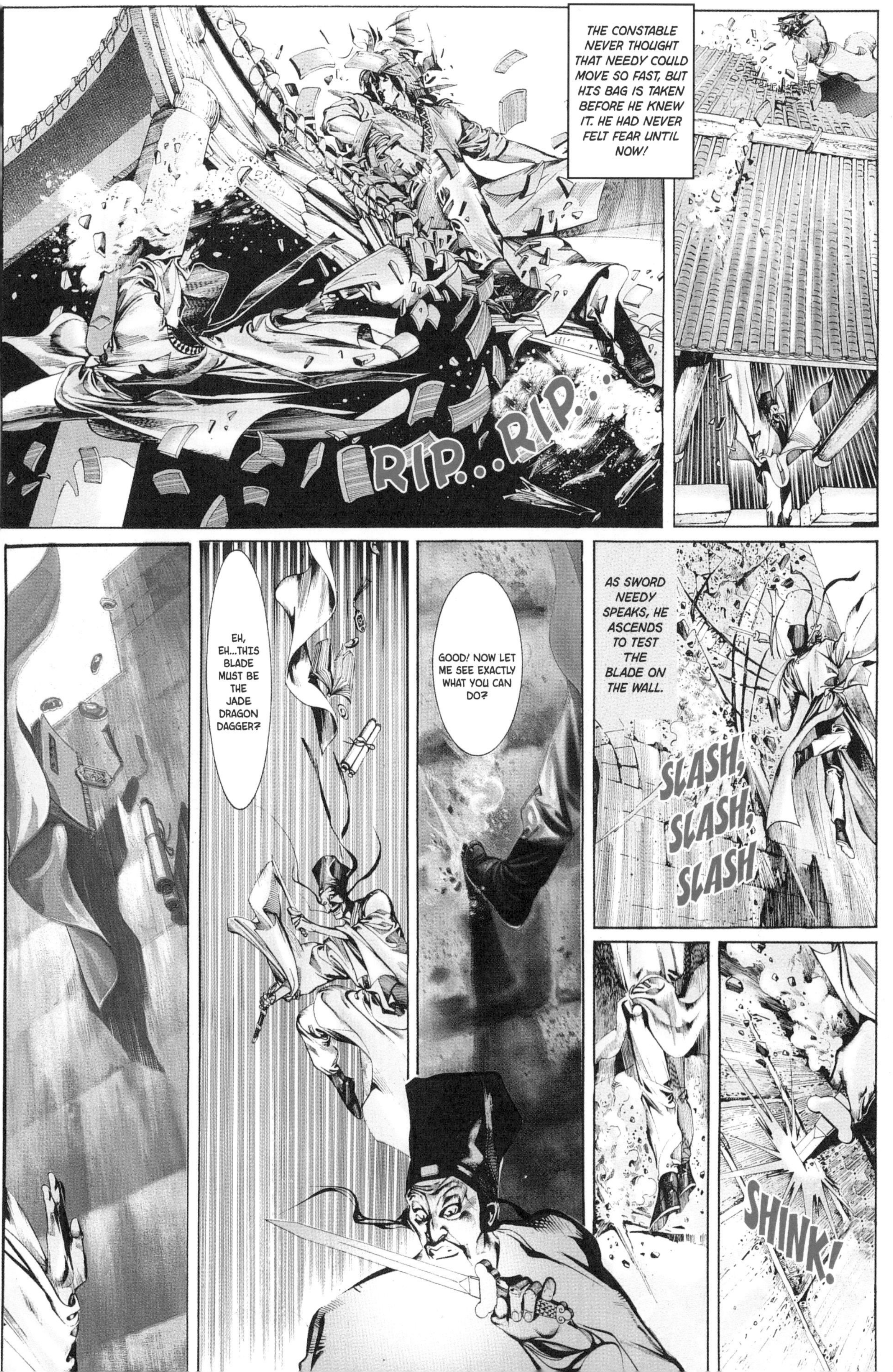
THE CONSTABLE NEVER THOUGHT THAT NEEDY COULD MOVE SO FAST, BUT HIS BAG IS TAKEN BEFORE HE KNEW IT. HE HAD NEVER FELT FEAR UNTIL NOW!
RIP...RIP...
EH, EH...THIS BLADE MUST BE THE JADE DRAGON DAGGER?
GOOD! NOW LET ME SEE EXACTLY WHAT YOU CAN DO?
AS SWORD NEEDY SPEAKS, HE ASCENDS TO TEST THE BLADE ON THE WALL.
SLASH, SLASH, SLASH
SHINK!

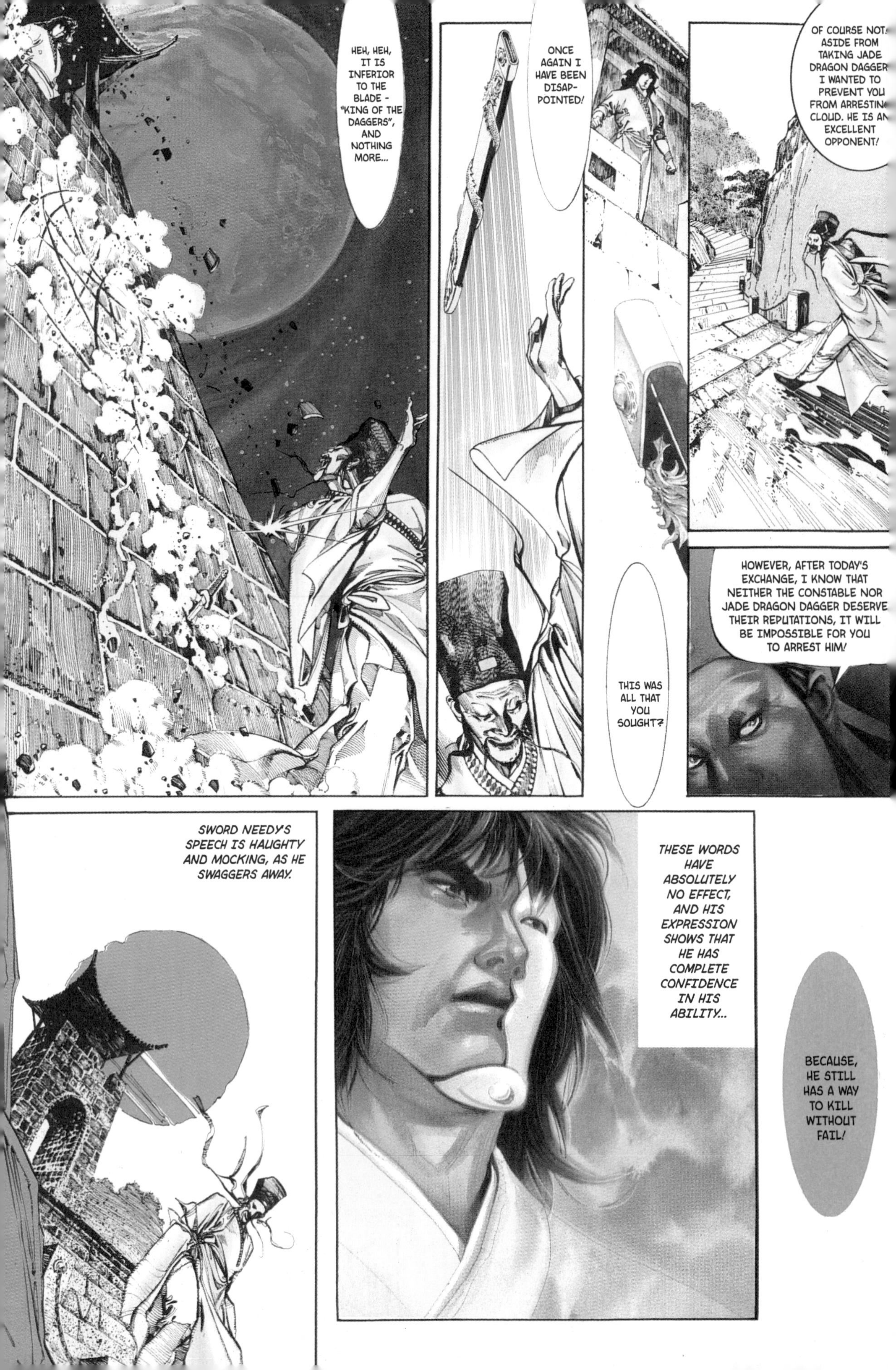
HEH, HEH, IT IS INFERIOR TO THE BLADE - "KING OF THE DAGGERS", AND NOTHING MORE...
ONCE AGAIN I HAVE BEEN DISAP-POINTED!
THIS WAS ALL THAT YOU SOUGHT?
OF COURSE NOT! ASIDE FROM TAKING JADE DRAGON DAGGER I WANTED TO PREVENT YOU FROM ARRESTING CLOUD. HE IS AN EXCELLENT OPPONENT!
HOWEVER, AFTER TODAY'S EXCHANGE, I KNOW THAT NEITHER THE CONSTABLE NOR JADE DRAGON DAGGER DESERVE THEIR REPUTATIONS, IT WILL BE IMPOSSIBLE FOR YOU TO ARREST HIM!
SWORD NEEDY'S SPEECH IS HAUGHTY AND MOCKING, AS HE SWAGGERS AWAY.
THESE WORDS HAVE ABSOLUTELY NO EFFECT, AND HIS EXPRESSION SHOWS THAT HE HAS COMPLETE CONFIDENCE IN HIS ABILITY...
BECAUSE, HE STILL HAS A WAY TO KILL WITHOUT FAIL!

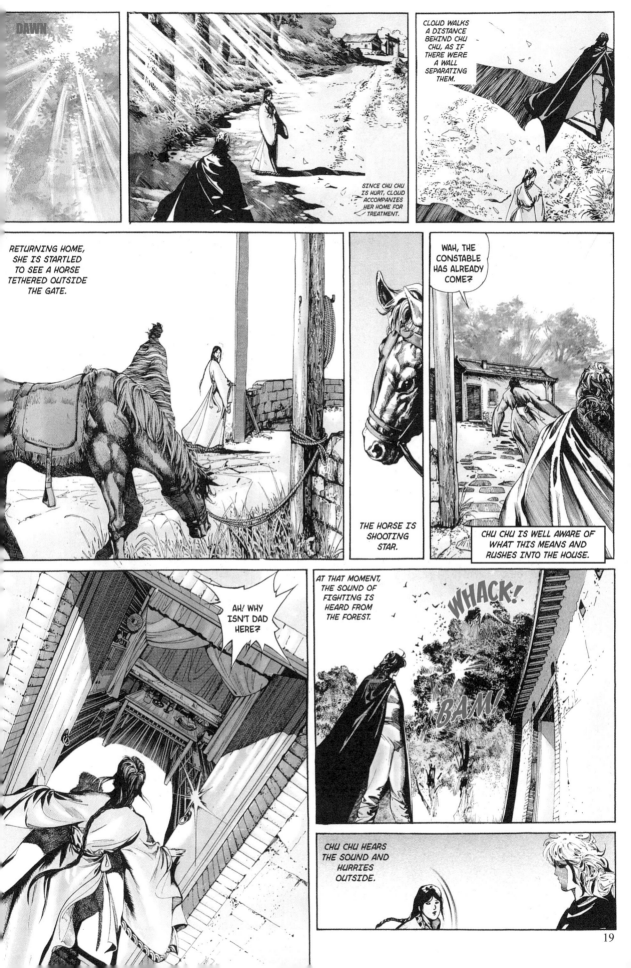

CLOUD WALKS A DISTANCE BEHIND CHU CHU, AS IF THERE WERE A WALL SEPARATING THEM.

SINCE CHU CHU IS HURT, CLOUD ACCOMPANIES HER HOME FOR TREATMENT.

RETURNING HOME, SHE IS STARTLED TO SEE A HORSE TETHERED OUTSIDE THE GATE.

THE HORSE IS SHOOTING STAR.

WAH, THE CONSTABLE HAS ALREADY COME?

CHU CHU IS WELL AWARE OF WHAT THIS MEANS AND RUSHES INTO THE HOUSE.

AH! WHY ISN'T DAD HERE?

AT THAT MOMENT, THE SOUND OF FIGHTING IS HEARD FROM THE FOREST.

WHACK!

BAM!

CHU CHU HEARS THE SOUND AND HURRIES OUTSIDE.

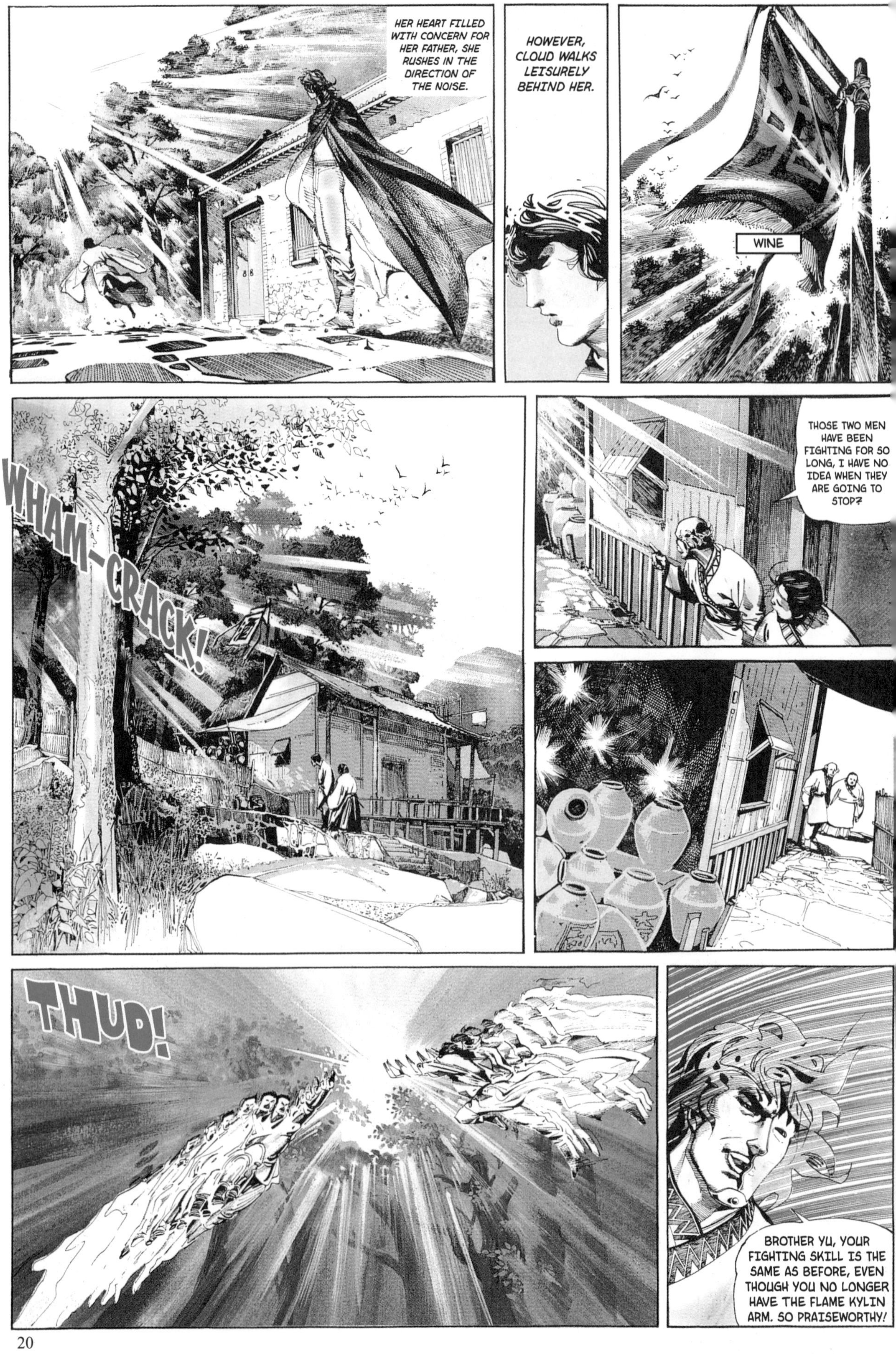
HER HEART FILLED WITH CONCERN FOR HER FATHER, SHE RUSHES IN THE DIRECTION OF THE NOISE.
HOWEVER, CLOUD WALKS LEISURELY BEHIND HER.
WINE
WHAM-CRACK!
THOSE TWO MEN HAVE BEEN FIGHTING FOR SO LONG, I HAVE NO IDEA WHEN THEY ARE GOING TO STOP?
THUD!
BROTHER YU, YOUR FIGHTING SKILL IS THE SAME AS BEFORE, EVEN THOUGH YOU NO LONGER HAVE THE FLAME KYLIN ARM. SO PRAISEWORTHY!

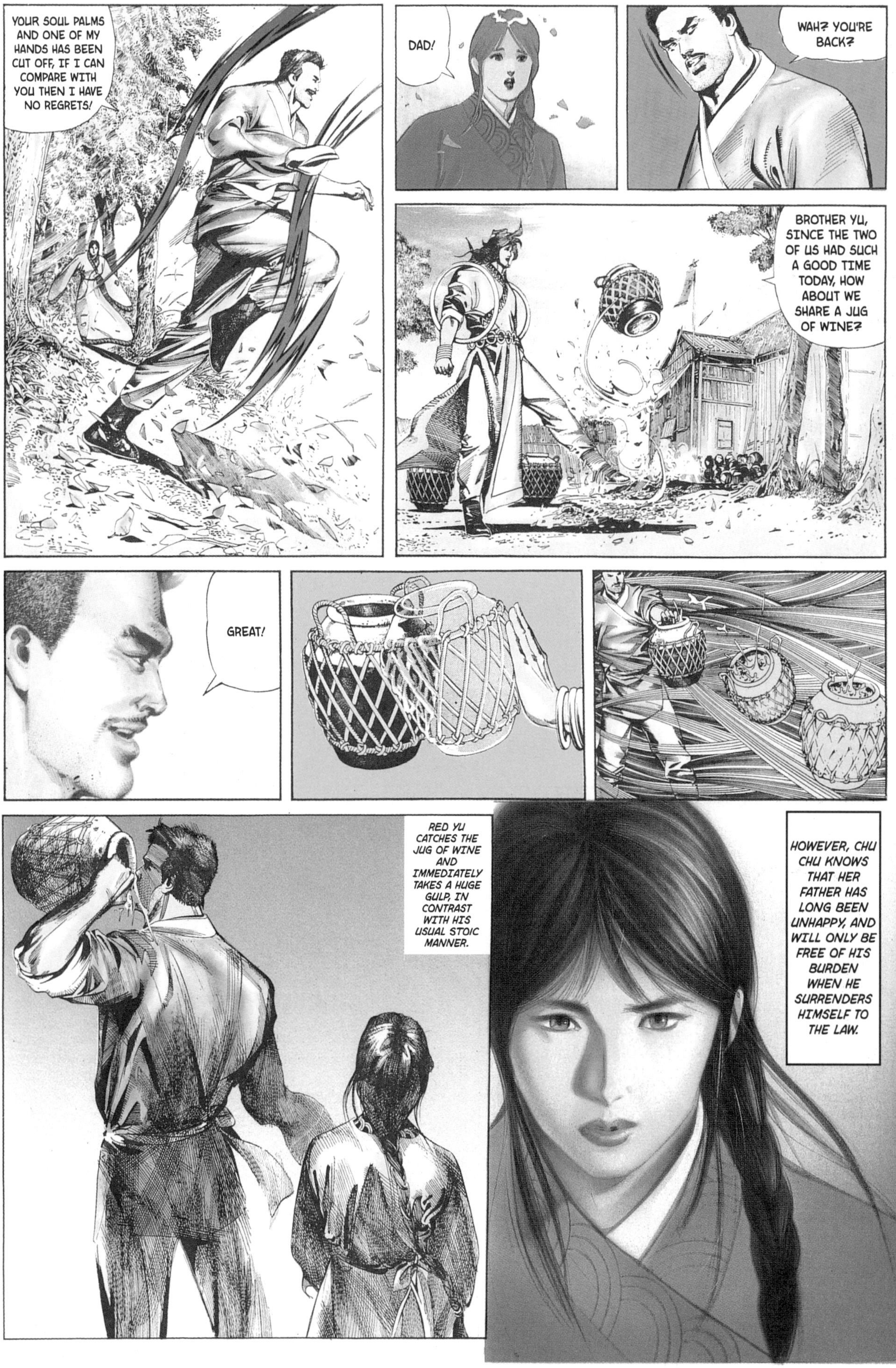
YOUR SOUL PALMS AND ONE OF MY HANDS HAS BEEN CUT OFF, IF I CAN COMPARE WITH YOU THEN I HAVE NO REGRETS!
DAD!
WAH? YOU'RE BACK?
BROTHER YU, SINCE THE TWO OF US HAD SUCH A GOOD TIME TODAY, HOW ABOUT WE SHARE A JUG OF WINE?
GREAT!
RED YU CATCHES THE JUG OF WINE AND IMMEDIATELY TAKES A HUGE GULP, IN CONTRAST WITH HIS USUAL STOIC MANNER.
HOWEVER, CHU CHU KNOWS THAT HER FATHER HAS LONG BEEN UNHAPPY, AND WILL ONLY BE FREE OF HIS BURDEN WHEN HE SURRENDERS HIMSELF TO THE LAW.

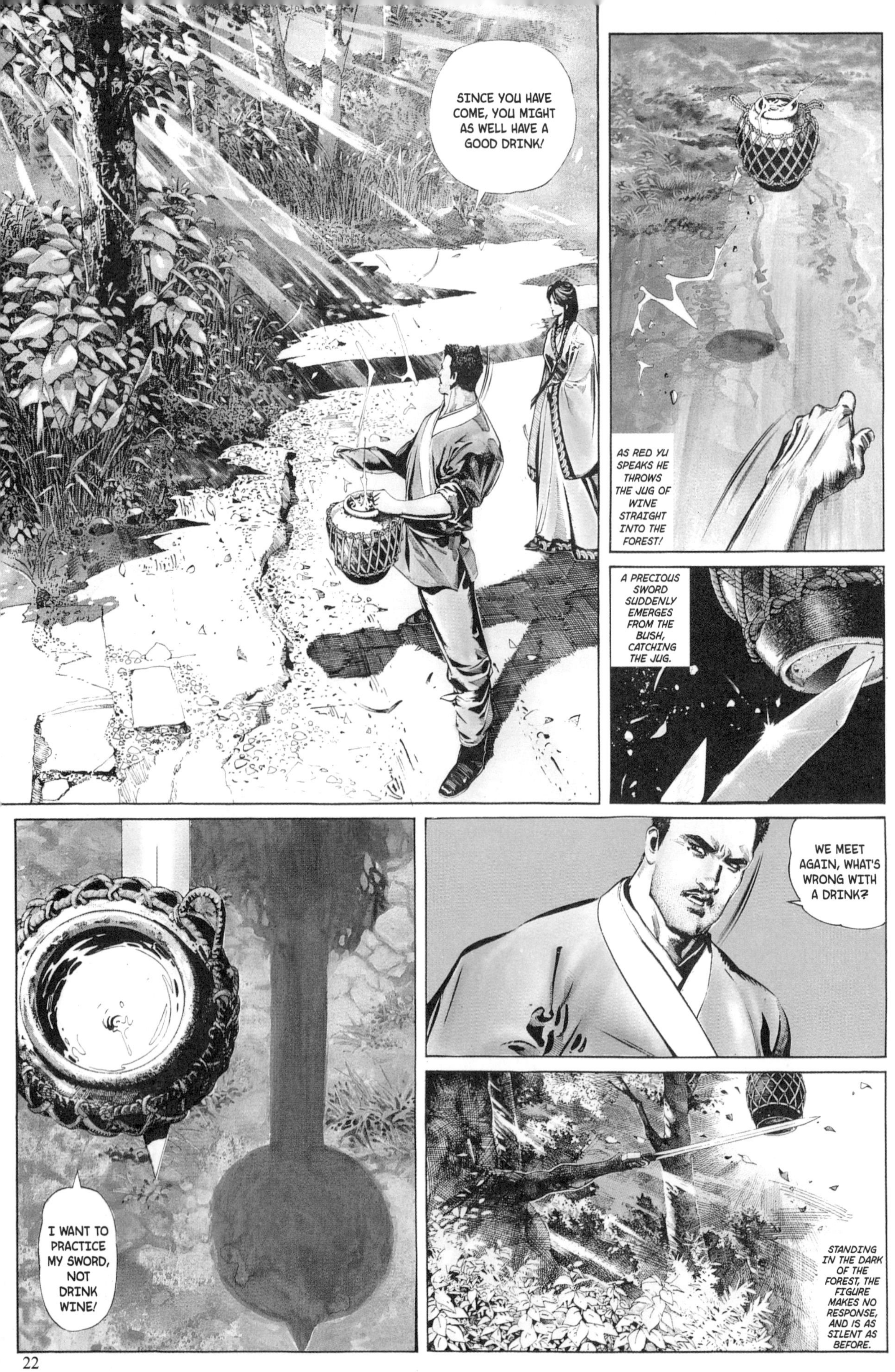
SINCE YOU HAVE COME, YOU MIGHT AS WELL HAVE A GOOD DRINK!
AS RED YU SPEAKS HE THROWS THE JUG OF WINE STRAIGHT INTO THE FOREST!
A PRECIOUS SWORD SUDDENLY EMERGES FROM THE BUSH, CATCHING THE JUG.
WE MEET AGAIN, WHAT'S WRONG WITH A DRINK?
I WANT TO PRACTICE MY SWORD, NOT DRINK WINE!
STANDING IN THE DARK OF THE FOREST, THE FIGURE MAKES NO RESPONSE, AND IS AS SILENT AS BEFORE.

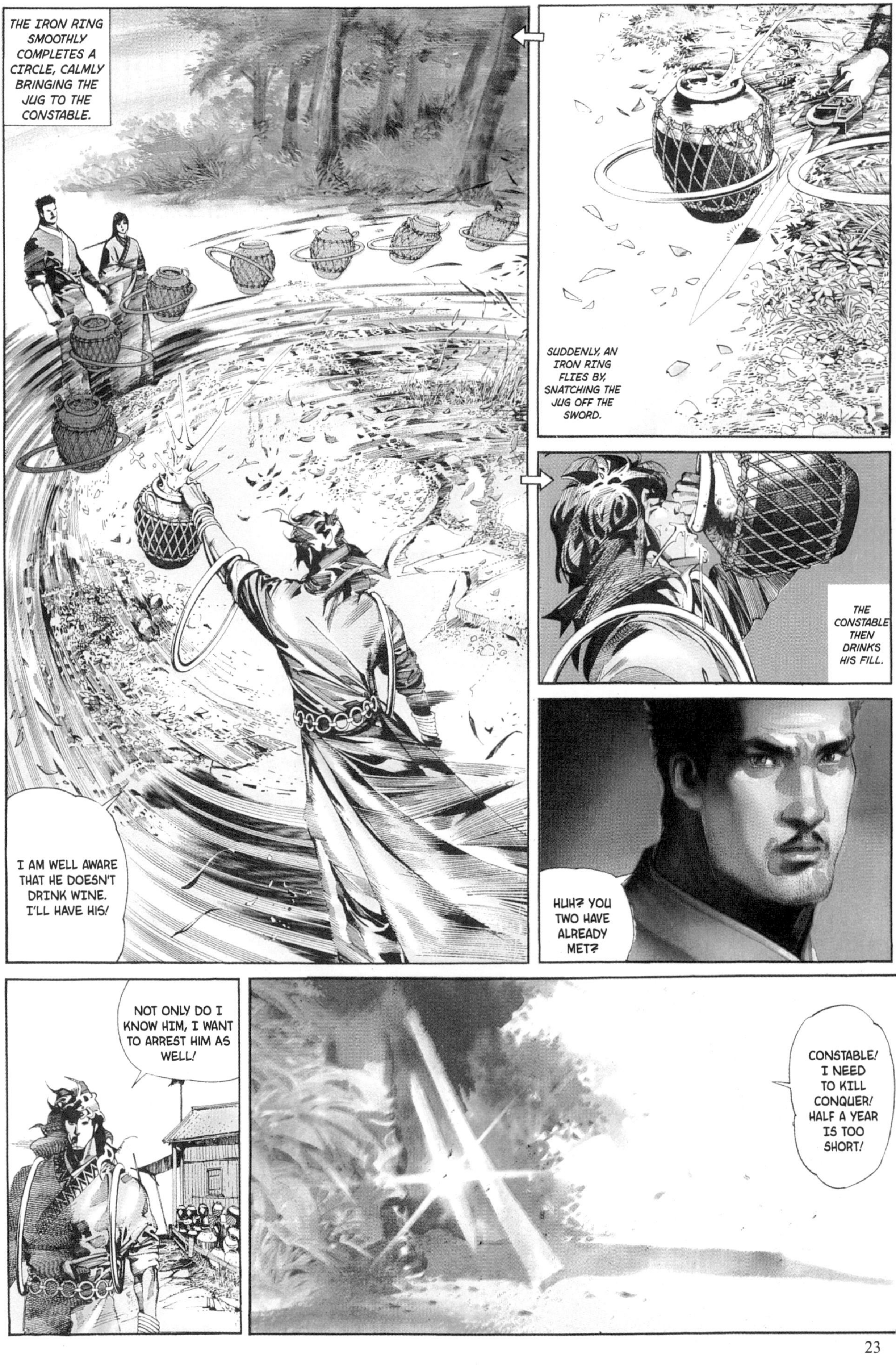

THE IRON RING SMOOTHLY COMPLETES A CIRCLE, CALMLY BRINGING THE JUG TO THE CONSTABLE.
I AM WELL AWARE THAT HE DOESN'T DRINK WINE. I'LL HAVE HIS!
SUDDENLY, AN IRON RING FLIES BY, SNATCHING THE JUG OFF THE SWORD.
THE CONSTABLE THEN DRINKS HIS FILL.
HUH? YOU TWO HAVE ALREADY MET?
NOT ONLY DO I KNOW HIM, I WANT TO ARREST HIM AS WELL!
CONSTABLE! I NEED TO KILL CONQUER! HALF A YEAR IS TOO SHORT!

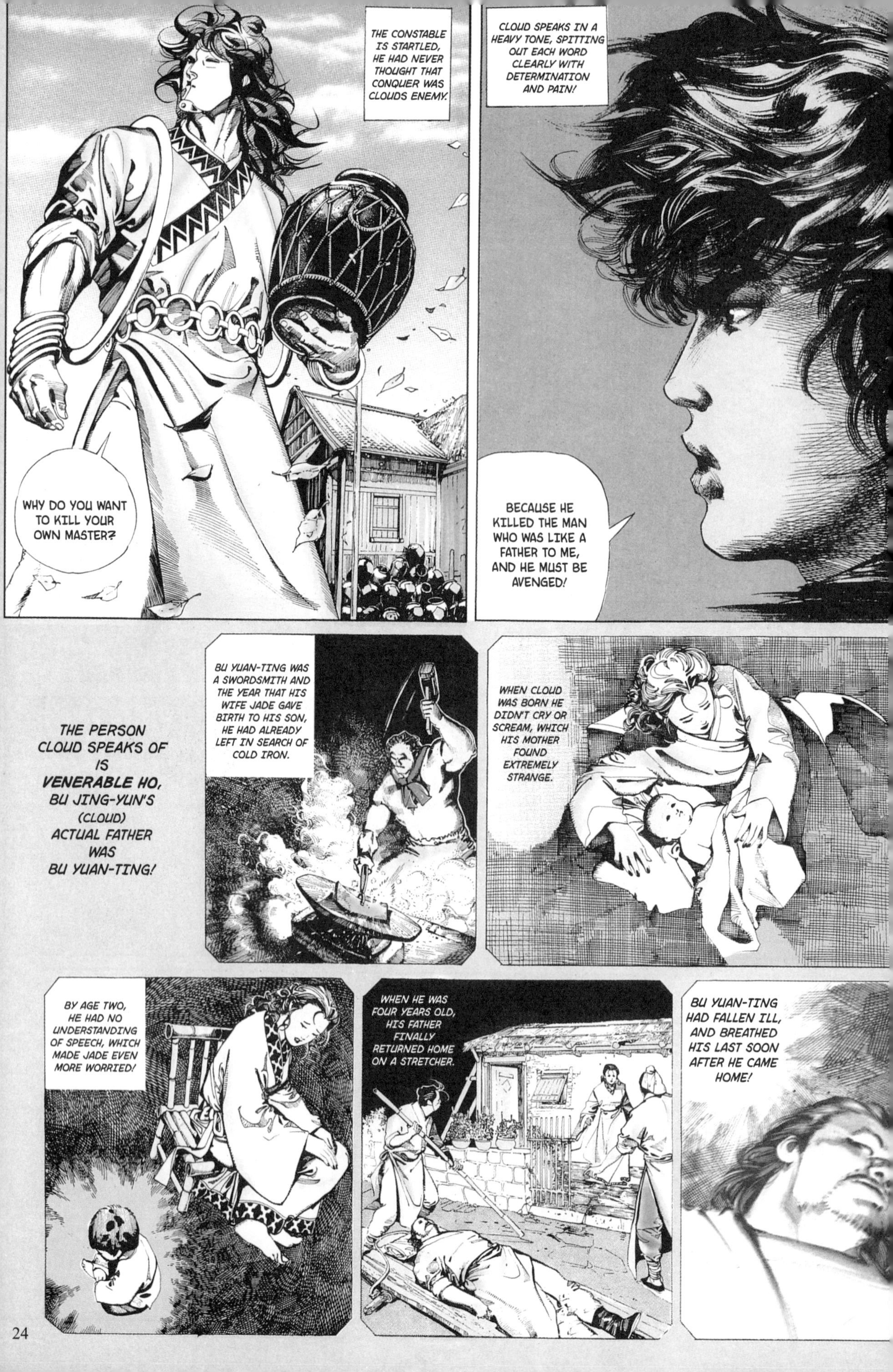
THE CONSTABLE IS STARTLED, HE HAD NEVER THOUGHT THAT CONQUER WAS CLOUDS ENEMY.
WHY DO YOU WANT TO KILL YOUR OWN MASTER?
CLOUD SPEAKS IN A HEAVY TONE, SPITTING OUT EACH WORD CLEARLY WITH DETERMINATION AND PAIN!
BECAUSE HE KILLED THE MAN WHO WAS LIKE A FATHER TO ME, AND HE MUST BE AVENGED!
THE PERSON CLOUD SPEAKS OF IS VENERABLE HO, BU JING-YUN'S (CLOUD) ACTUAL FATHER WAS BU YUAN-TING!
BU YUAN-TING WAS A SWORDSMITH AND THE YEAR THAT HIS WIFE JADE GAVE BIRTH TO HIS SON, HE HAD ALREADY LEFT IN SEARCH OF COLD IRON.
WHEN CLOUD WAS BORN HE DIDN'T CRY OR SCREAM, WHICH HIS MOTHER FOUND EXTREMELY STRANGE.
BY AGE TWO, HE HAD NO UNDERSTANDING OF SPEECH, WHICH MADE JADE EVEN MORE WORRIED!
WHEN HE WAS FOUR YEARS OLD, HIS FATHER FINALLY RETURNED HOME ON A STRETCHER.
BU YUAN-TING HAD FALLEN ILL, AND BREATHED HIS LAST SOON AFTER HE CAME HOME!

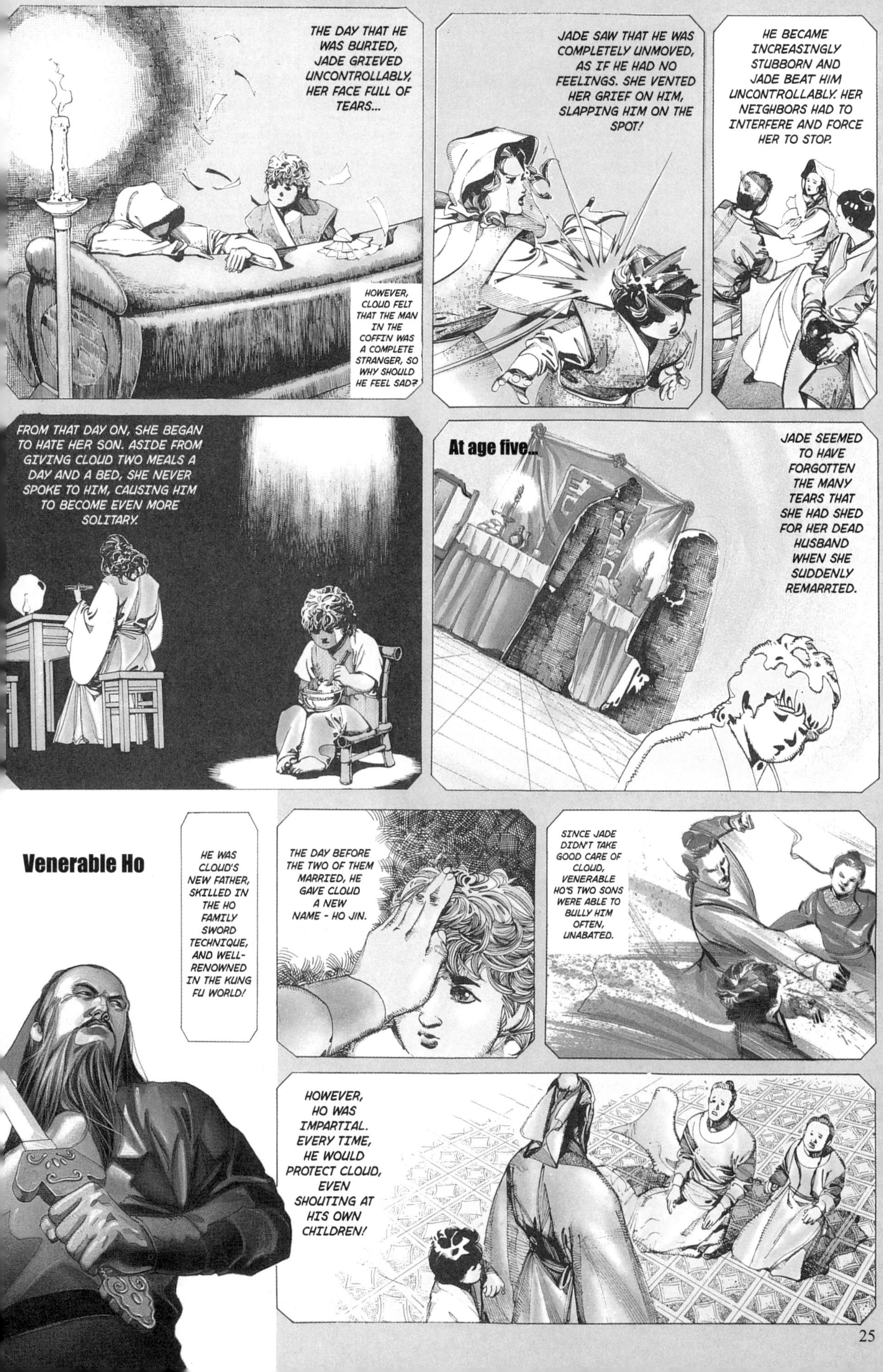
THE DAY THAT HE WAS BURIED, JADE GRIEVED UNCONTROLLABLY, HER FACE FULL OF TEARS...
HOWEVER, CLOUD FELT THAT THE MAN IN THE COFFIN WAS A COMPLETE STRANGER, SO WHY SHOULD HE FEEL SAD?
JADE SAW THAT HE WAS COMPLETELY UNMOVED, AS IF HE HAD NO FEELINGS. SHE VENTED HER GRIEF ON HIM, SLAPPING HIM ON THE SPOT!
HE BECAME INCREASINGLY STUBBORN AND JADE BEAT HIM UNCONTROLLABLY. HER NEIGHBORS HAD TO INTERFERE AND FORCE HER TO STOP.
FROM THAT DAY ON, SHE BEGAN TO HATE HER SON. ASIDE FROM GIVING CLOUD TWO MEALS A DAY AND A BED, SHE NEVER SPOKE TO HIM, CAUSING HIM TO BECOME EVEN MORE SOLITARY.
At age five...
JADE SEEMED TO HAVE FORGOTTEN THE MANY TEARS THAT SHE HAD SHED FOR HER DEAD HUSBAND WHEN SHE SUDDENLY REMARRIED.
Venerable Ho
HE WAS CLOUD'S NEW FATHER, SKILLED IN THE HO FAMILY SWORD TECHNIQUE, AND WELL-RENOWNED IN THE KUNG FU WORLD!
THE DAY BEFORE THE TWO OF THEM MARRIED, HE GAVE CLOUD A NEW NAME - HO JIN.
SINCE JADE DIDN'T TAKE GOOD CARE OF CLOUD, VENERABLE HO'S TWO SONS WERE ABLE TO BULLY HIM OFTEN, UNABATED.
HOWEVER, HO WAS IMPARTIAL. EVERY TIME, HE WOULD PROTECT CLOUD, EVEN SHOUTING AT HIS OWN CHILDREN!

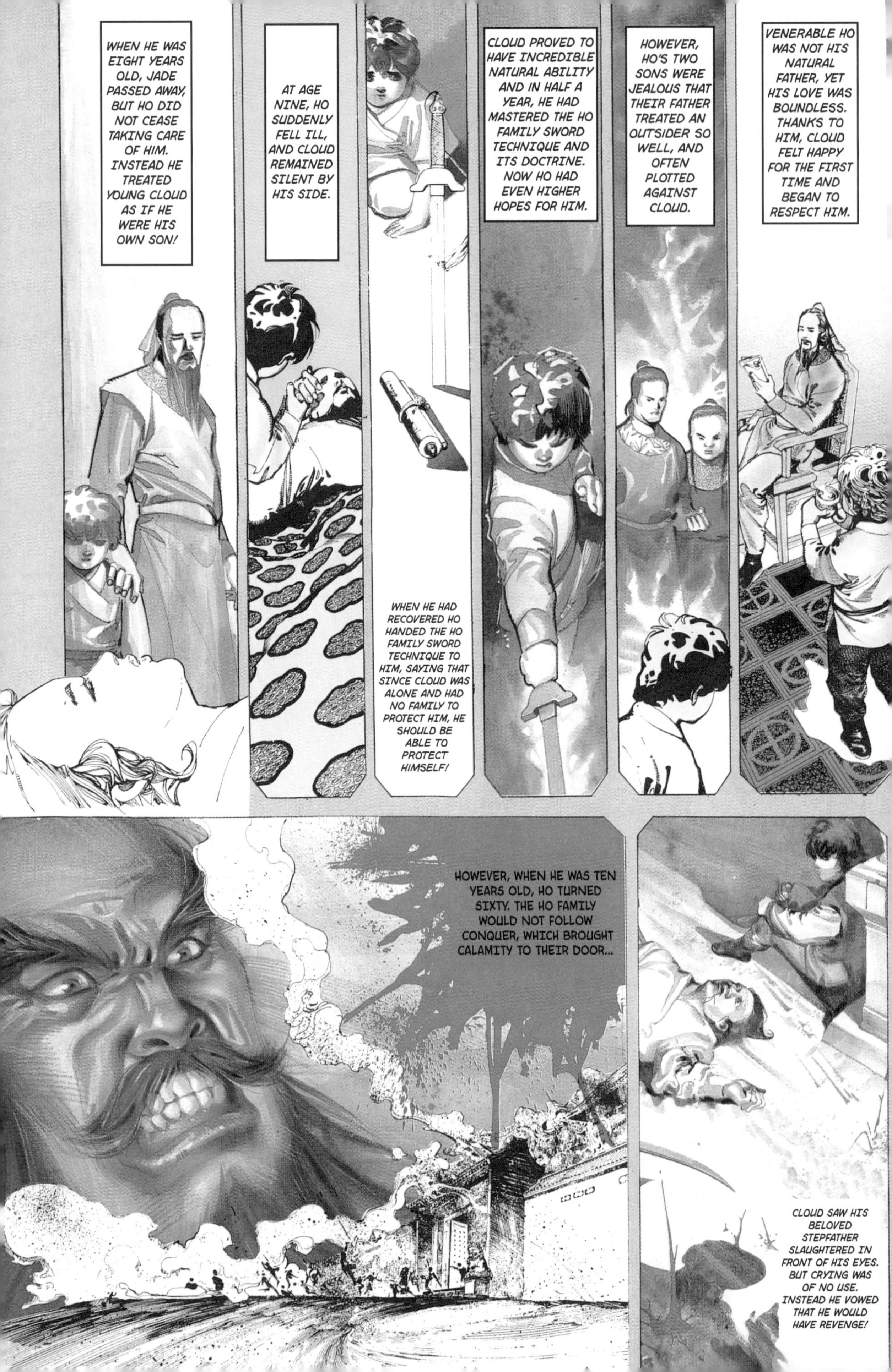
WHEN HE WAS EIGHT YEARS OLD, JADE PASSED AWAY, BUT HO DID NOT CEASE TAKING CARE OF HIM. INSTEAD HE TREATED YOUNG CLOUD AS IF HE WERE HIS OWN SON!
AT AGE NINE, HO SUDDENLY FELL ILL, AND CLOUD REMAINED SILENT BY HIS SIDE.
WHEN HE HAD RECOVERED HO HANDED THE HO FAMILY SWORD TECHNIQUE TO HIM, SAYING THAT SINCE CLOUD WAS ALONE AND HAD NO FAMILY TO PROTECT HIM, HE SHOULD BE ABLE TO PROTECT HIMSELF!
CLOUD PROVED TO HAVE INCREDIBLE NATURAL ABILITY AND IN HALF A YEAR, HE HAD MASTERED THE HO FAMILY SWORD TECHNIQUE AND ITS DOCTRINE. NOW HO HAD EVEN HIGHER HOPES FOR HIM.
HOWEVER, HO'S TWO SONS WERE JEALOUS THAT THEIR FATHER TREATED AN OUTSIDER SO WELL, AND OFTEN PLOTTED AGAINST CLOUD.
VENERABLE HO WAS NOT HIS NATURAL FATHER, YET HIS LOVE WAS BOUNDLESS. THANKS TO HIM, CLOUD FELT HAPPY FOR THE FIRST TIME AND BEGAN TO RESPECT HIM.
HOWEVER, WHEN HE WAS TEN YEARS OLD, HO TURNED SIXTY. THE HO FAMILY WOULD NOT FOLLOW CONQUER, WHICH BROUGHT CALAMITY TO THEIR DOOR...
CLOUD SAW HIS BELOVED STEPFATHER SLAUGHTERED IN FRONT OF HIS EYES. BUT CRYING WAS OF NO USE. INSTEAD HE VOWED THAT HE WOULD HAVE REVENGE!

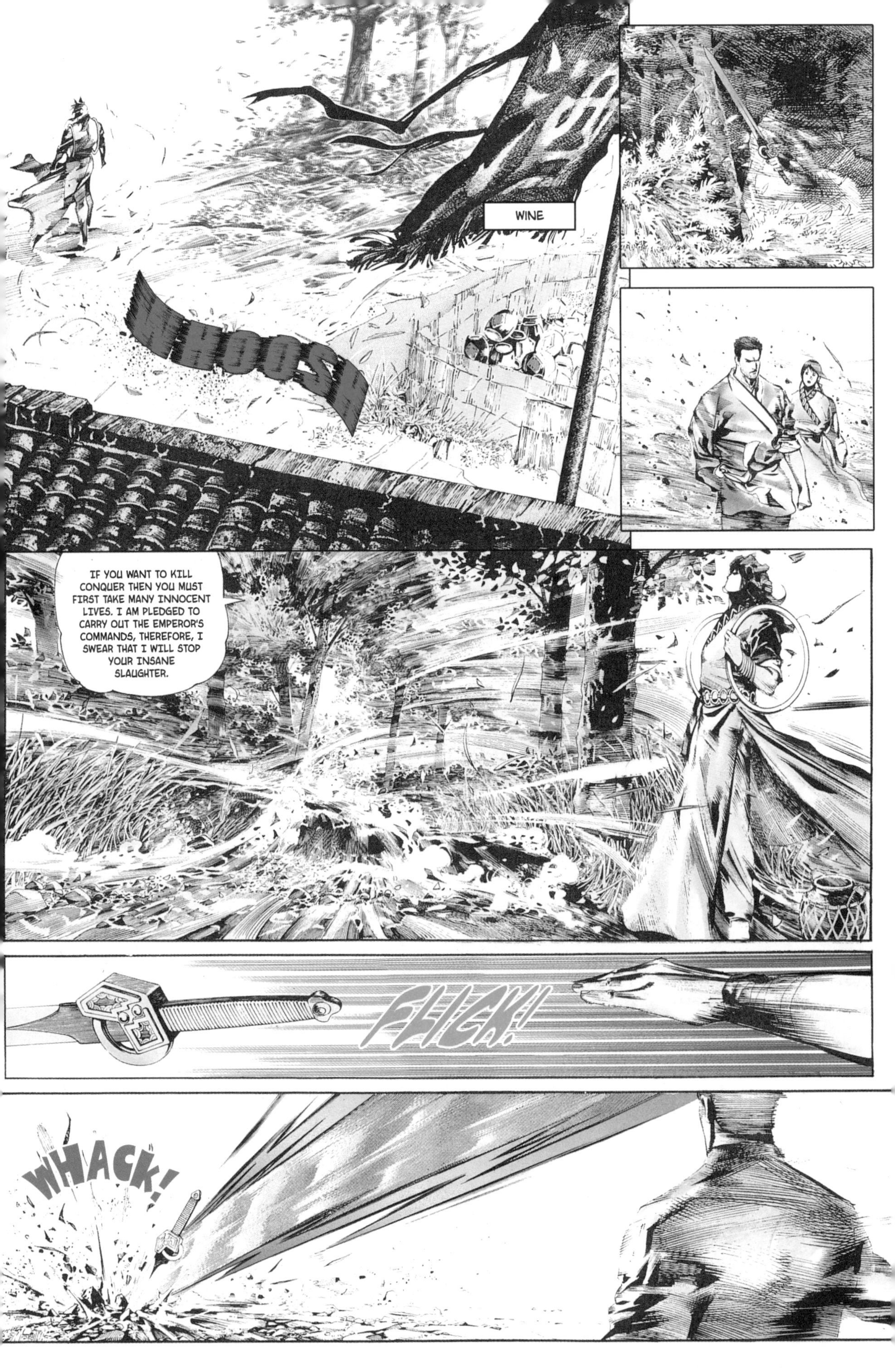
WINE
WHOOSH
IF YOU WANT TO KILL CONQUER THEN YOU MUST FIRST TAKE MANY INNOCENT LIVES. I AM PLEDGED TO CARRY OUT THE EMPEROR'S COMMANDS, THEREFORE, I SWEAR THAT I WILL STOP YOUR INSANE SLAUGHTER.
FLICK!
WHACK!

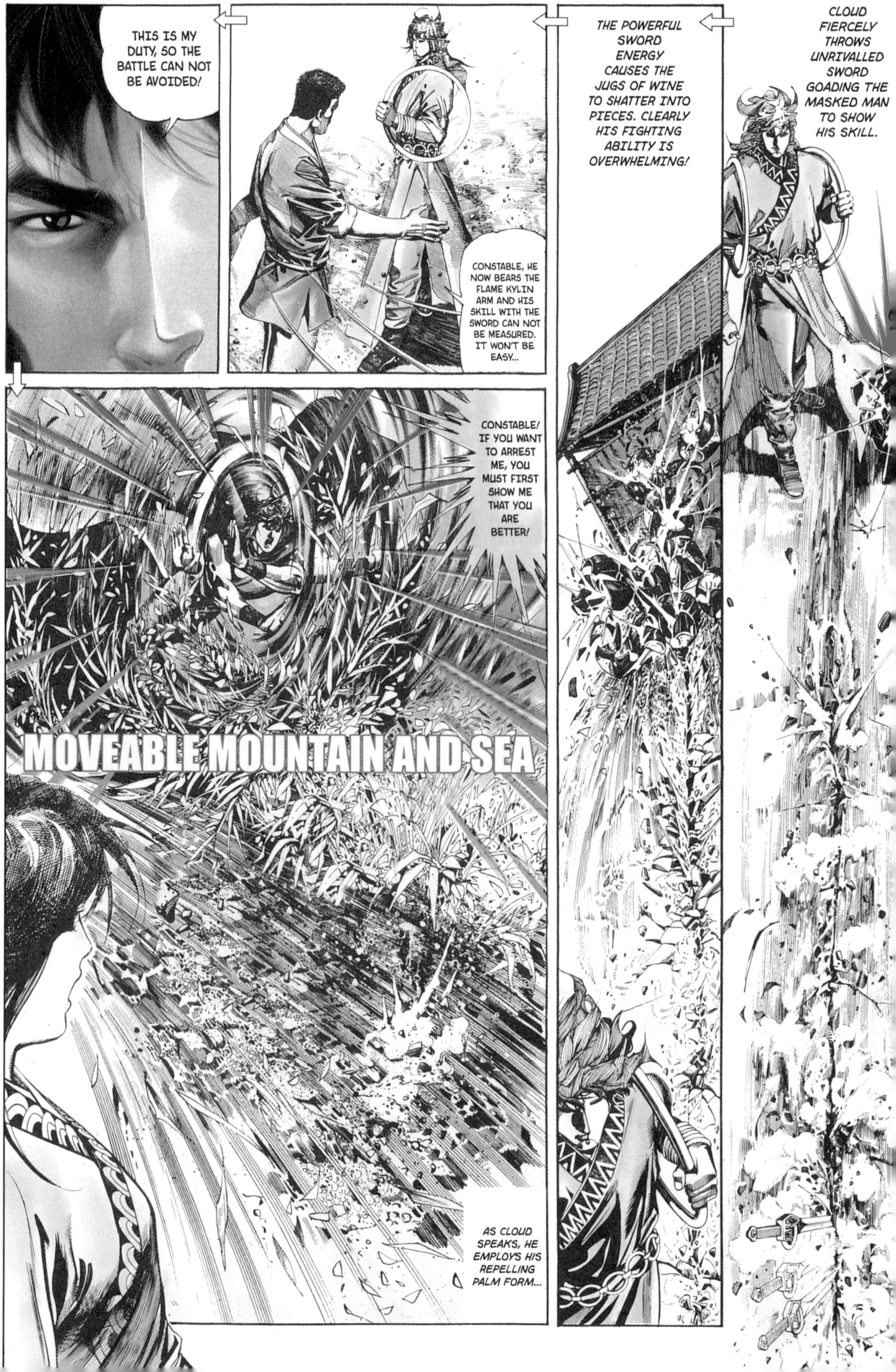

CLOUD FIERCELY THROWS UNRIVALLED SWORD GOADING THE MASKED MAN TO SHOW HIS SKILL.
THE POWERFUL SWORD ENERGY CAUSES THE JUGS OF WINE TO SHATTER INTO PIECES. CLEARLY HIS FIGHTING ABILITY IS OVERWHELMING!
CONSTABLE, HE NOW BEARS THE FLAME KYLIN ARM AND HIS SKILL WITH THE SWORD CAN NOT BE MEASURED. IT WON'T BE EASY...
THIS IS MY DUTY, SO THE BATTLE CAN NOT BE AVOIDED!
CONSTABLE! IF YOU WANT TO ARREST ME, YOU MUST FIRST SHOW ME THAT YOU ARE BETTER!
MOVEABLE MOUNTAIN AND SEA
AS CLOUD SPEAKS, HE EMPLOYS HIS REPELLING PALM FORM...

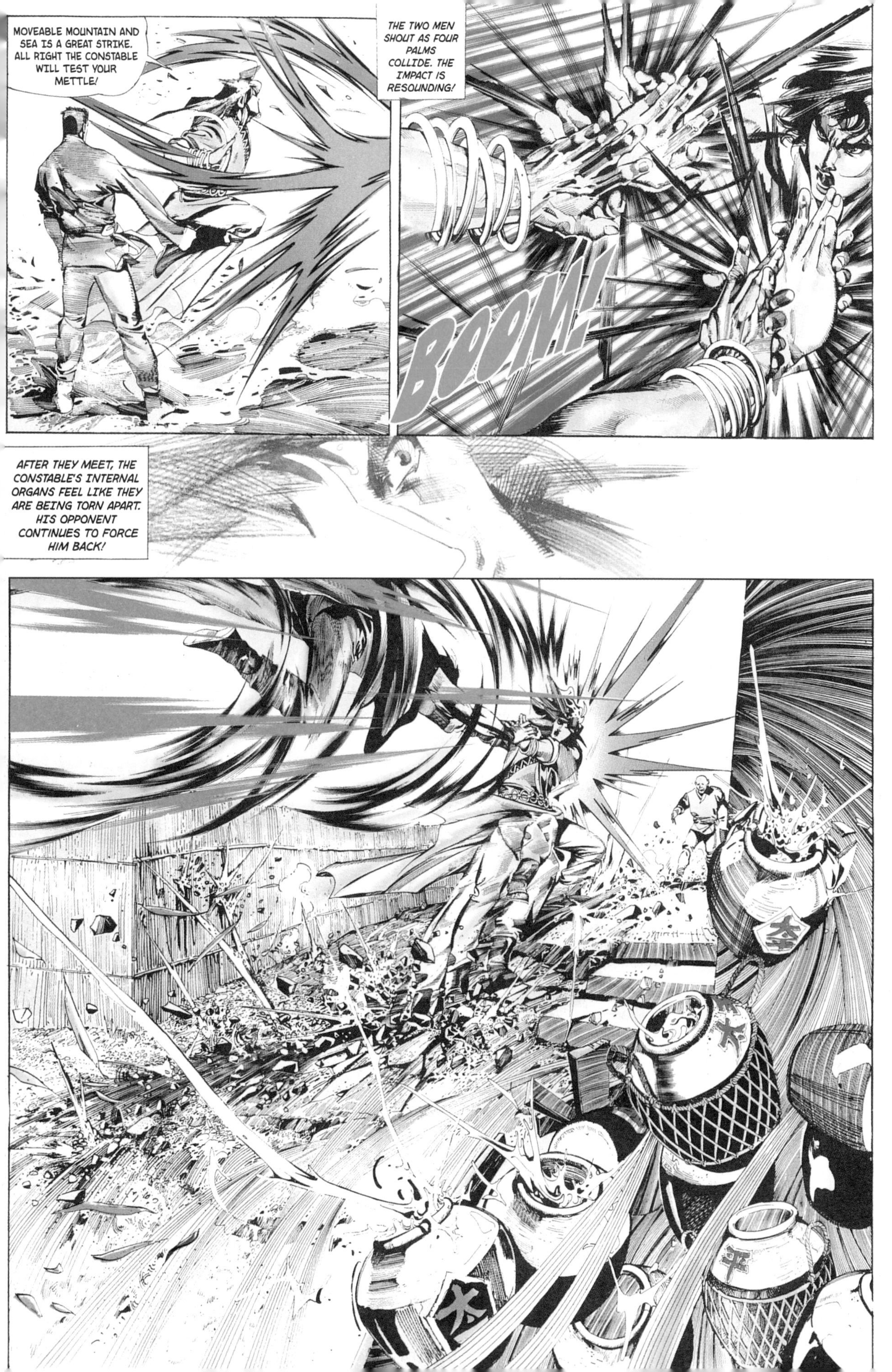
MOVEABLE MOUNTAIN AND SEA IS A GREAT STRIKE. ALL RIGHT THE CONSTABLE WILL TEST YOUR METTLE!
THE TWO MEN SHOUT AS FOUR PALMS COLLIDE. THE IMPACT IS RESOUNDING!
BOOM!
AFTER THEY MEET, THE CONSTABLE'S INTERNAL ORGANS FEEL LIKE THEY ARE BEING TORN APART. HIS OPPONENT CONTINUES TO FORCE HIM BACK!

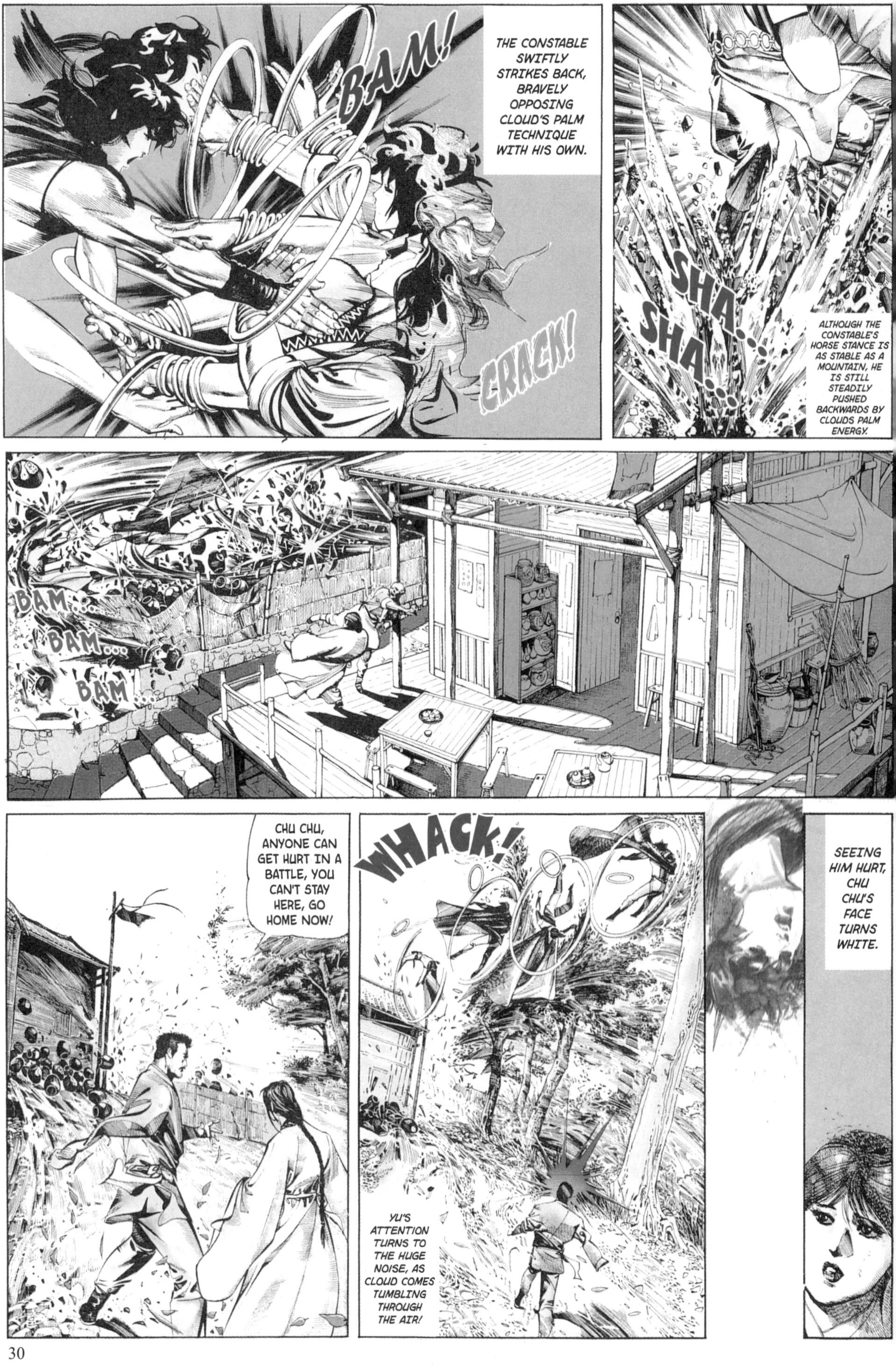
BAM!
THE CONSTABLE SWIFTLY STRIKES BACK, BRAVELY OPPOSING CLOUD'S PALM TECHNIQUE WITH HIS OWN.
CRACK!
SHA... SHA...
ALTHOUGH THE CONSTABLE'S HORSE STANCE IS AS STABLE AS A MOUNTAIN, HE IS STILL STEADILY PUSHED BACKWARDS BY CLOUDS PALM ENERGY.
BAM... BAM... BAM...
CHU CHU, ANYONE CAN GET HURT IN A BATTLE, YOU CAN'T STAY HERE, GO HOME NOW!
WHACK!
YU'S ATTENTION TURNS TO THE HUGE NOISE, AS CLOUD COMES TUMBLING THROUGH THE AIR!
SEEING HIM HURT, CHU CHU'S FACE TURNS WHITE.

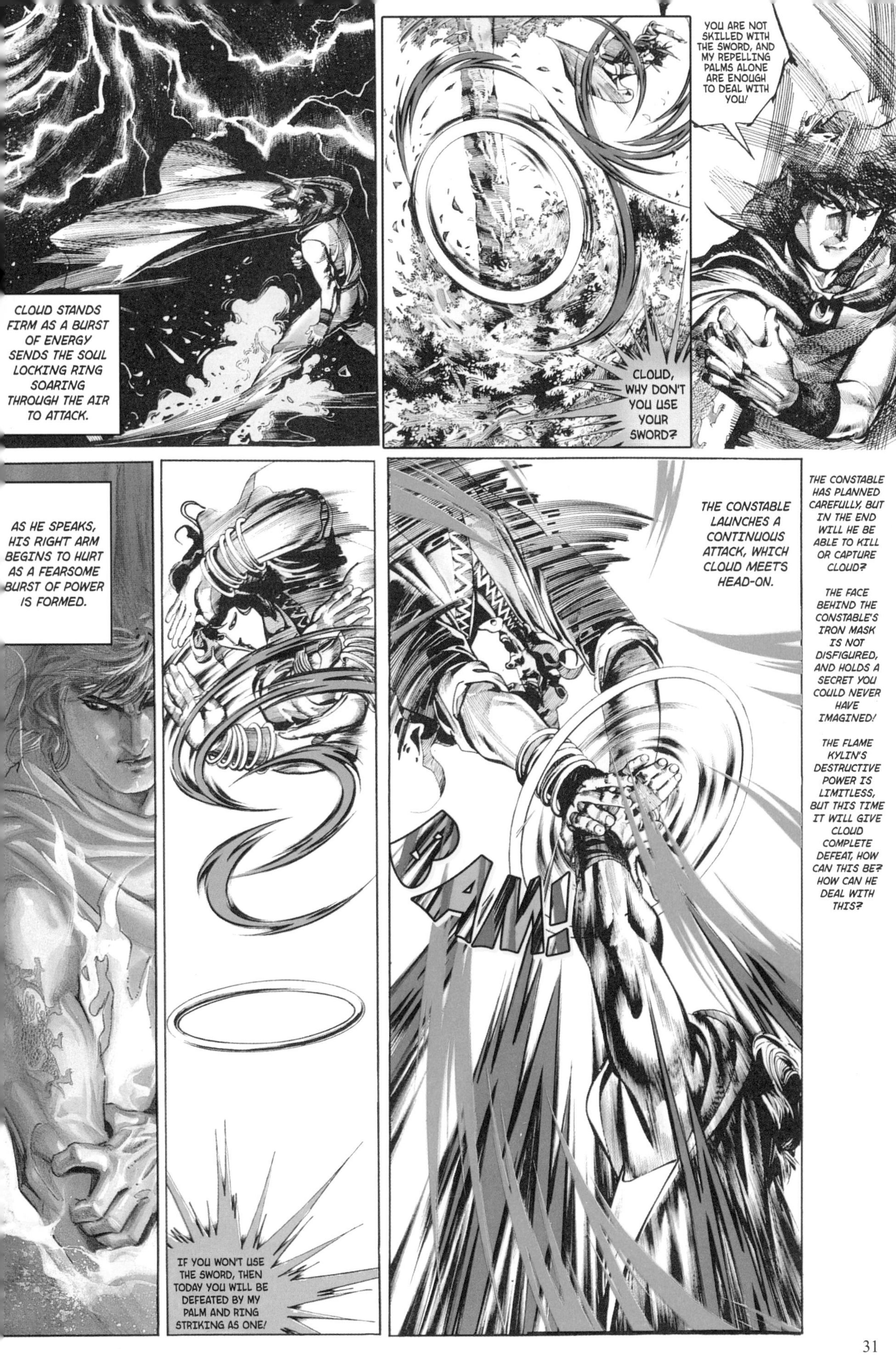
CLOUD STANDS FIRM AS A BURST OF ENERGY SENDS THE SOUL LOCKING RING SOARING THROUGH THE AIR TO ATTACK.
CLOUD, WHY DON'T YOU USE YOUR SWORD?
YOU ARE NOT SKILLED WITH THE SWORD, AND MY REPELLING PALMS ALONE ARE ENOUGH TO DEAL WITH YOU!
AS HE SPEAKS, HIS RIGHT ARM BEGINS TO HURT AS A FEARSOME BURST OF POWER IS FORMED.
IF YOU WON'T USE THE SWORD, THEN TODAY YOU WILL BE DEFEATED BY MY PALM AND RING STRIKING AS ONE!
THE CONSTABLE LAUNCHES A CONTINUOUS ATTACK, WHICH CLOUD MEETS HEAD-ON.
BAM!
THE CONSTABLE HAS PLANNED CAREFULLY, BUT IN THE END WILL HE BE ABLE TO KILL OR CAPTURE CLOUD?
THE FACE BEHIND THE CONSTABLE'S IRON MASK IS NOT DISFIGURED, AND HOLDS A SECRET YOU COULD NEVER HAVE IMAGINED!
THE FLAME KYLIN'S DESTRUCTIVE POWER IS LIMITLESS, BUT THIS TIME IT WILL GIVE CLOUD COMPLETE DEFEAT, HOW CAN THIS BE? HOW CAN HE DEAL WITH THIS?

# CHAPTER 41: THE SWORD BEHIND THE IRON MASK

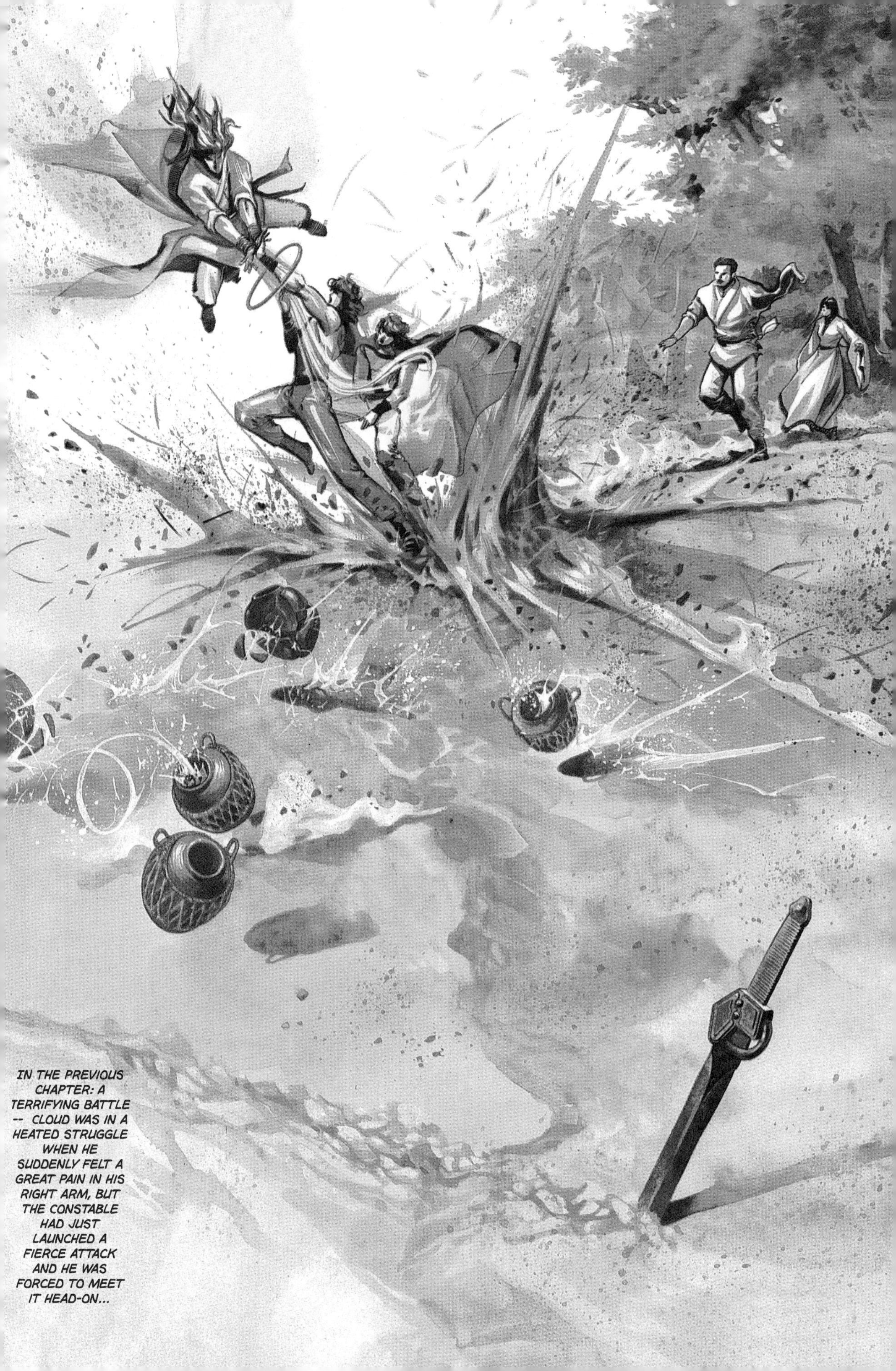
IN THE PREVIOUS CHAPTER: A TERRIFYING BATTLE -- CLOUD WAS IN A HEATED STRUGGLE WHEN HE SUDDENLY FELT A GREAT PAIN IN HIS RIGHT ARM, BUT THE CONSTABLE HAD JUST LAUNCHED A FIERCE ATTACK AND HE WAS FORCED TO MEET IT HEAD-ON...

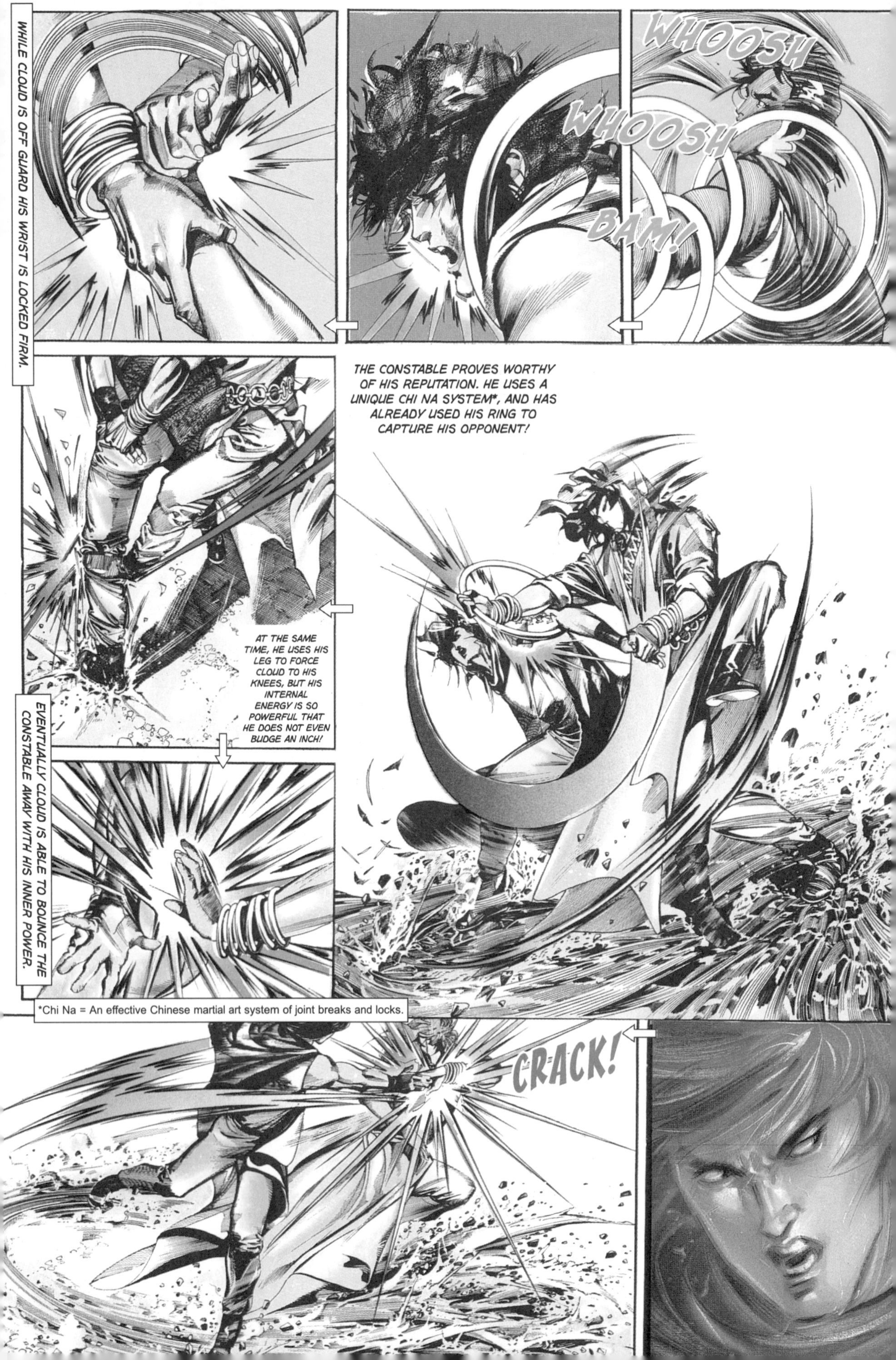
WHILE CLOUD IS OFF GUARD HIS WRIST IS LOCKED FIRM.
WHOOSH
WHOOSH
BAM!
THE CONSTABLE PROVES WORTHY OF HIS REPUTATION. HE USES A UNIQUE CHI NA SYSTEM*, AND HAS ALREADY USED HIS RING TO CAPTURE HIS OPPONENT!
AT THE SAME TIME, HE USES HIS LEG TO FORCE CLOUD TO HIS KNEES, BUT HIS INTERNAL ENERGY IS SO POWERFUL THAT HE DOES NOT EVEN BUDGE AN INCH!
EVENTUALLY CLOUD IS ABLE TO BOUNCE THE CONSTABLE AWAY WITH HIS INNER POWER.
*Chi Na = An effective Chinese martial art system of joint breaks and locks.
CRACK!

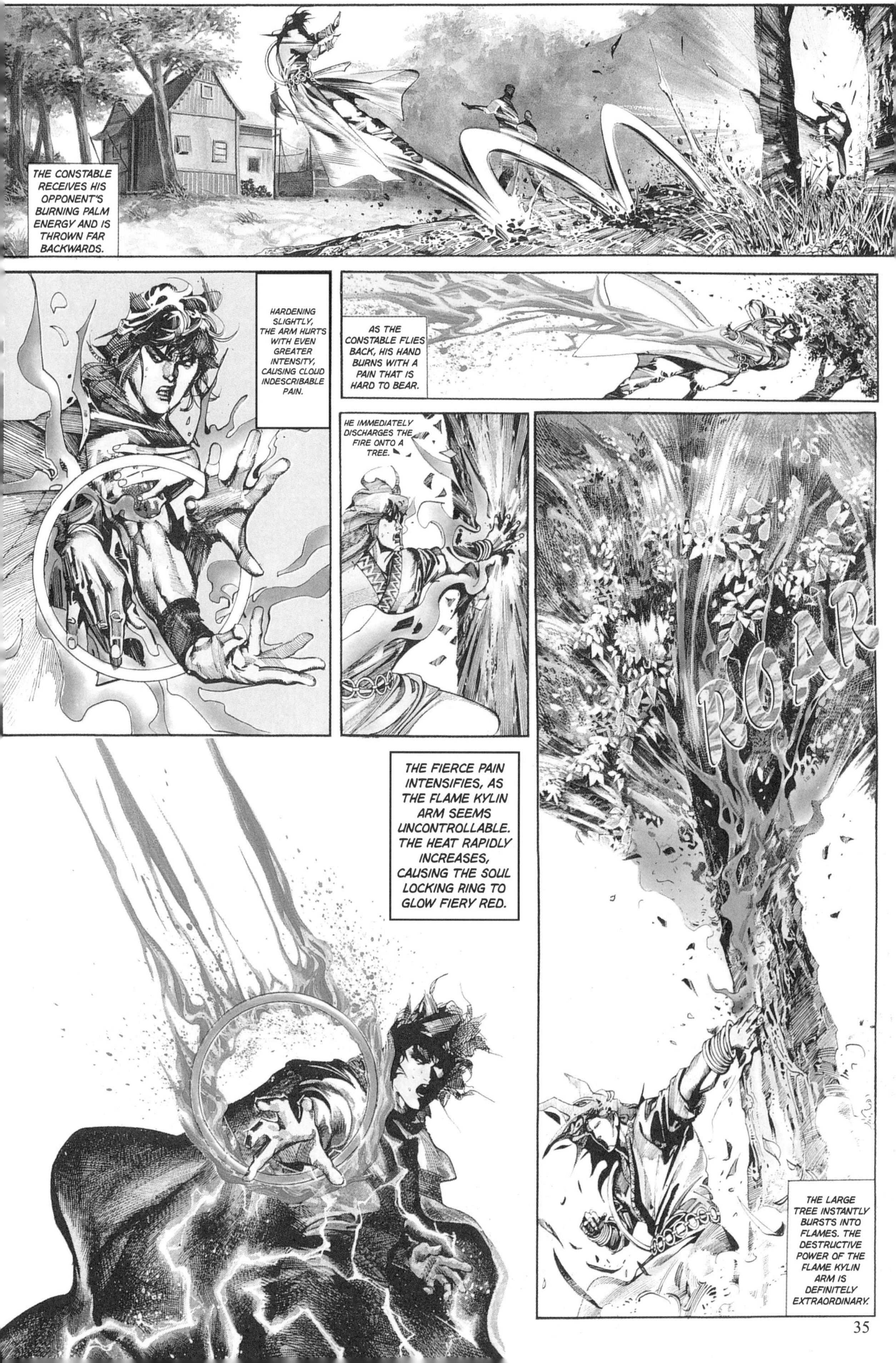
THE CONSTABLE RECEIVES HIS OPPONENT'S BURNING PALM ENERGY AND IS THROWN FAR BACKWARDS.
HARDENING SLIGHTLY, THE ARM HURTS WITH EVEN GREATER INTENSITY, CAUSING CLOUD INDESCRIBABLE PAIN.
AS THE CONSTABLE FLIES BACK, HIS HAND BURNS WITH A PAIN THAT IS HARD TO BEAR.
HE IMMEDIATELY DISCHARGES THE FIRE ONTO A TREE.
ROAR
THE LARGE TREE INSTANTLY BURSTS INTO FLAMES. THE DESTRUCTIVE POWER OF THE FLAME KYLIN ARM IS DEFINITELY EXTRAORDINARY.
THE FIERCE PAIN INTENSIFIES, AS THE FLAME KYLIN ARM SEEMS UNCONTROLLABLE. THE HEAT RAPIDLY INCREASES, CAUSING THE SOUL LOCKING RING TO GLOW FIERY RED.

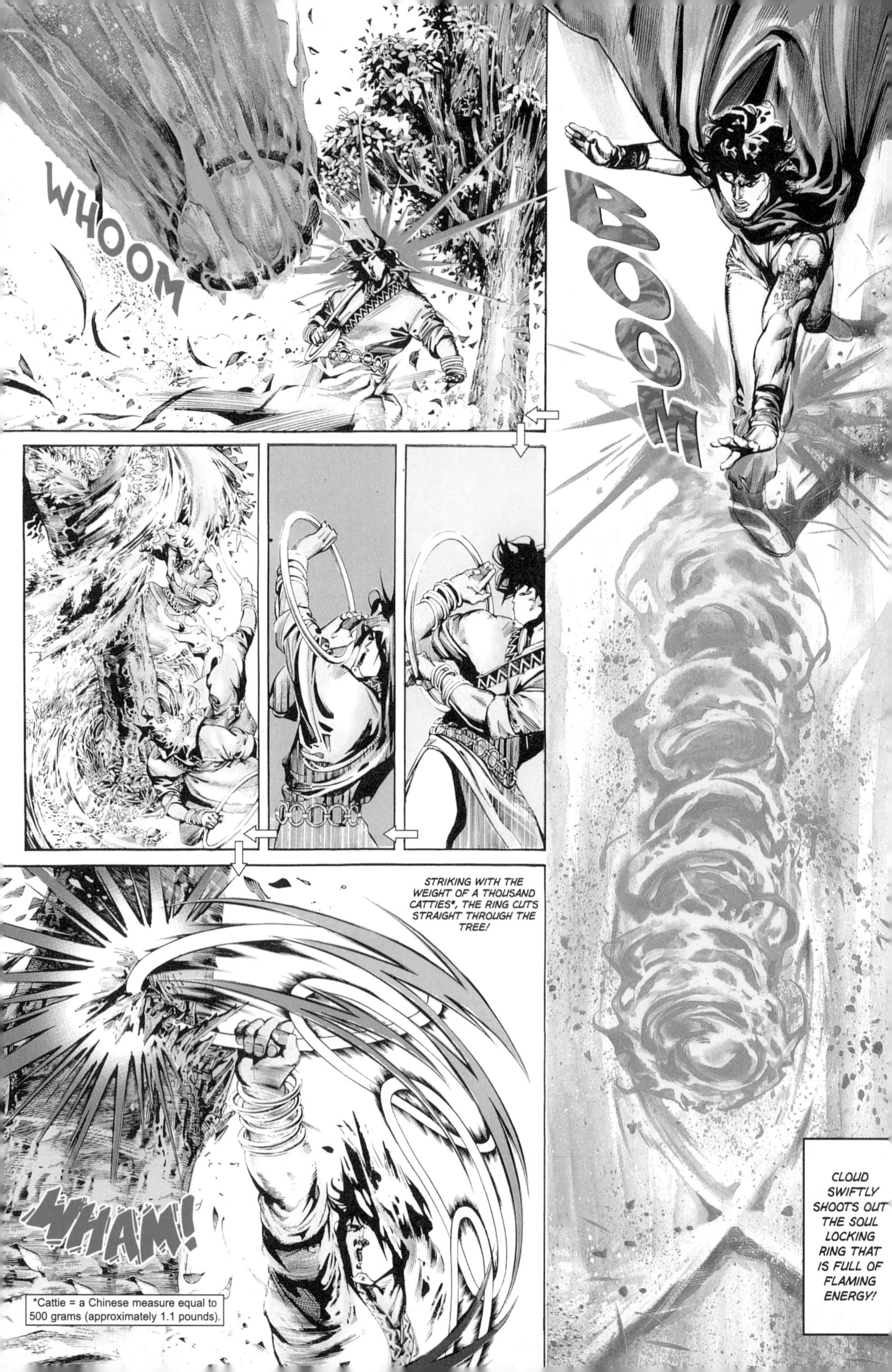
BOOM
CLOUD SWIFTLY SHOOTS OUT THE SOUL LOCKING RING THAT IS FULL OF FLAMING ENERGY!
WHOOM
STRIKING WITH THE WEIGHT OF A THOUSAND CATTIES*, THE RING CUTS STRAIGHT THROUGH THE TREE!
WHAM!

*Cattie = a Chinese measure equal to 500 grams (approximately 1.1 pounds).

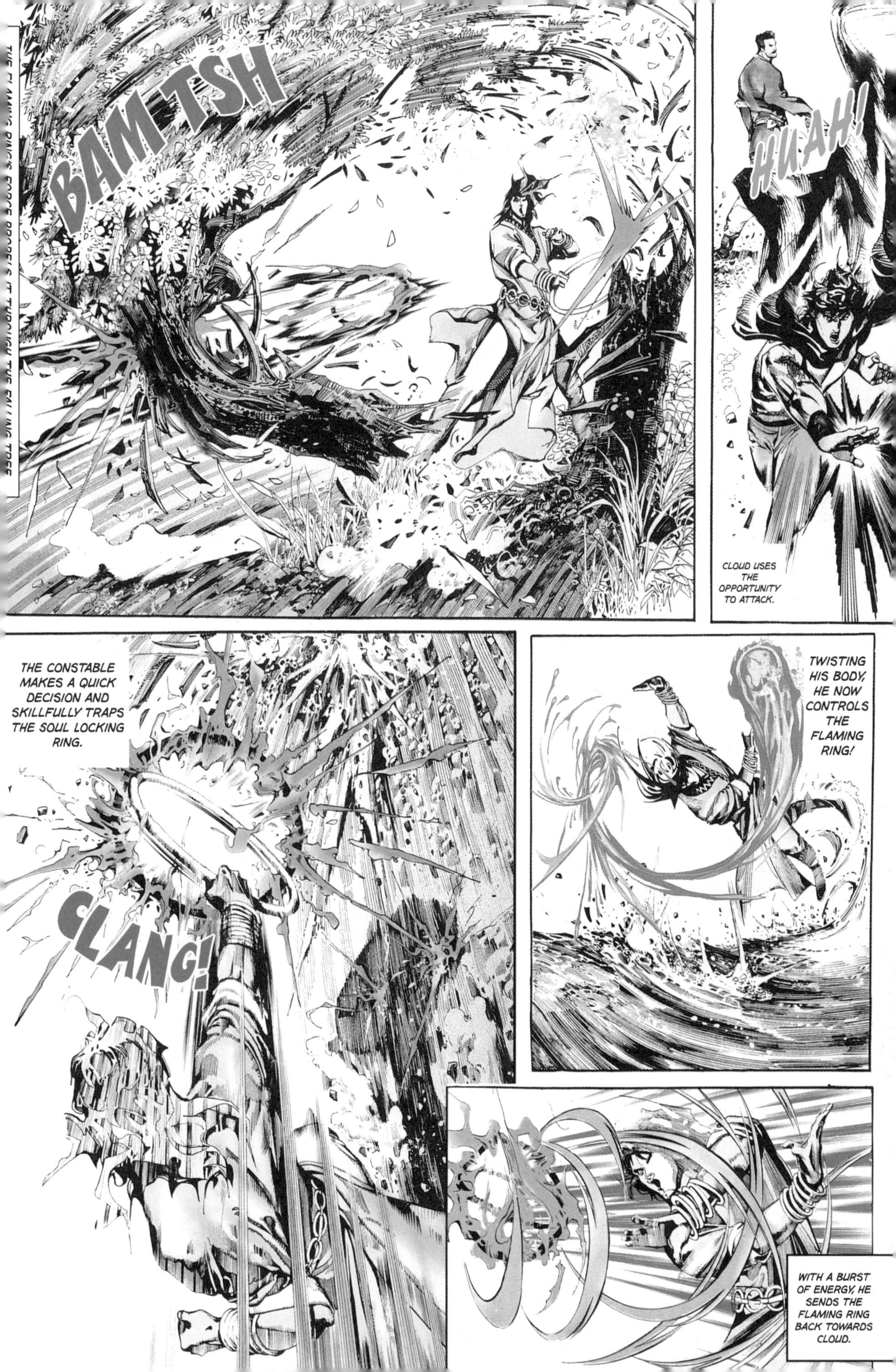
THE FLAMING RING'S FORCE PROPELS IT THROUGH THE FALLING TREE
BAM TSH
HUAH!
CLOUD USES THE OPPORTUNITY TO ATTACK.
THE CONSTABLE MAKES A QUICK DECISION AND SKILLFULLY TRAPS THE SOUL LOCKING RING.
CLANG!
TWISTING HIS BODY, HE NOW CONTROLS THE FLAMING RING!
WITH A BURST OF ENERGY, HE SENDS THE FLAMING RING BACK TOWARDS CLOUD.

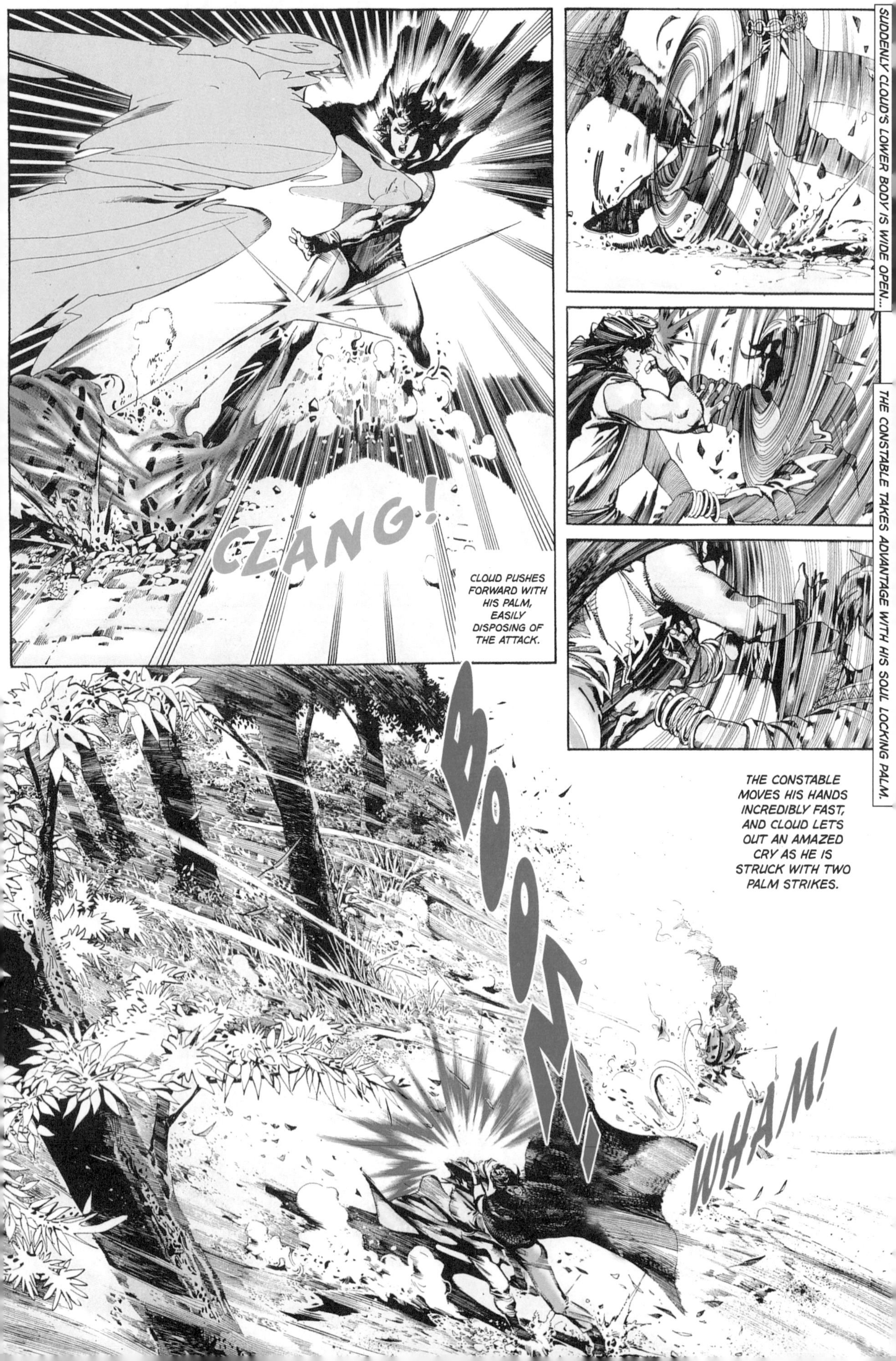
CLANG!
CLOUD PUSHES FORWARD WITH HIS PALM, EASILY DISPOSING OF THE ATTACK.
SUDDENLY CLOUD'S LOWER BODY IS WIDE OPEN...
THE CONSTABLE TAKES ADVANTAGE WITH HIS SOUL LOCKING PALM.
THE CONSTABLE MOVES HIS HANDS INCREDIBLY FAST, AND CLOUD LETS OUT AN AMAZED CRY AS HE IS STRUCK WITH TWO PALM STRIKES.
BOOOM!
WHAM!

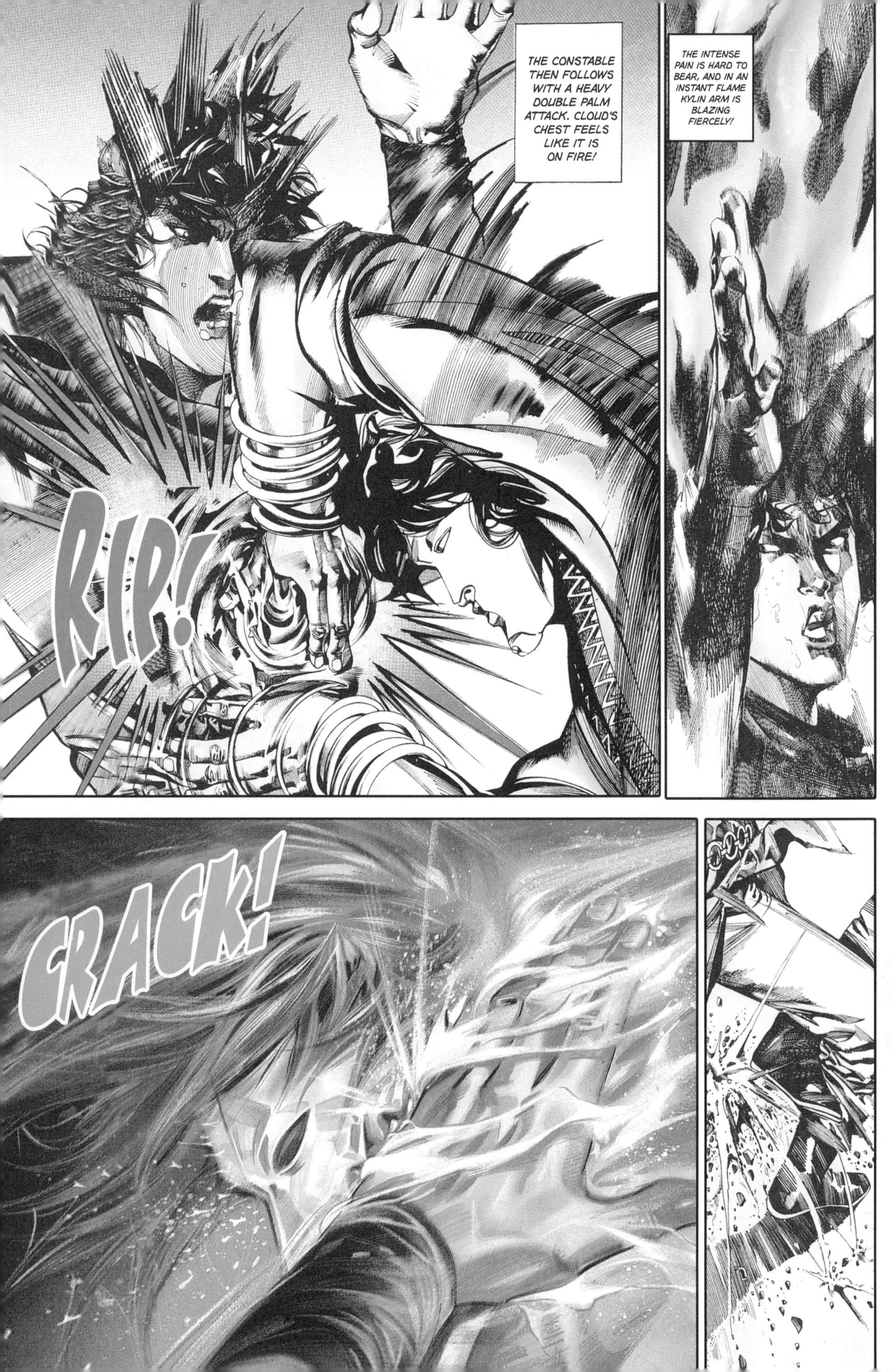
THE CONSTABLE THEN FOLLOWS WITH A HEAVY DOUBLE PALM ATTACK. CLOUD'S CHEST FEELS LIKE IT IS ON FIRE!
THE INTENSE PAIN IS HARD TO BEAR, AND IN AN INSTANT FLAME KYLIN ARM IS BLAZING FIERCELY!
RIP!
CRACK!

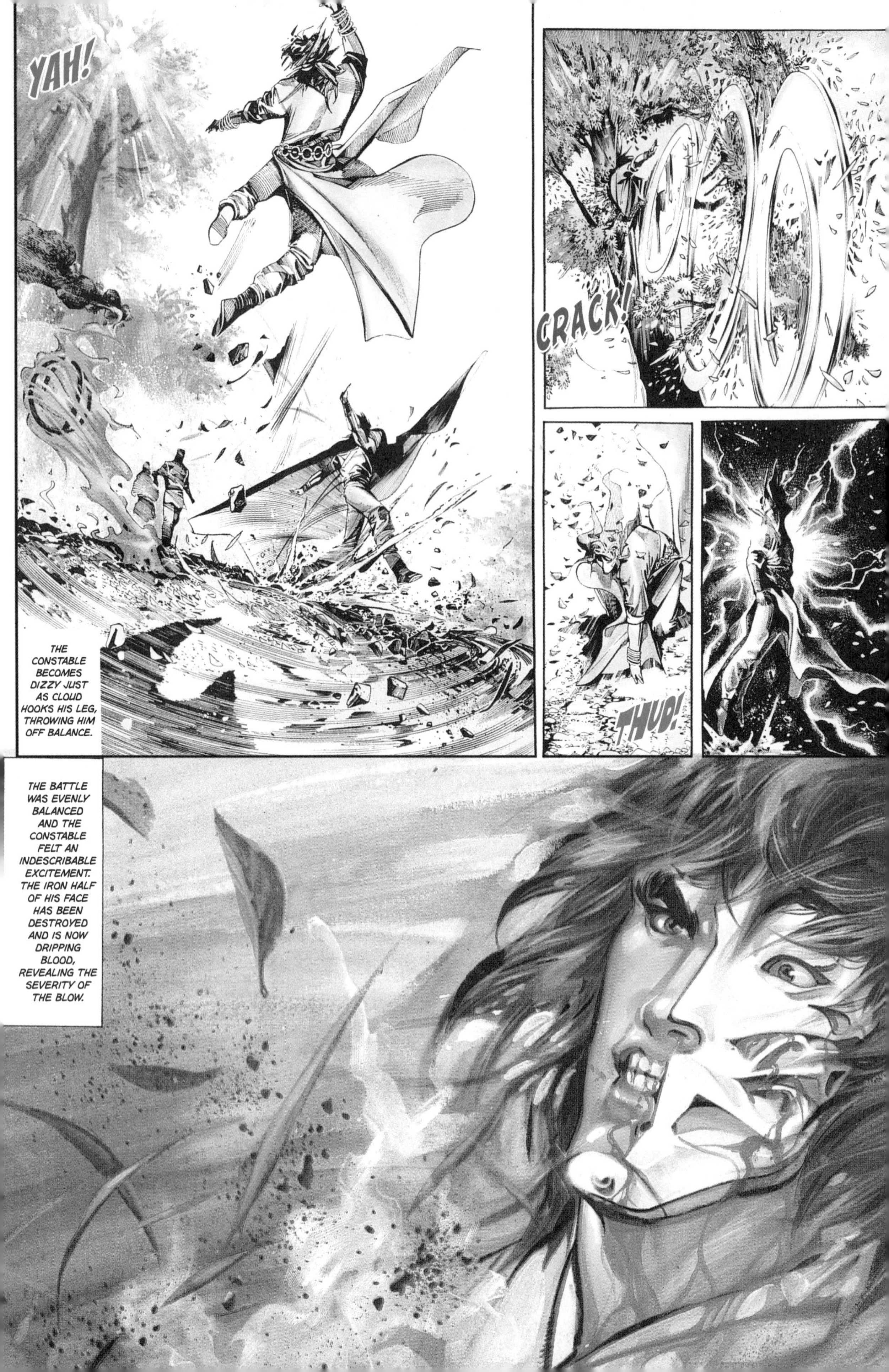
YAH!
CRACK!
THE CONSTABLE BECOMES DIZZY JUST AS CLOUD HOOKS HIS LEG, THROWING HIM OFF BALANCE.
THUD!
THE BATTLE WAS EVENLY BALANCED AND THE CONSTABLE FELT AN INDESCRIBABLE EXCITEMENT. THE IRON HALF OF HIS FACE HAS BEEN DESTROYED AND IS NOW DRIPPING BLOOD, REVEALING THE SEVERITY OF THE BLOW.

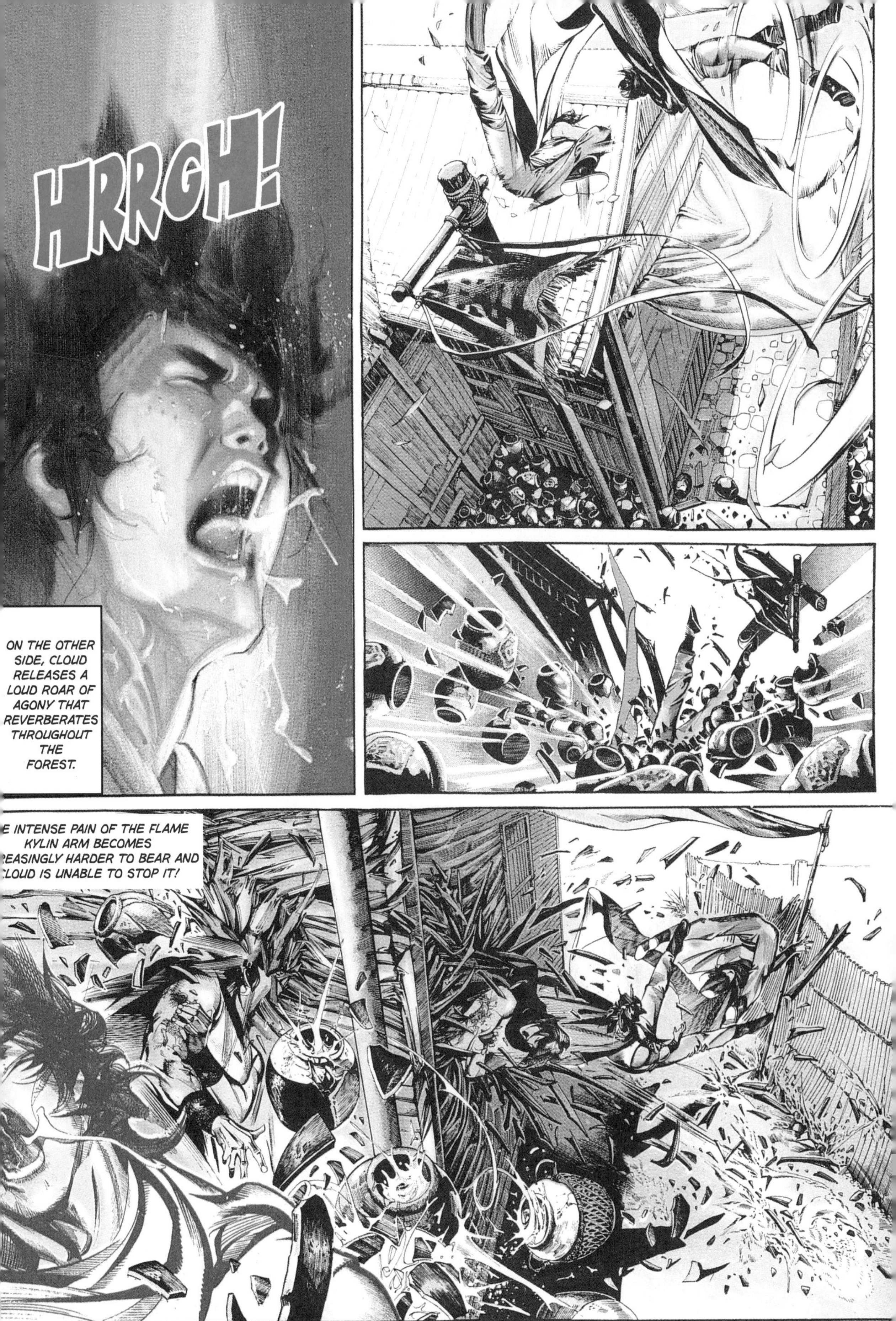
HRRGH!
ON THE OTHER SIDE, CLOUD RELEASES A LOUD ROAR OF AGONY THAT REVERBERATES THROUGHOUT THE FOREST.
E INTENSE PAIN OF THE FLAME KYLIN ARM BECOMES REASINGLY HARDER TO BEAR AND CLOUD IS UNABLE TO STOP IT!

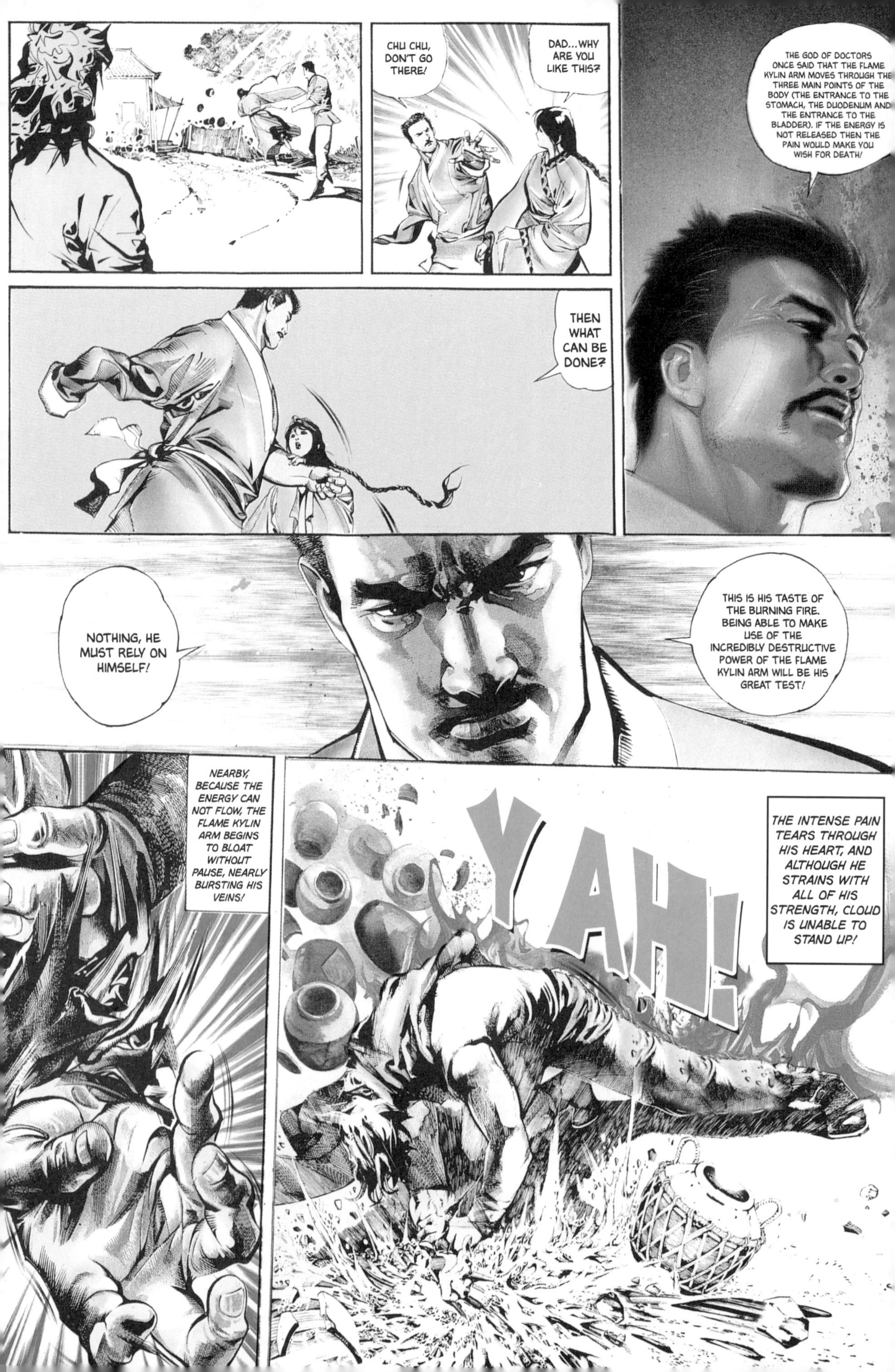
CHU CHU, DON'T GO THERE!
DAD... WHY ARE YOU LIKE THIS?
THE GOD OF DOCTORS ONCE SAID THAT THE FLAME KYLIN ARM MOVES THROUGH THE THREE MAIN POINTS OF THE BODY (THE ENTRANCE TO THE STOMACH, THE DUODENUM AND THE ENTRANCE TO THE BLADDER). IF THE ENERGY IS NOT RELEASED THEN THE PAIN WOULD MAKE YOU WISH FOR DEATH!
THEN WHAT CAN BE DONE?
NOTHING, HE MUST RELY ON HIMSELF!
THIS IS HIS TASTE OF THE BURNING FIRE. BEING ABLE TO MAKE USE OF THE INCREDIBLY DESTRUCTIVE POWER OF THE FLAME KYLIN ARM WILL BE HIS GREAT TEST!
NEARBY, BECAUSE THE ENERGY CAN NOT FLOW, THE FLAME KYLIN ARM BEGINS TO BLOAT WITHOUT PAUSE, NEARLY BURSTING HIS VEINS!
YAH!
THE INTENSE PAIN TEARS THROUGH HIS HEART, AND ALTHOUGH HE STRAINS WITH ALL OF HIS STRENGTH, CLOUD IS UNABLE TO STAND UP!

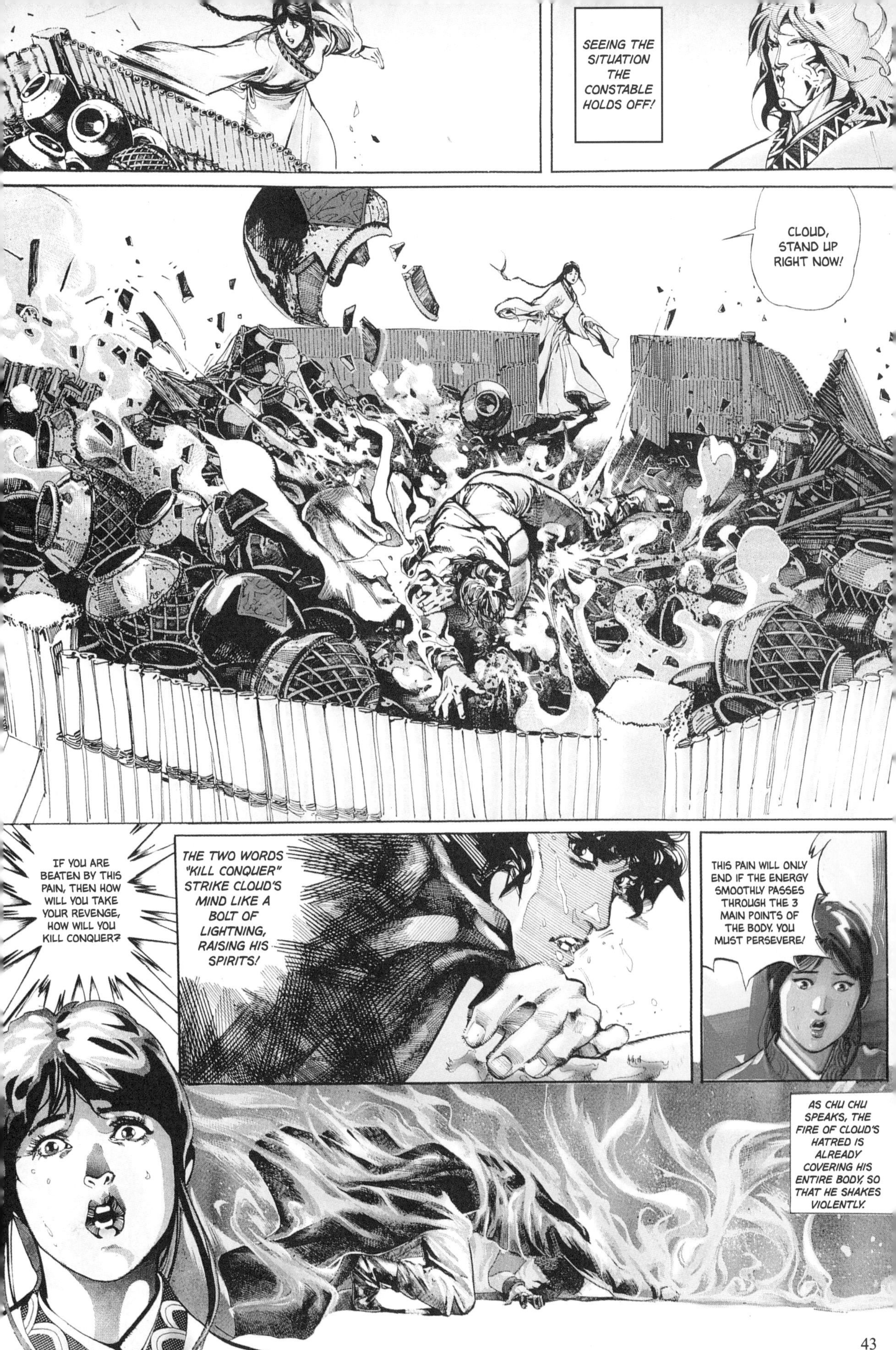

SEEING THE SITUATION THE CONSTABLE HOLDS OFF!
CLOUD, STAND UP RIGHT NOW!
IF YOU ARE BEATEN BY THIS PAIN, THEN HOW WILL YOU TAKE YOUR REVENGE, HOW WILL YOU KILL CONQUER?
THE TWO WORDS "KILL CONQUER" STRIKE CLOUD'S MIND LIKE A BOLT OF LIGHTNING, RAISING HIS SPIRITS!
THIS PAIN WILL ONLY END IF THE ENERGY SMOOTHLY PASSES THROUGH THE 3 MAIN POINTS OF THE BODY. YOU MUST PERSEVERE!
AS CHU CHU SPEAKS, THE FIRE OF CLOUD'S HATRED IS ALREADY COVERING HIS ENTIRE BODY, SO THAT HE SHAKES VIOLENTLY.

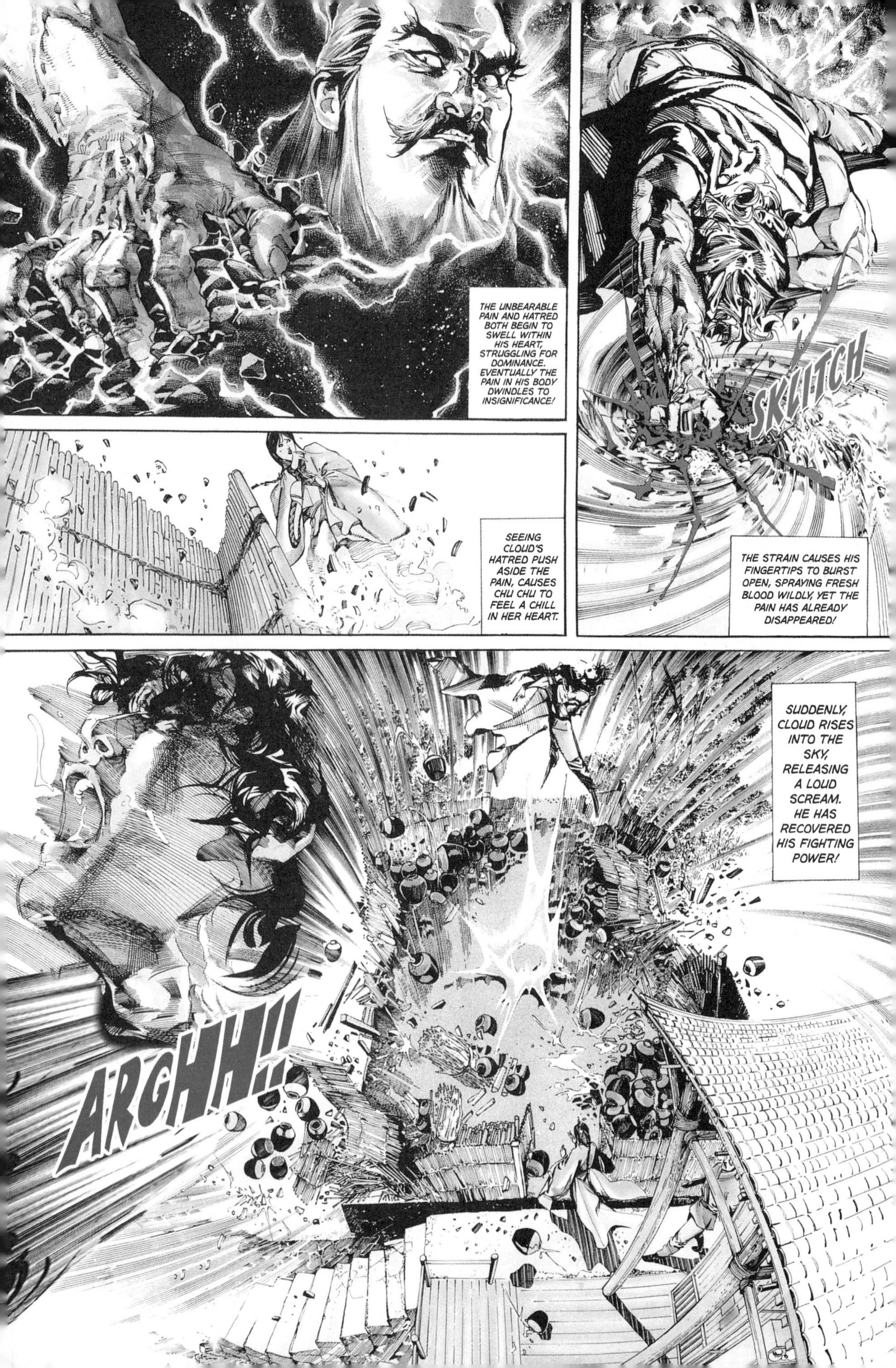
THE UNBEARABLE PAIN AND HATRED BOTH BEGIN TO SWELL WITHIN HIS HEART, STRUGGLING FOR DOMINANCE. EVENTUALLY THE PAIN IN HIS BODY DWINDLES TO INSIGNIFICANCE!
SKLITCH
SEEING CLOUD'S HATRED PUSH ASIDE THE PAIN, CAUSES CHU CHU TO FEEL A CHILL IN HER HEART.
THE STRAIN CAUSES HIS FINGERTIPS TO BURST OPEN, SPRAYING FRESH BLOOD WILDLY, YET THE PAIN HAS ALREADY DISAPPEARED!
SUDDENLY, CLOUD RISES INTO THE SKY, RELEASING A LOUD SCREAM. HE HAS RECOVERED HIS FIGHTING POWER!
ARGHH!!

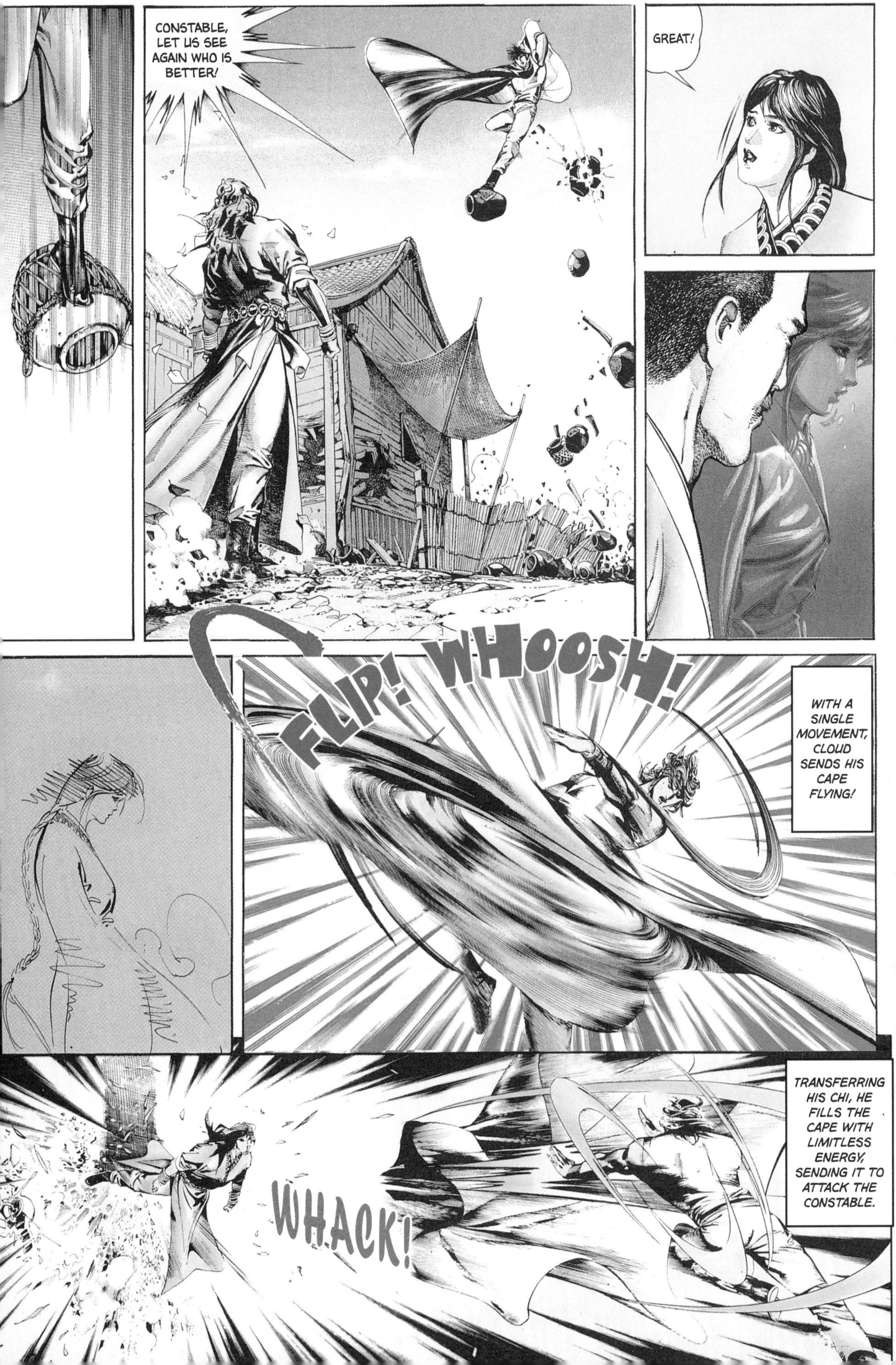
CONSTABLE, LET US SEE AGAIN WHO IS BETTER!
GREAT!
FLIP! WHOOSH!
WITH A SINGLE MOVEMENT, CLOUD SENDS HIS CAPE FLYING!
TRANSFERRING HIS CHI, HE FILLS THE CAPE WITH LIMITLESS ENERGY, SENDING IT TO ATTACK THE CONSTABLE.
WHACK!

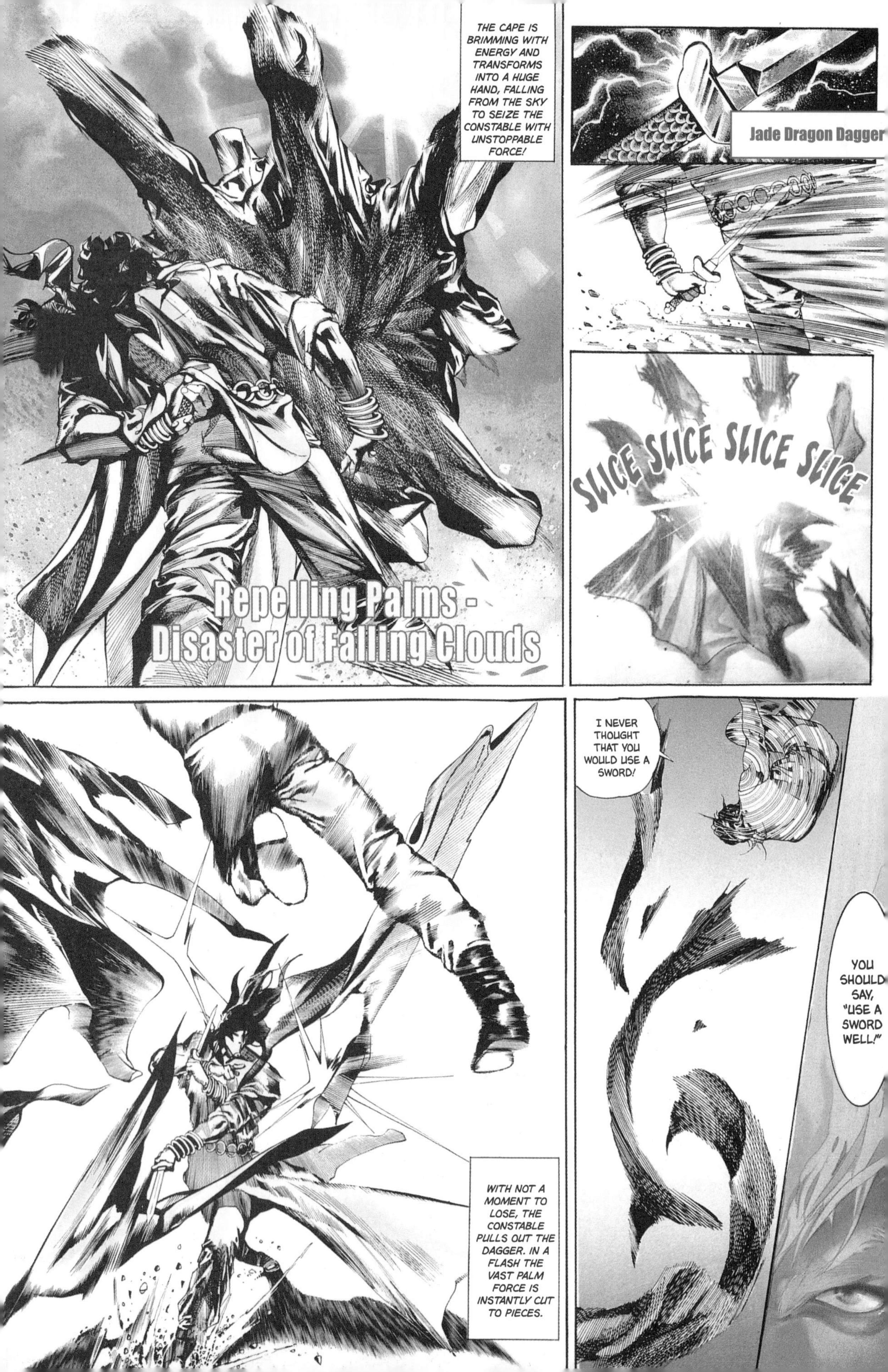
THE CAPE IS BRIMMING WITH ENERGY AND TRANSFORMS INTO A HUGE HAND, FALLING FROM THE SKY TO SEIZE THE CONSTABLE WITH UNSTOPPABLE FORCE!
Repelling Palms - Disaster of Falling Clouds
Jade Dragon Dagger
SLICE SLICE SLICE SLICE
WITH NOT A MOMENT TO LOSE, THE CONSTABLE PULLS OUT THE DAGGER. IN A FLASH THE VAST PALM FORCE IS INSTANTLY CUT TO PIECES.
I NEVER THOUGHT THAT YOU WOULD USE A SWORD!
YOU SHOULD SAY, "USE A SWORD WELL!"

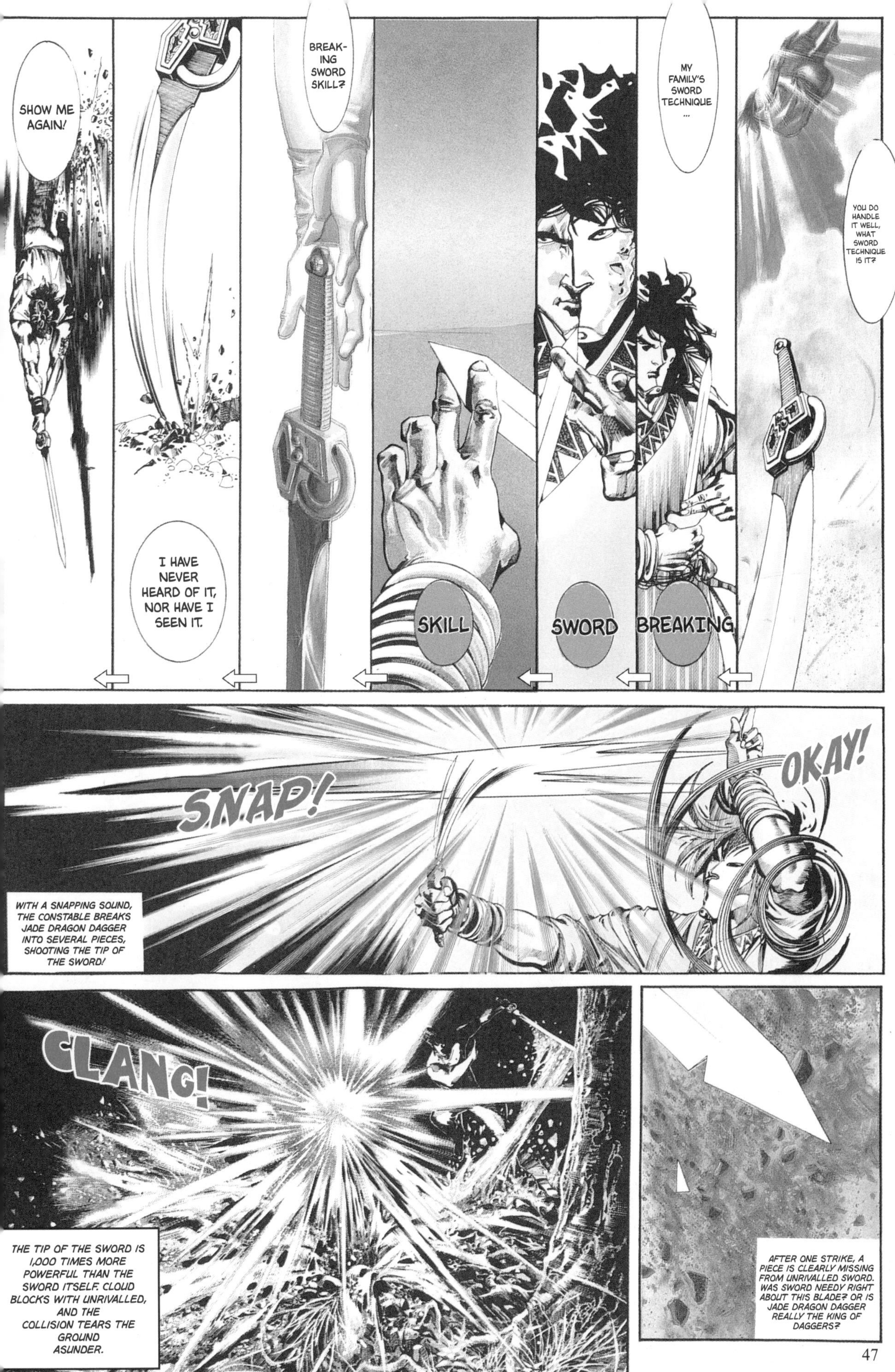
YOU DO HANDLE IT WELL, WHAT SWORD TECHNIQUE IS IT?
BREAKING
MY FAMILY'S SWORD TECHNIQUE ...
SWORD
SKILL
BREAKING SWORD SKILL?
I HAVE NEVER HEARD OF IT, NOR HAVE I SEEN IT.
SHOW ME AGAIN!
OKAY!
SNAP!
WITH A SNAPPING SOUND, THE CONSTABLE BREAKS JADE DRAGON DAGGER INTO SEVERAL PIECES, SHOOTING THE TIP OF THE SWORD!
CLANG!
THE TIP OF THE SWORD IS 1,000 TIMES MORE POWERFUL THAN THE SWORD ITSELF. CLOUD BLOCKS WITH UNRIVALLED, AND THE COLLISION TEARS THE GROUND ASUNDER.
AFTER ONE STRIKE, A PIECE IS CLEARLY MISSING FROM UNRIVALLED SWORD. WAS SWORD NEEDY RIGHT ABOUT THIS BLADE? OR IS JADE DRAGON DAGGER REALLY THE KING OF DAGGERS?

CLOUD! WHEN THE STRONGEST SWORDSMAN USES HIS SWORD, THEN IT IS NECESSARY TO USE - "SEVERED LOVE SEVERED PRINCIPLE"

PREPARE YOURSELF!

Severed Love Severed Principle

AS THE CONSTABLE SPEAKS HE LAUNCHED THE ATTACK

WITH A SINGLE STRIKE, THE SWORD ENERGY SLICES THROUGH EVERYTHING WITHIN RANGE!

"SEVERED LOVE SEVERED PRINCIPLE" IS LIKE A ROARING WAVE SURGING TOWARDS CLOUD. YET, HE MOVES HIS SWORD IN A COMPLETE CIRCLE IN ORDER TO BLOCK THE ATTACK!

THIS IS THE CONSTABLE'S TECHNIQUE THAT KILLS WITHOUT FAIL! HE HAS PRACTICED IT FOR A LONG TIME, BUT HAD HOPED THAT HE WOULD NEVER HAVE TO USE IT, FOR A REASON THAT HE CAN NOT TELL OTHERS!

THE SWORD ENERGY IS AS POWERFUL AS MOUNTAIN SO YU AND CHU CHU FLEE TO SAFETY!

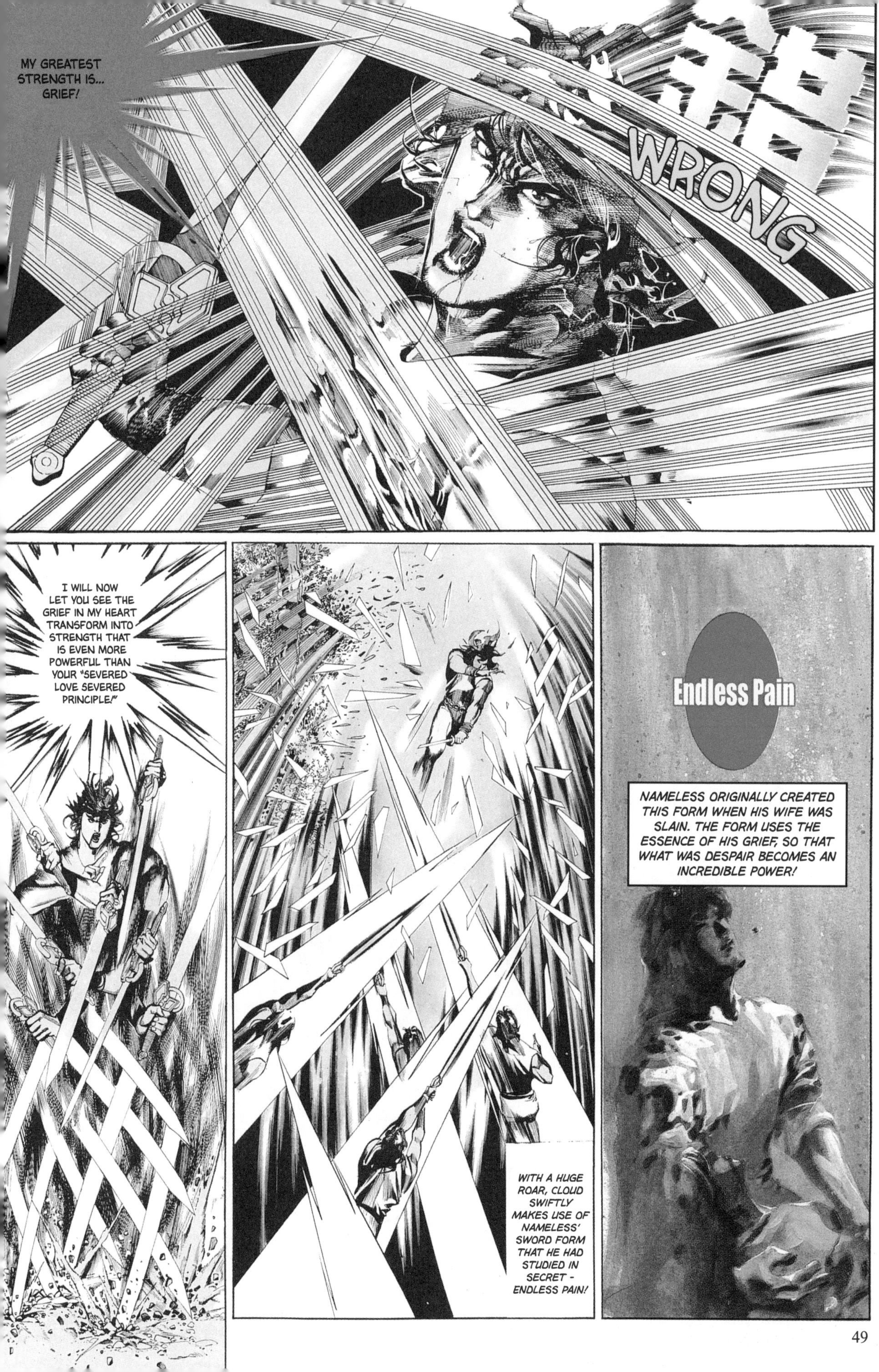
MY GREATEST STRENGTH IS... GRIEF!
WRONG
I WILL NOW LET YOU SEE THE GRIEF IN MY HEART TRANSFORM INTO STRENGTH THAT IS EVEN MORE POWERFUL THAN YOUR "SEVERED LOVE SEVERED PRINCIPLE!"
WITH A HUGE ROAR, CLOUD SWIFTLY MAKES USE OF NAMELESS' SWORD FORM THAT HE HAD STUDIED IN SECRET - ENDLESS PAIN!
Endless Pain
NAMELESS ORIGINALLY CREATED THIS FORM WHEN HIS WIFE WAS SLAIN. THE FORM USES THE ESSENCE OF HIS GRIEF, SO THAT WHAT WAS DESPAIR BECOMES AN INCREDIBLE POWER!

CLOUD HAS BEEN PRACTICING THIS FORM SINCE HE WAS TEN, AND HAS GAINED FULL MASTERY. A LIFETIME OF SADNESS, THE DEATH OF HIS MASTER, LOSING KONG CHI... HIS GRIEF IS NOW AT ITS PEAK, GREATLY INCREASING HIS DESTRUCTIVE POWER!

CLOUD PUTS ALL HIS PAIN AND TRAGEDY INTO THE ATTACK. THE FORM CREATES AN INDESCRIBABLE NET OF BLADES THAT HOME IN ON THE CONSTABLE.

AT THAT MOMENT, THE CONSTABLE SUDDENLY LOCKS EYES WITH CLOUD AND IMMEDIATELY FEELS HIS UNENDING GRIEF AND PAIN, THAT IS THE SOURCE OF CLOUD'S IMMEASURABLE POWER!

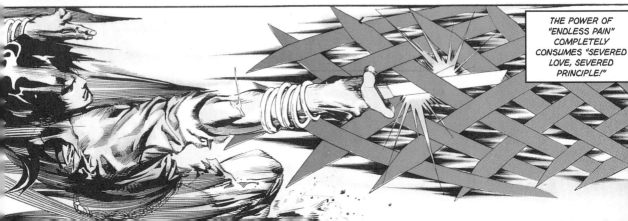

THE POWER OF "ENDLESS PAIN" COMPLETELY CONSUMES "SEVERED LOVE, SEVERED PRINCIPLE!"

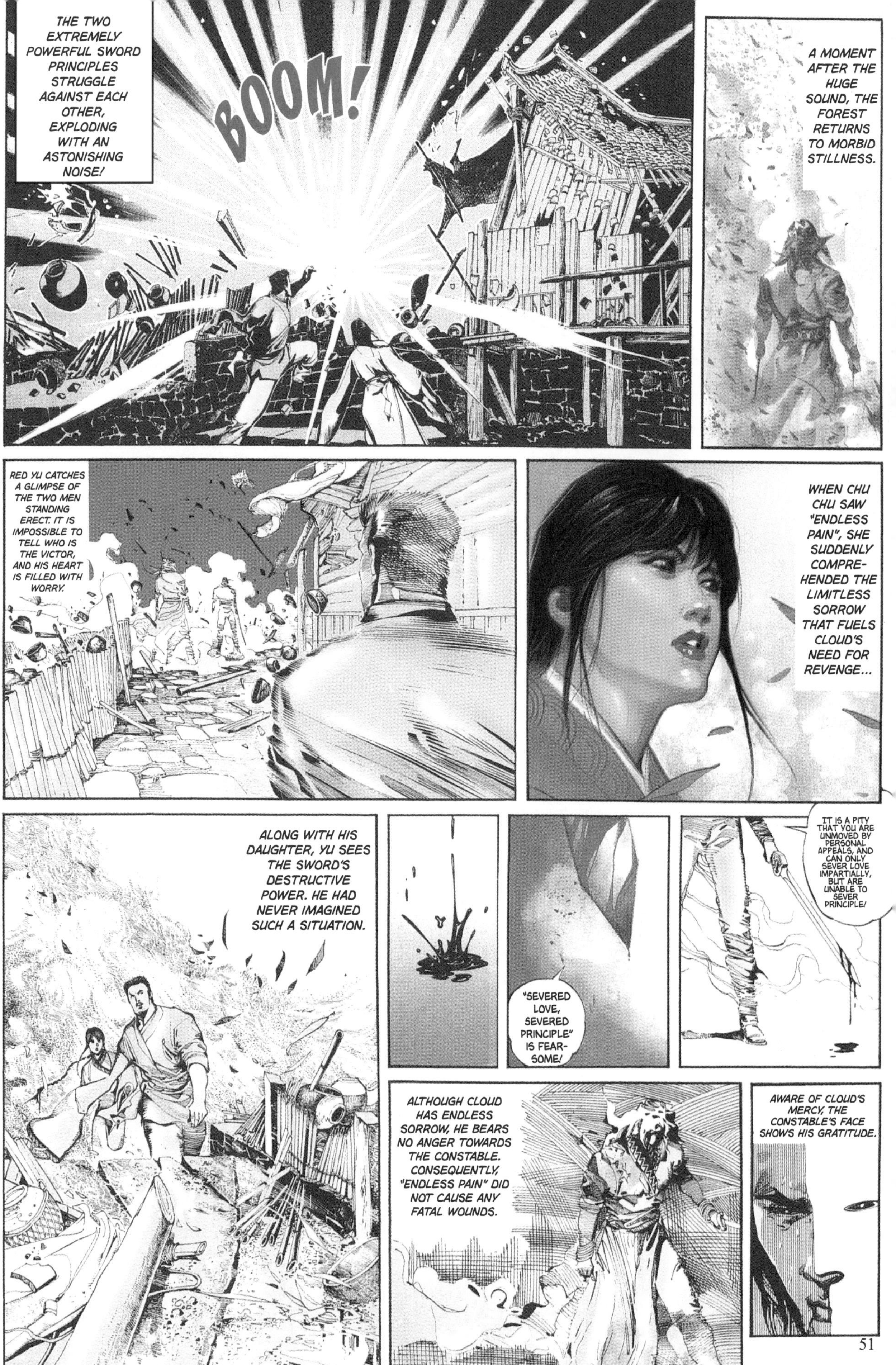
THE TWO EXTREMELY POWERFUL SWORD PRINCIPLES STRUGGLE AGAINST EACH OTHER, EXPLODING WITH AN ASTONISHING NOISE!
BOOM!
A MOMENT AFTER THE HUGE SOUND, THE FOREST RETURNS TO MORBID STILLNESS.
RED YU CATCHES A GLIMPSE OF THE TWO MEN STANDING ERECT. IT IS IMPOSSIBLE TO TELL WHO IS THE VICTOR, AND HIS HEART IS FILLED WITH WORRY.
WHEN CHU CHU SAW "ENDLESS PAIN", SHE SUDDENLY COMPRE-HENDED THE LIMITLESS SORROW THAT FUELS CLOUD'S NEED FOR REVENGE...
ALONG WITH HIS DAUGHTER, YU SEES THE SWORD'S DESTRUCTIVE POWER. HE HAD NEVER IMAGINED SUCH A SITUATION.
"SEVERED LOVE, SEVERED PRINCIPLE" IS FEAR-SOME!
IT IS A PITY THAT YOU ARE UNMOVED BY PERSONAL APPEALS, AND CAN ONLY SEVER LOVE IMPARTIALLY, BUT ARE UNABLE TO SEVER PRINCIPLE!
ALTHOUGH CLOUD HAS ENDLESS SORROW, HE BEARS NO ANGER TOWARDS THE CONSTABLE. CONSEQUENTLY, "ENDLESS PAIN" DID NOT CAUSE ANY FATAL WOUNDS.
AWARE OF CLOUD'S MERCY, THE CONSTABLE'S FACE SHOWS HIS GRATITUDE.

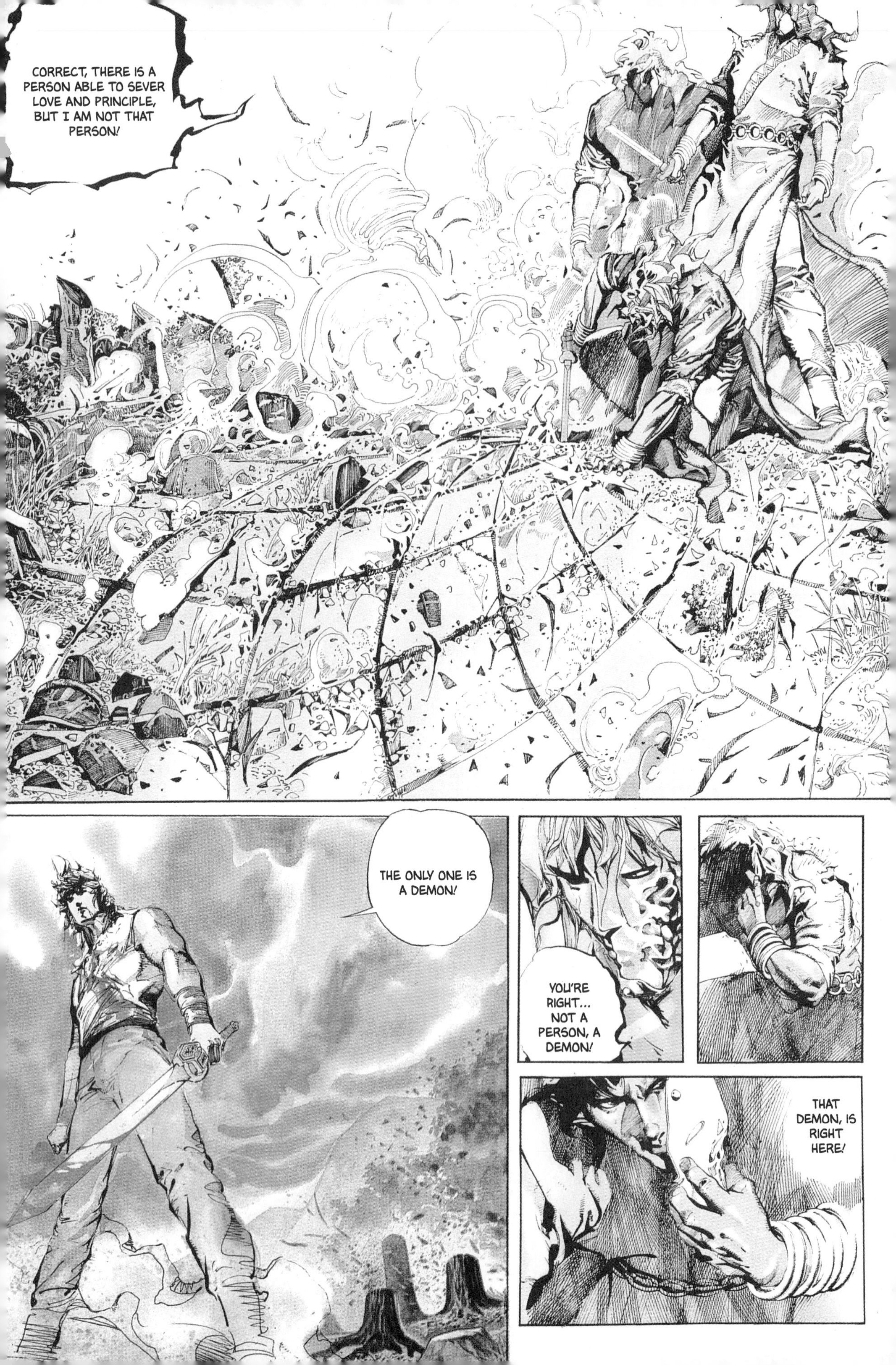
CORRECT, THERE IS A PERSON ABLE TO SEVER LOVE AND PRINCIPLE, BUT I AM NOT THAT PERSON!
THE ONLY ONE IS A DEMON!
YOU'RE RIGHT... NOT A PERSON, A DEMON!
THAT DEMON, IS RIGHT HERE!

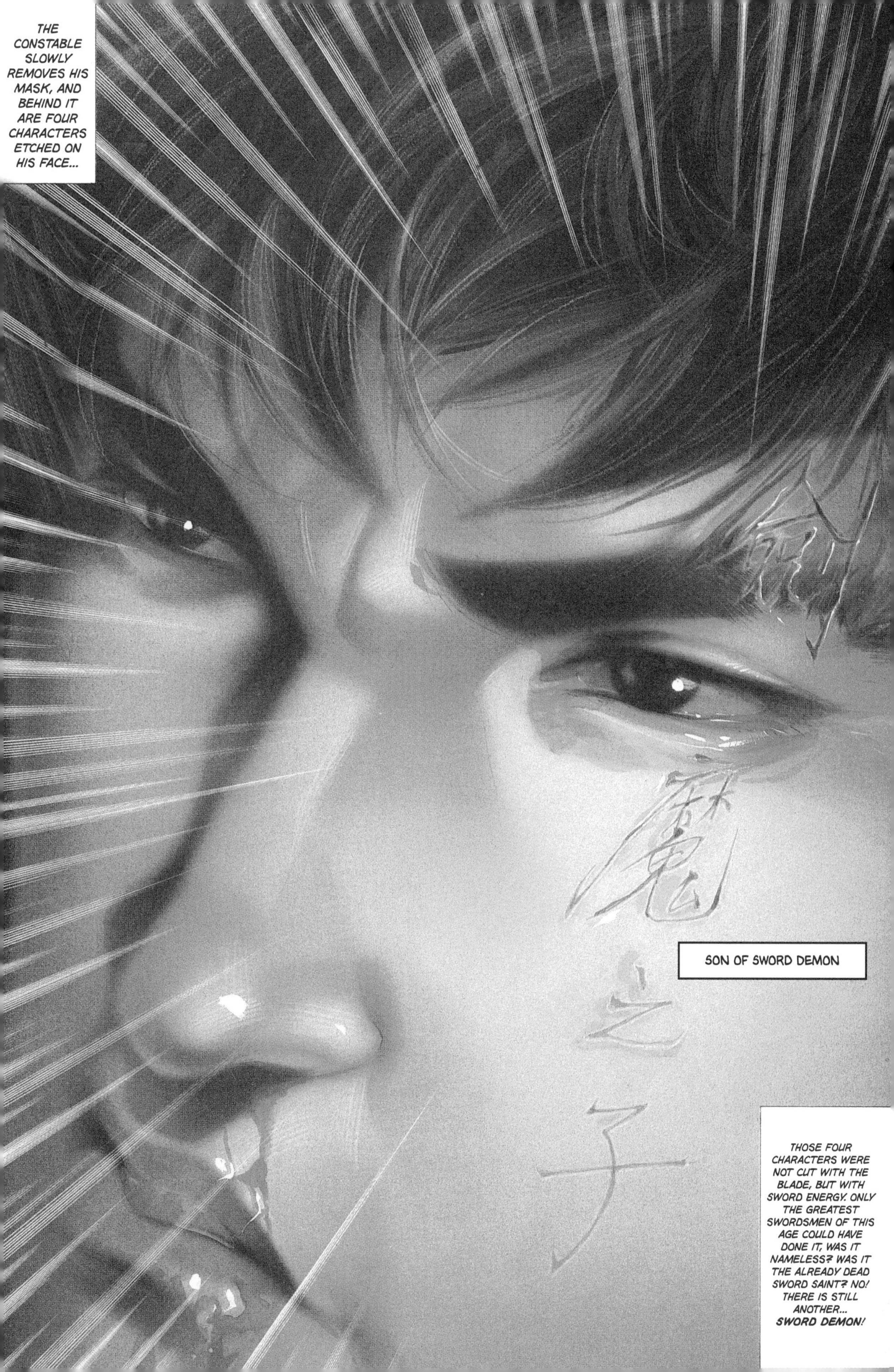
THE CONSTABLE SLOWLY REMOVES HIS MASK, AND BEHIND IT ARE FOUR CHARACTERS ETCHED ON HIS FACE...
SON OF SWORD DEMON
THOSE FOUR CHARACTERS WERE NOT CUT WITH THE BLADE, BUT WITH SWORD ENERGY. ONLY THE GREATEST SWORDSMEN OF THIS AGE COULD HAVE DONE IT, WAS IT NAMELESS? WAS IT THE ALREADY DEAD SWORD SAINT? NO! THERE IS STILL ANOTHER... SWORD DEMON!

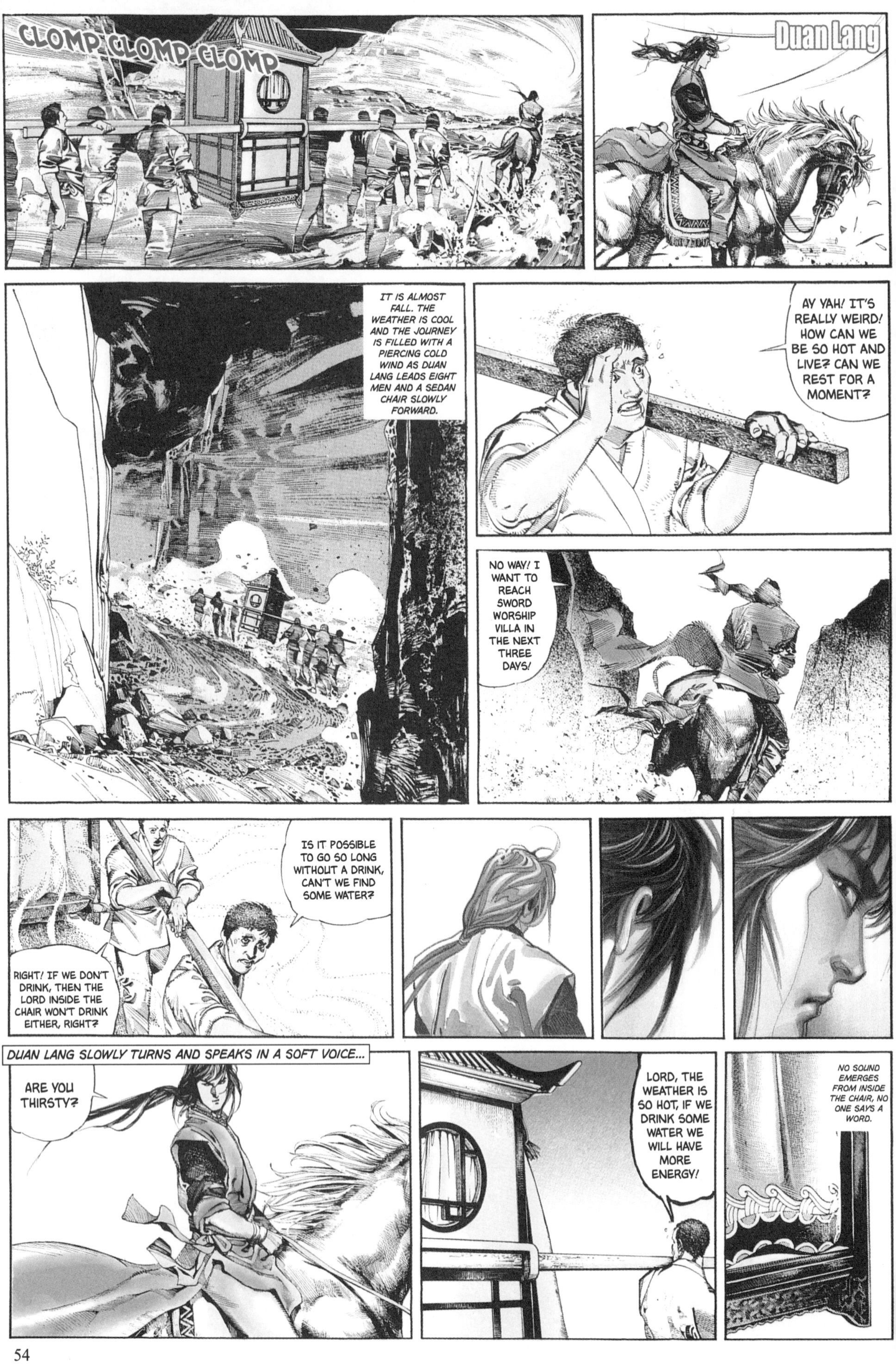
CLOMP CLOMP CLOMP
Duan Lang
IT IS ALMOST FALL. THE WEATHER IS COOL AND THE JOURNEY IS FILLED WITH A PIERCING COLD WIND AS DUAN LANG LEADS EIGHT MEN AND A SEDAN CHAIR SLOWLY FORWARD.
AY YAH! IT'S REALLY WEIRD! HOW CAN WE BE SO HOT AND LIVE? CAN WE REST FOR A MOMENT?
NO WAY! I WANT TO REACH SWORD WORSHIP VILLA IN THE NEXT THREE DAYS!
IS IT POSSIBLE TO GO SO LONG WITHOUT A DRINK, CAN'T WE FIND SOME WATER?
RIGHT! IF WE DON'T DRINK, THEN THE LORD INSIDE THE CHAIR WON'T DRINK EITHER, RIGHT?
DUAN LANG SLOWLY TURNS AND SPEAKS IN A SOFT VOICE...
ARE YOU THIRSTY?
LORD, THE WEATHER IS SO HOT, IF WE DRINK SOME WATER WE WILL HAVE MORE ENERGY!
NO SOUND EMERGES FROM INSIDE THE CHAIR, NO ONE SAYS A WORD.

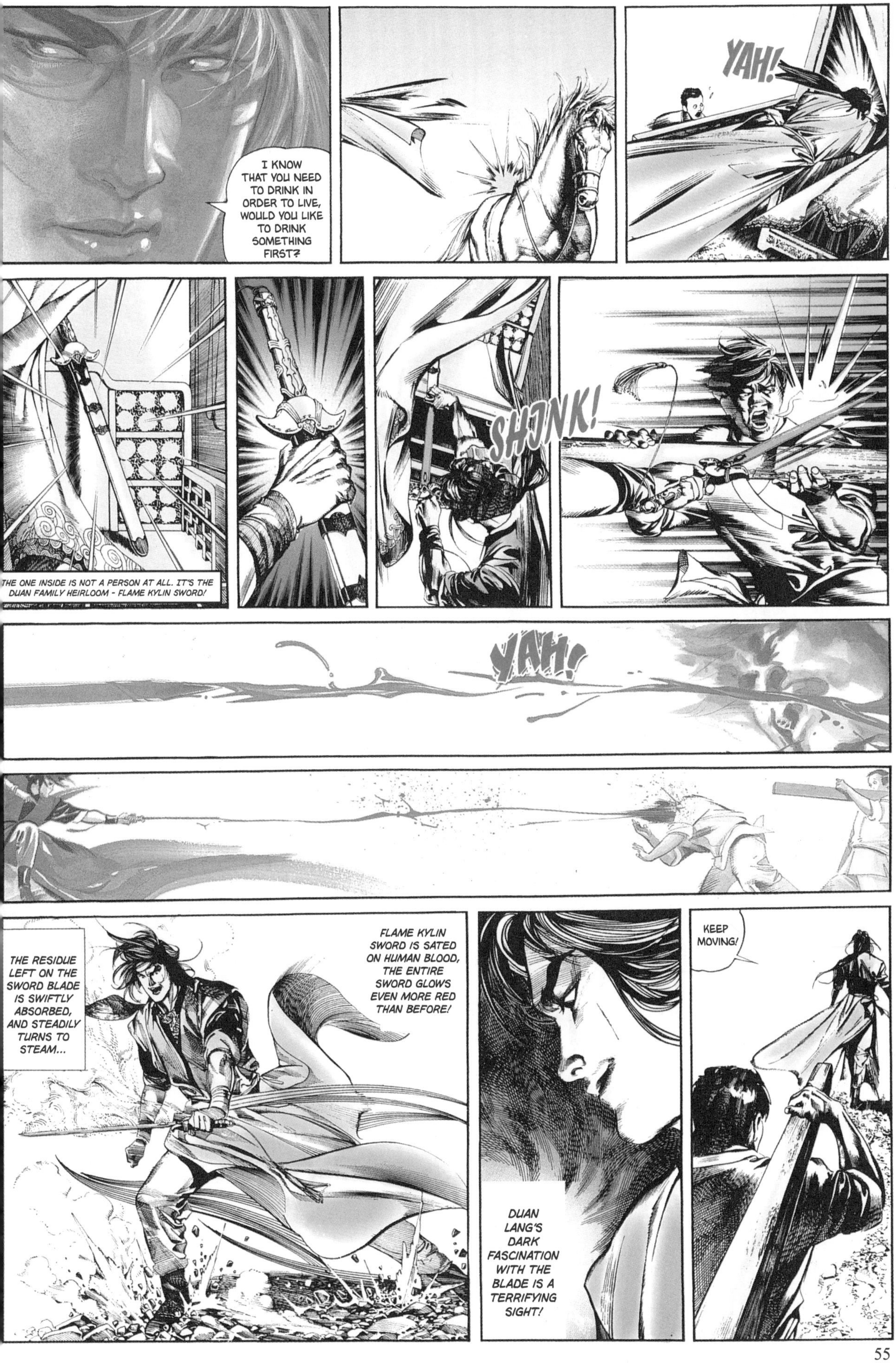
I KNOW THAT YOU NEED TO DRINK IN ORDER TO LIVE, WOULD YOU LIKE TO DRINK SOMETHING FIRST?
YAH!
THE ONE INSIDE IS NOT A PERSON AT ALL. IT'S THE DUAN FAMILY HEIRLOOM - FLAME KYLIN SWORD!
SHINK!
YAH!
THE RESIDUE LEFT ON THE SWORD BLADE IS SWIFTLY ABSORBED, AND STEADILY TURNS TO STEAM...
FLAME KYLIN SWORD IS SATED ON HUMAN BLOOD, THE ENTIRE SWORD GLOWS EVEN MORE RED THAN BEFORE!
DUAN LANG'S DARK FASCINATION WITH THE BLADE IS A TERRIFYING SIGHT!
KEEP MOVING!

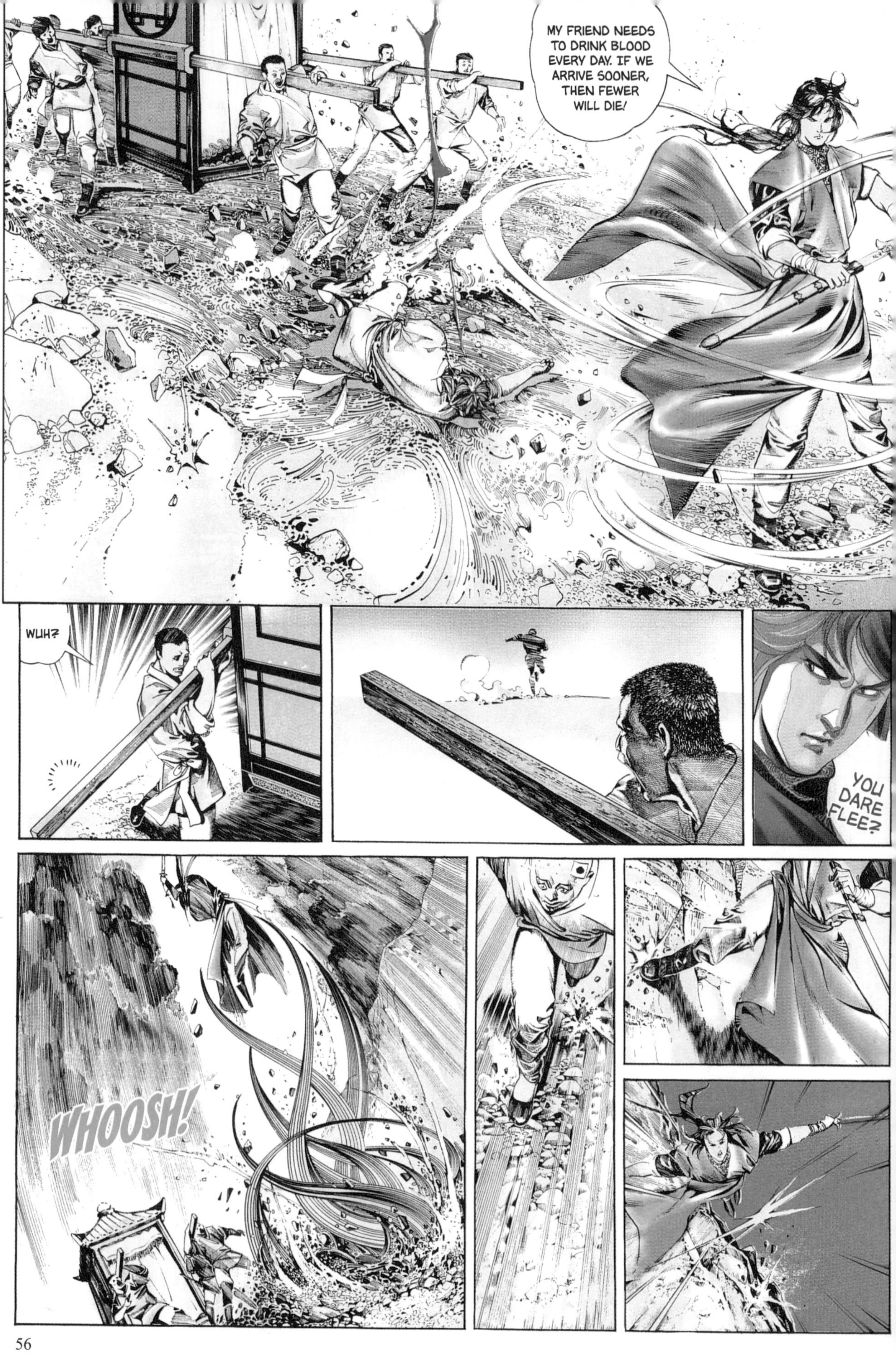
MY FRIEND NEEDS TO DRINK BLOOD EVERY DAY. IF WE ARRIVE SOONER, THEN FEWER WILL DIE!
WUH?
YOU DARE FLEE?
WHOOSH!

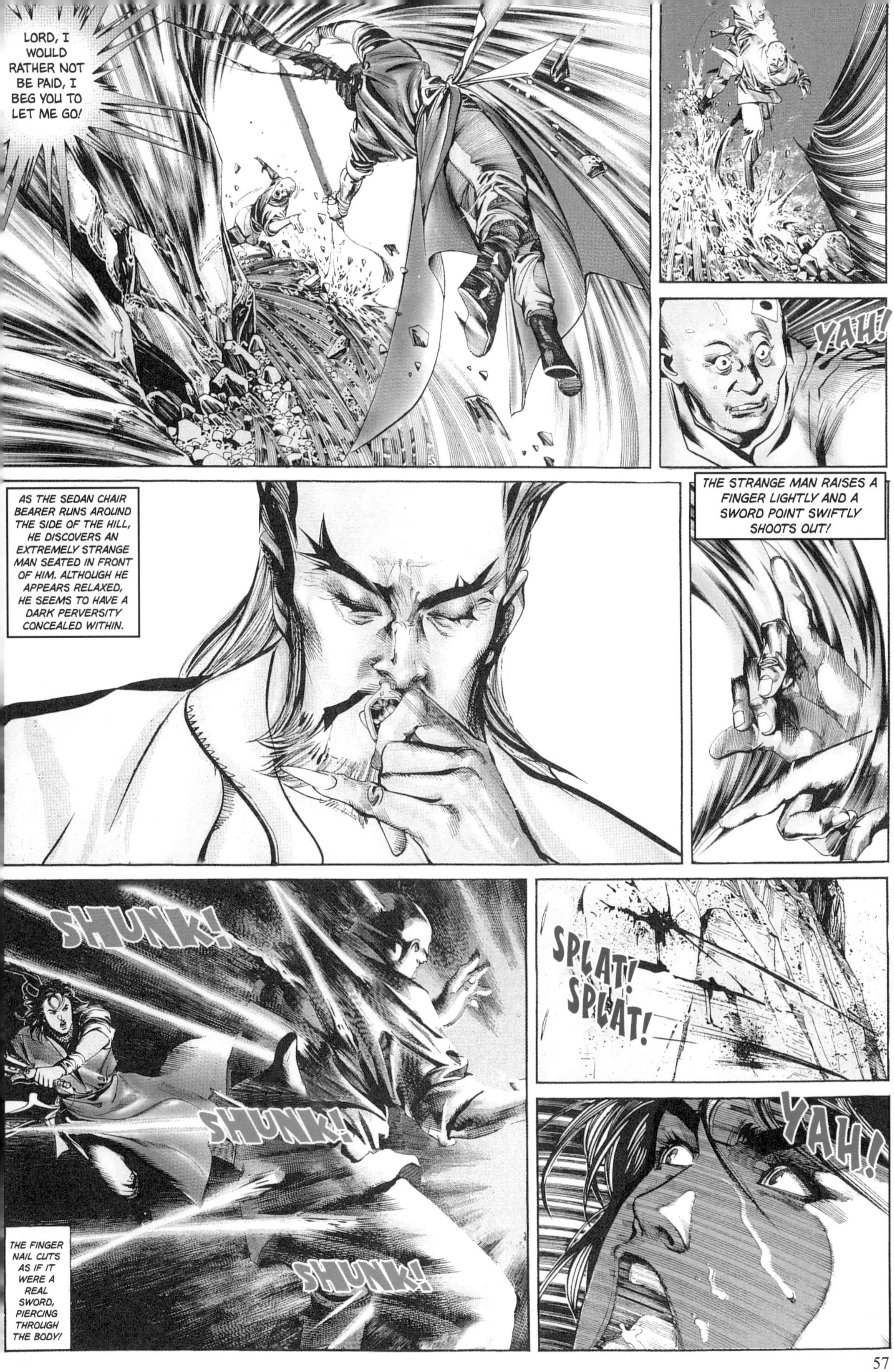

LORD, I WOULD RATHER NOT BE PAID, I BEG YOU TO LET ME GO!
YAH!
AS THE SEDAN CHAIR BEARER RUNS AROUND THE SIDE OF THE HILL, HE DISCOVERS AN EXTREMELY STRANGE MAN SEATED IN FRONT OF HIM. ALTHOUGH HE APPEARS RELAXED, HE SEEMS TO HAVE A DARK PERVERSITY CONCEALED WITHIN.
THE STRANGE MAN RAISES A FINGER LIGHTLY AND A SWORD POINT SWIFTLY SHOOTS OUT!
SHUNK!
SHUNK!
SHUNK!
THE FINGER NAIL CUTS AS IF IT WERE A REAL SWORD, PIERCING THROUGH THE BODY!
SPLAT! SPLAT!
YAH!

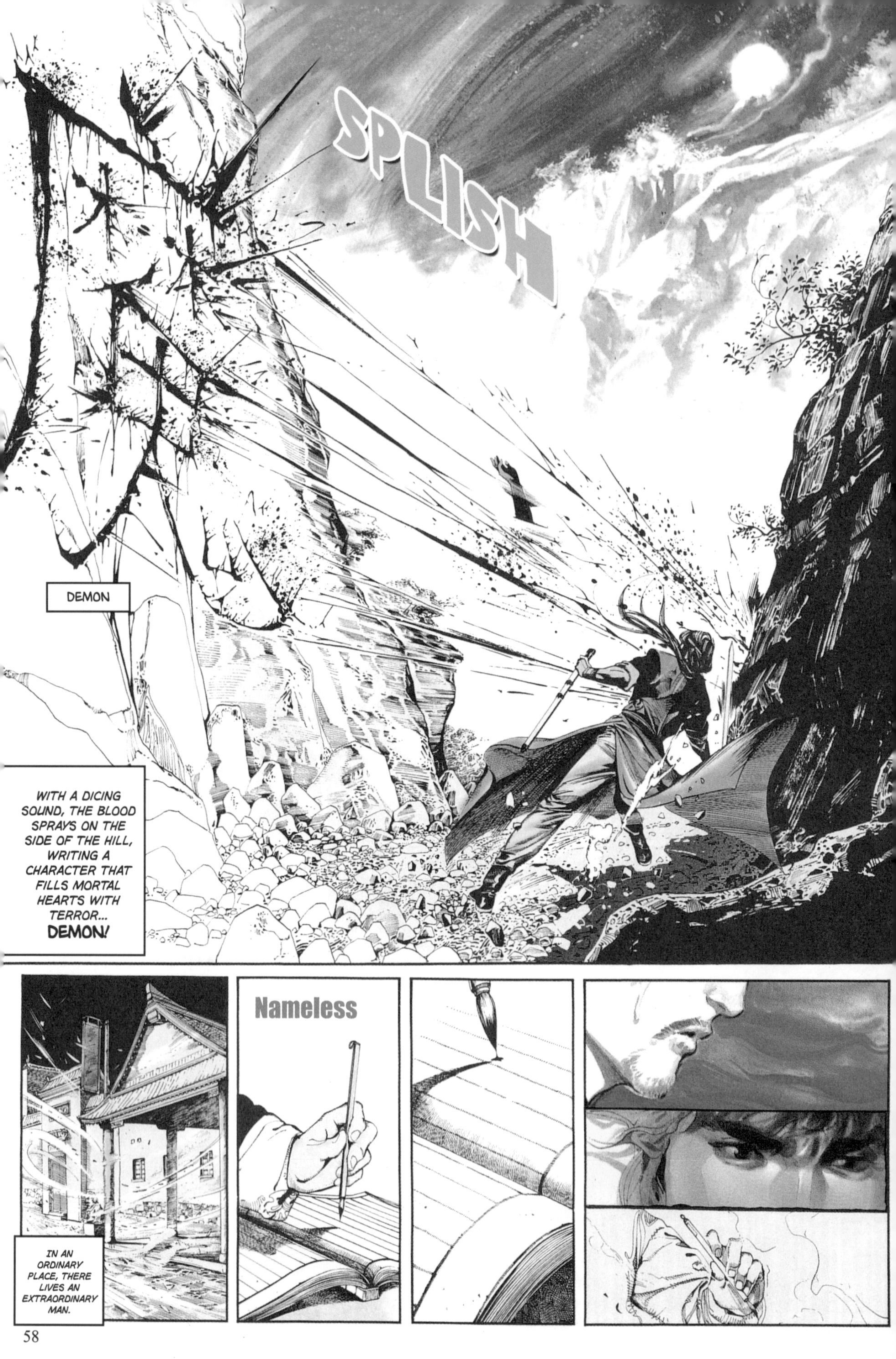
SPLISH
DEMON
WITH A DICING SOUND, THE BLOOD SPRAYS ON THE SIDE OF THE HILL, WRITING A CHARACTER THAT FILLS MORTAL HEARTS WITH TERROR... DEMON!
IN AN ORDINARY PLACE, THERE LIVES AN EXTRAORDINARY MAN.
Nameless

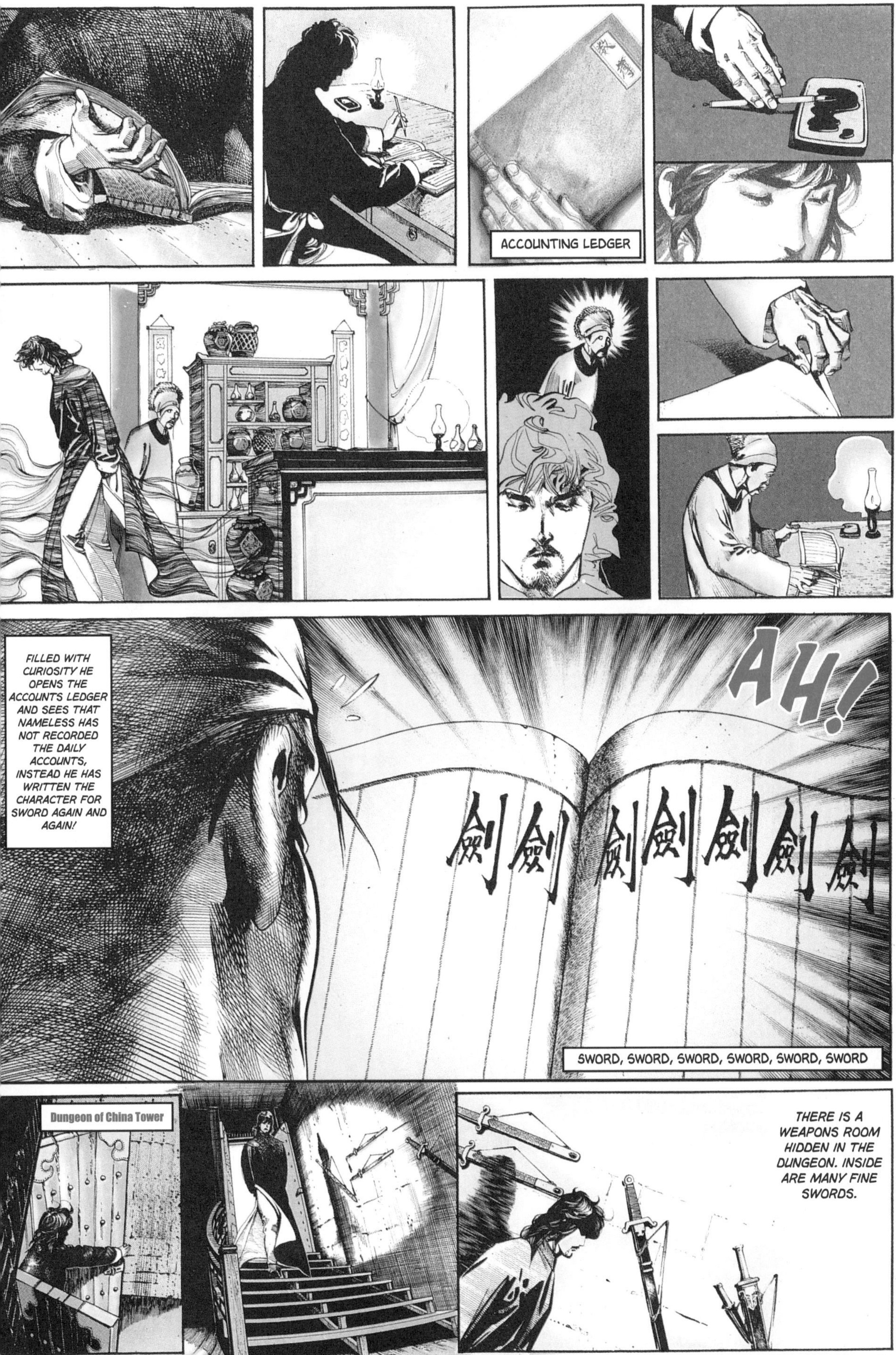

ACCOUNTING LEDGER
FILLED WITH CURIOSITY HE OPENS THE ACCOUNTS LEDGER AND SEES THAT NAMELESS HAS NOT RECORDED THE DAILY ACCOUNTS, INSTEAD HE HAS WRITTEN THE CHARACTER FOR SWORD AGAIN AND AGAIN!
AH!
劍劍劍劍劍劍劍
SWORD, SWORD, SWORD, SWORD, SWORD, SWORD
Dungeon of China Tower
THERE IS A WEAPONS ROOM HIDDEN IN THE DUNGEON. INSIDE ARE MANY FINE SWORDS.

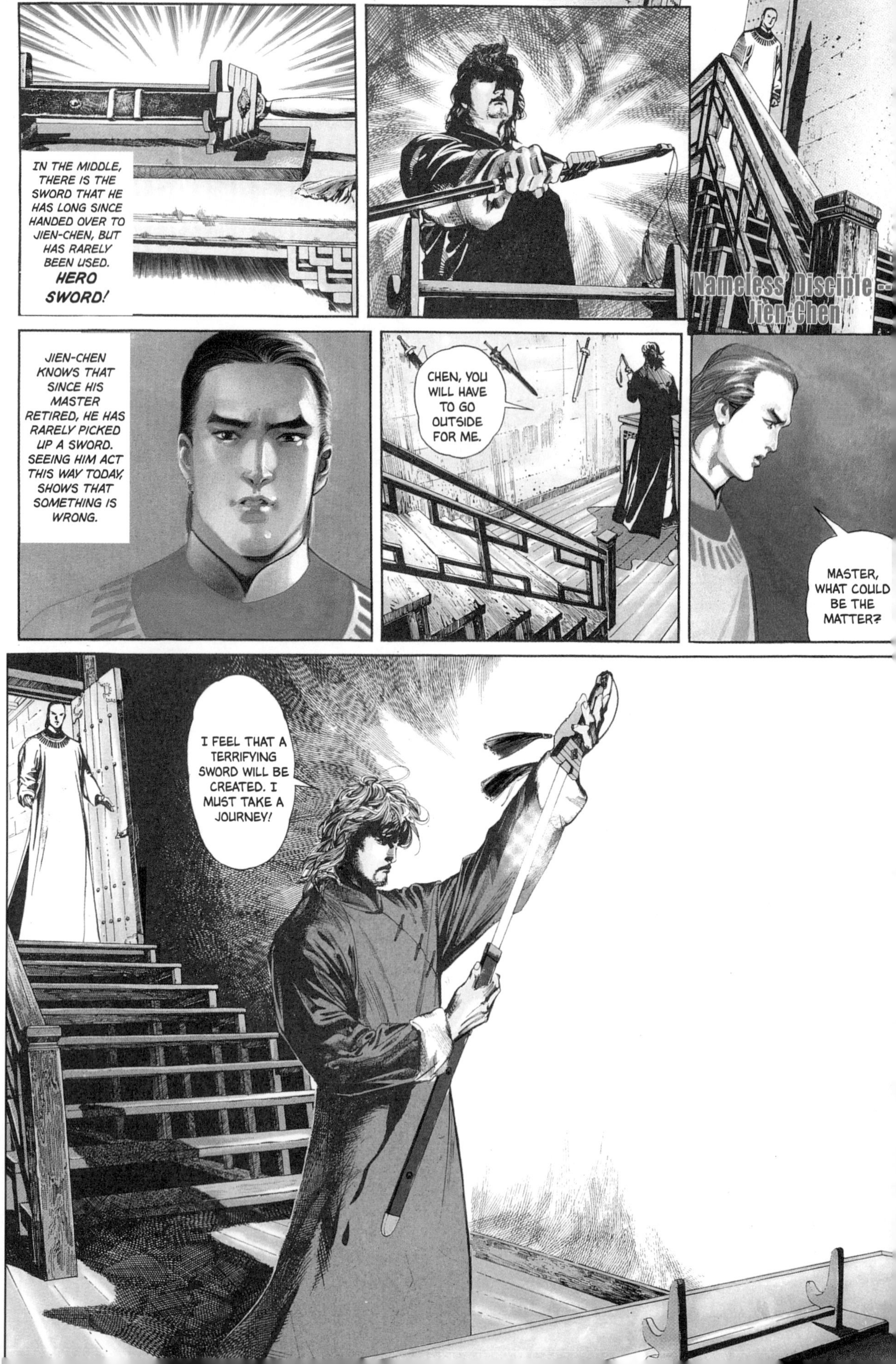
IN THE MIDDLE, THERE IS THE SWORD THAT HE HAS LONG SINCE HANDED OVER TO JIEN-CHEN, BUT HAS RARELY BEEN USED.
HERO SWORD!
Nameless' Disciple -- Jien-Chen
JIEN-CHEN KNOWS THAT SINCE HIS MASTER RETIRED, HE HAS RARELY PICKED UP A SWORD. SEEING HIM ACT THIS WAY TODAY, SHOWS THAT SOMETHING IS WRONG.
CHEN, YOU WILL HAVE TO GO OUTSIDE FOR ME.
MASTER, WHAT COULD BE THE MATTER?
I FEEL THAT A TERRIFYING SWORD WILL BE CREATED. I MUST TAKE A JOURNEY!

# CHAPTER 42: SWORD DEMON

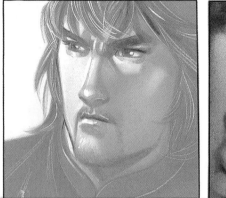

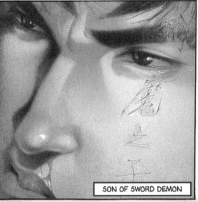

SON OF SWORD DEMON

SWORD, SWORD, SWORD, SWORD

SWORD!
SWORD!
SWORD! WHAT
KIND OF
RECORD IS
THE BOSS
MAKING?

AH!

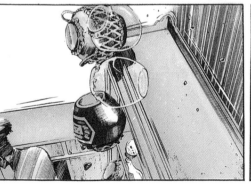

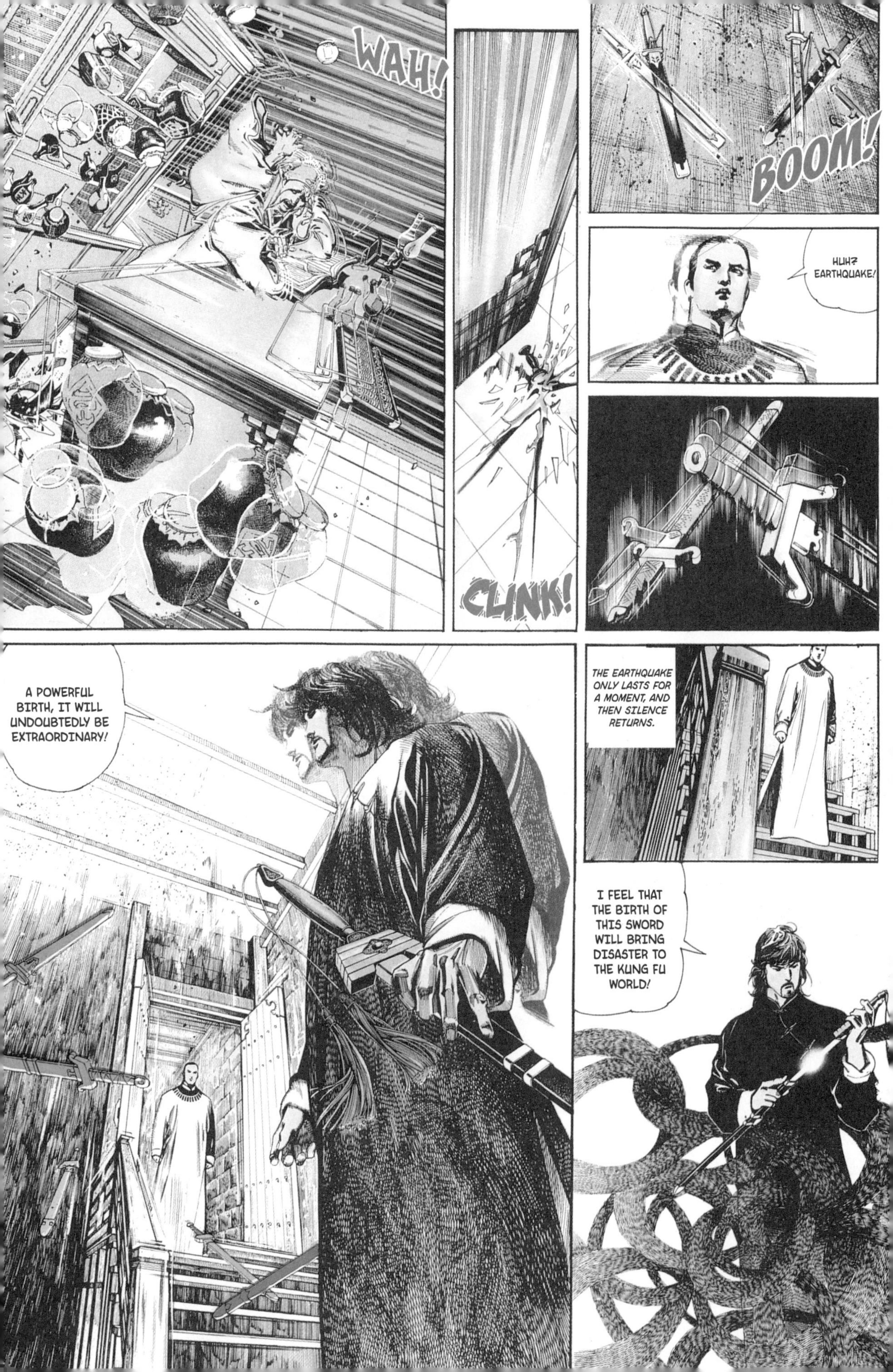
WAH!
CLINK!
BOOM!
HUH? EARTHQUAKE!
A POWERFUL BIRTH, IT WILL UNDOUBTEDLY BE EXTRAORDINARY!
THE EARTHQUAKE ONLY LASTS FOR A MOMENT, AND THEN SILENCE RETURNS.
I FEEL THAT THE BIRTH OF THIS SWORD WILL BRING DISASTER TO THE KUNG FU WORLD!

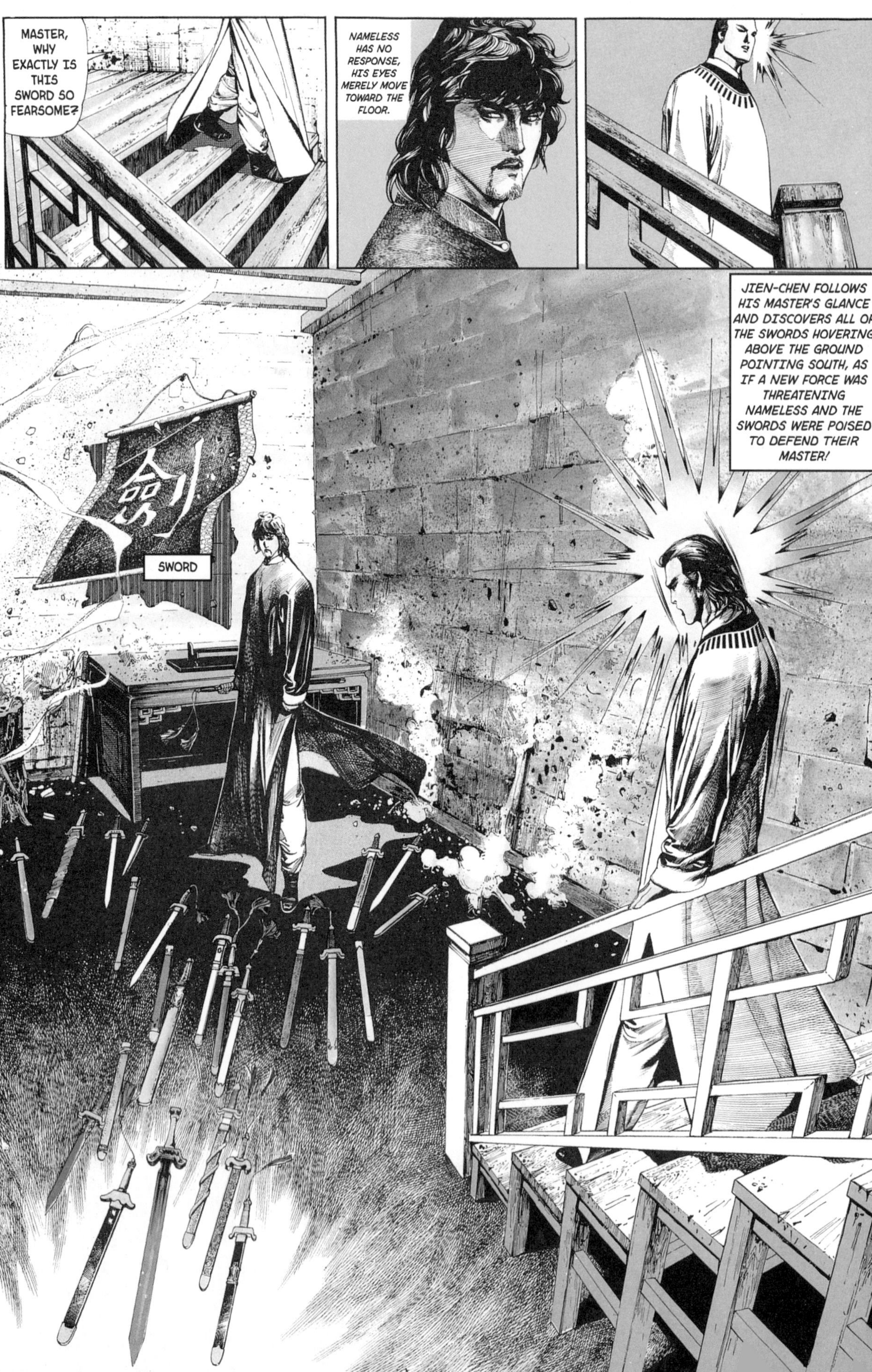
MASTER, WHY EXACTLY IS THIS SWORD SO FEARSOME?
NAMELESS HAS NO RESPONSE, HIS EYES MERELY MOVE TOWARD THE FLOOR.
JIEN-CHEN FOLLOWS HIS MASTER'S GLANCE AND DISCOVERS ALL OF THE SWORDS HOVERING ABOVE THE GROUND POINTING SOUTH, AS IF A NEW FORCE WAS THREATENING NAMELESS AND THE SWORDS WERE POISED TO DEFEND THEIR MASTER!
劍
SWORD

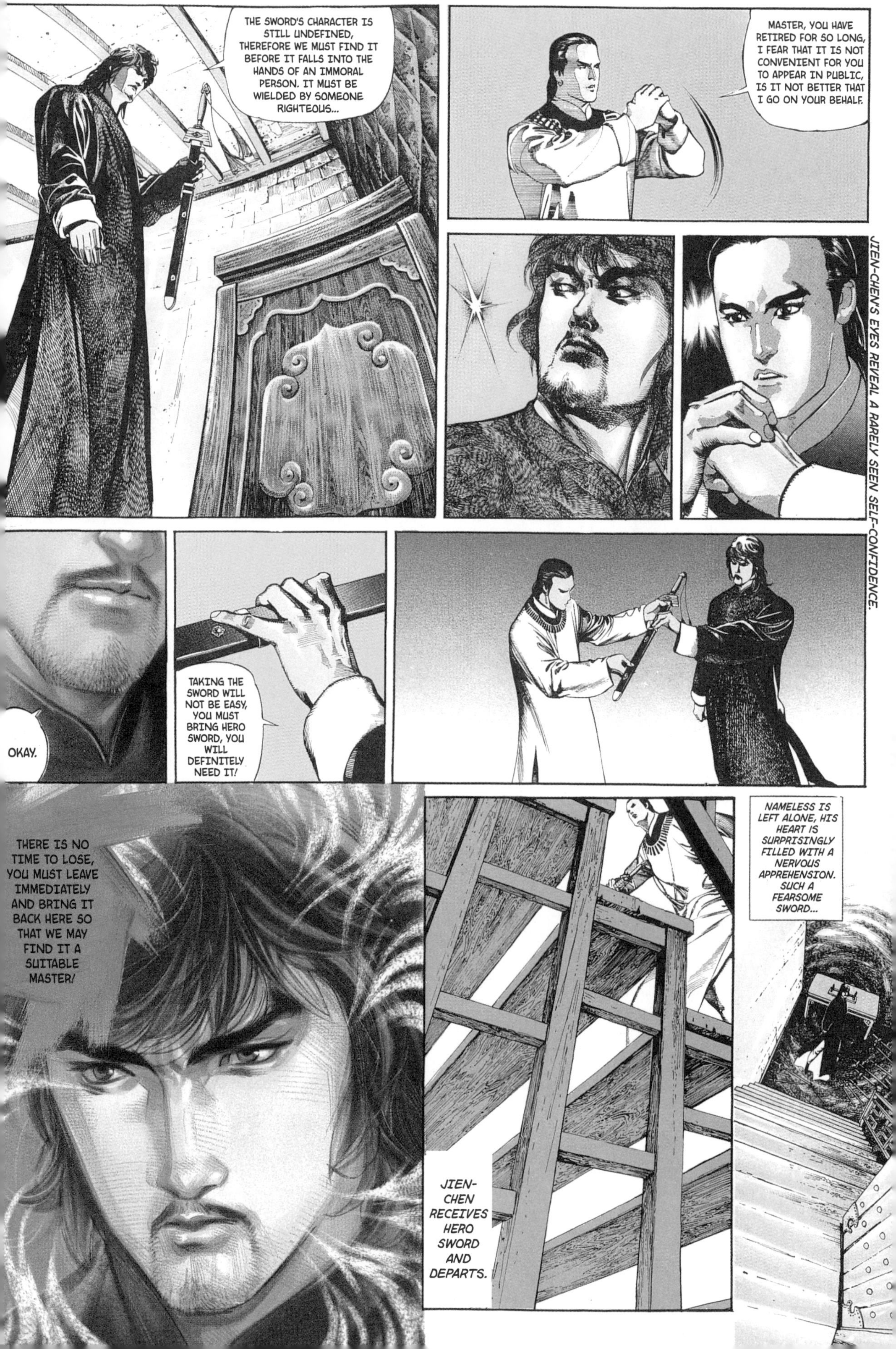
THE SWORD'S CHARACTER IS STILL UNDEFINED, THEREFORE WE MUST FIND IT BEFORE IT FALLS INTO THE HANDS OF AN IMMORAL PERSON. IT MUST BE WIELDED BY SOMEONE RIGHTEOUS...
MASTER, YOU HAVE RETIRED FOR SO LONG, I FEAR THAT IT IS NOT CONVENIENT FOR YOU TO APPEAR IN PUBLIC, IS IT NOT BETTER THAT I GO ON YOUR BEHALF.
JIEN-CHEN'S EYES REVEAL A RARELY SEEN SELF-CONFIDENCE.
OKAY.
TAKING THE SWORD WILL NOT BE EASY, YOU MUST BRING HERO SWORD, YOU WILL DEFINITELY NEED IT!
THERE IS NO TIME TO LOSE, YOU MUST LEAVE IMMEDIATELY AND BRING IT BACK HERE SO THAT WE MAY FIND IT A SUITABLE MASTER!
JIEN-CHEN RECEIVES HERO SWORD AND DEPARTS.
NAMELESS IS LEFT ALONE, HIS HEART IS SURPRISINGLY FILLED WITH A NERVOUS APPREHENSION. SUCH A FEARSOME SWORD...

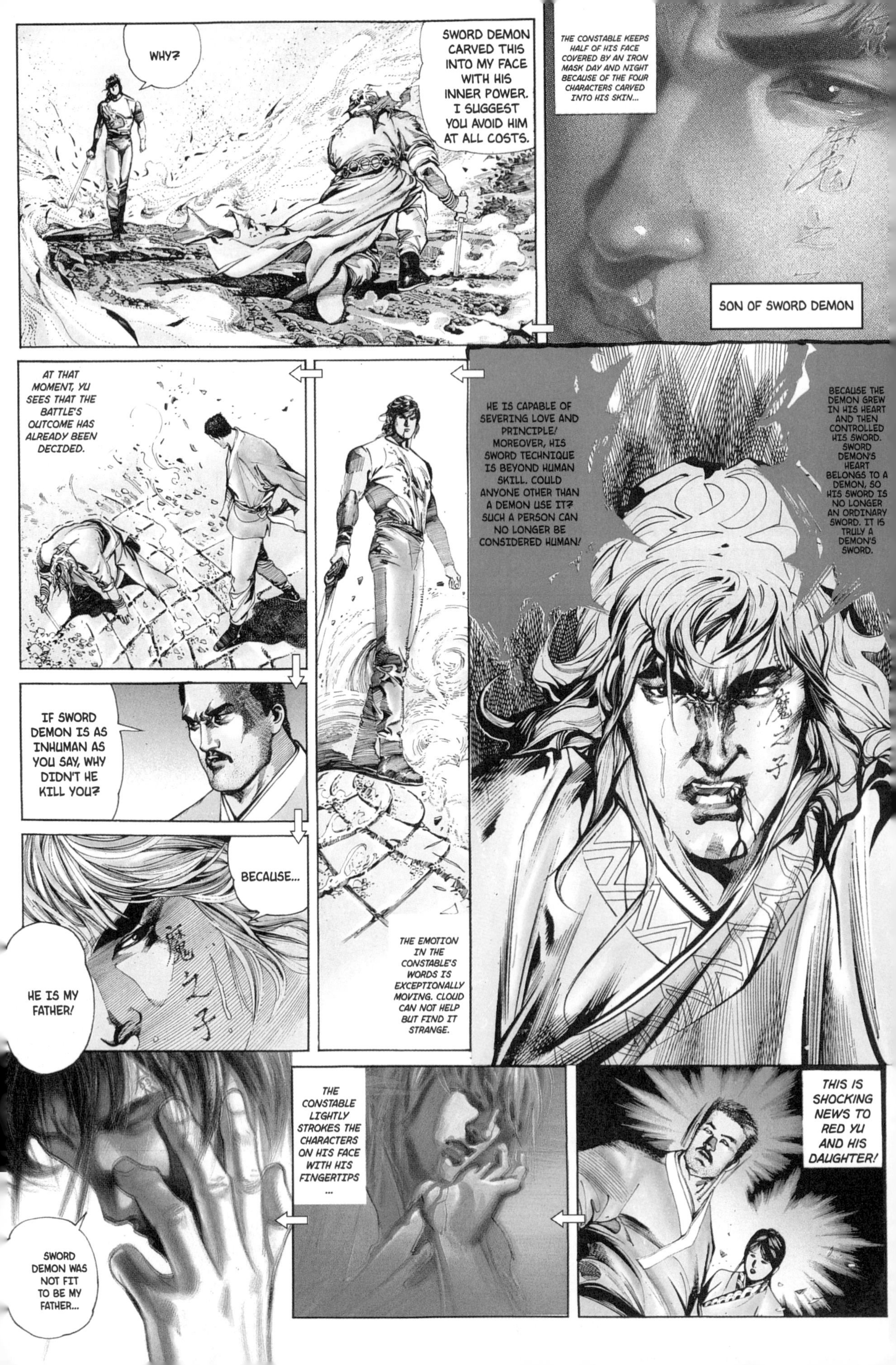
WHY?
SWORD DEMON CARVED THIS INTO MY FACE WITH HIS INNER POWER. I SUGGEST YOU AVOID HIM AT ALL COSTS.
THE CONSTABLE KEEPS HALF OF HIS FACE COVERED BY AN IRON MASK DAY AND NIGHT BECAUSE OF THE FOUR CHARACTERS CARVED INTO HIS SKIN...
SON OF SWORD DEMON
HE IS CAPABLE OF SEVERING LOVE AND PRINCIPLE! MOREOVER, HIS SWORD TECHNIQUE IS BEYOND HUMAN SKILL. COULD ANYONE OTHER THAN A DEMON USE IT? SUCH A PERSON CAN NO LONGER BE CONSIDERED HUMAN!
BECAUSE THE DEMON GREW IN HIS HEART AND THEN CONTROLLED HIS SWORD. SWORD DEMON'S HEART BELONGS TO A DEMON, SO HIS SWORD IS NO LONGER AN ORDINARY SWORD. IT IS TRULY A DEMON'S SWORD.
AT THAT MOMENT, YU SEES THAT THE BATTLE'S OUTCOME HAS ALREADY BEEN DECIDED.
IF SWORD DEMON IS AS INHUMAN AS YOU SAY, WHY DIDN'T HE KILL YOU?
BECAUSE...
HE IS MY FATHER!
THE EMOTION IN THE CONSTABLE'S WORDS IS EXCEPTIONALLY MOVING. CLOUD CAN NOT HELP BUT FIND IT STRANGE.
THIS IS SHOCKING NEWS TO RED YU AND HIS DAUGHTER!
THE CONSTABLE LIGHTLY STROKES THE CHARACTERS ON HIS FACE WITH HIS FINGERTIPS ...
SWORD DEMON WAS NOT FIT TO BE MY FATHER...

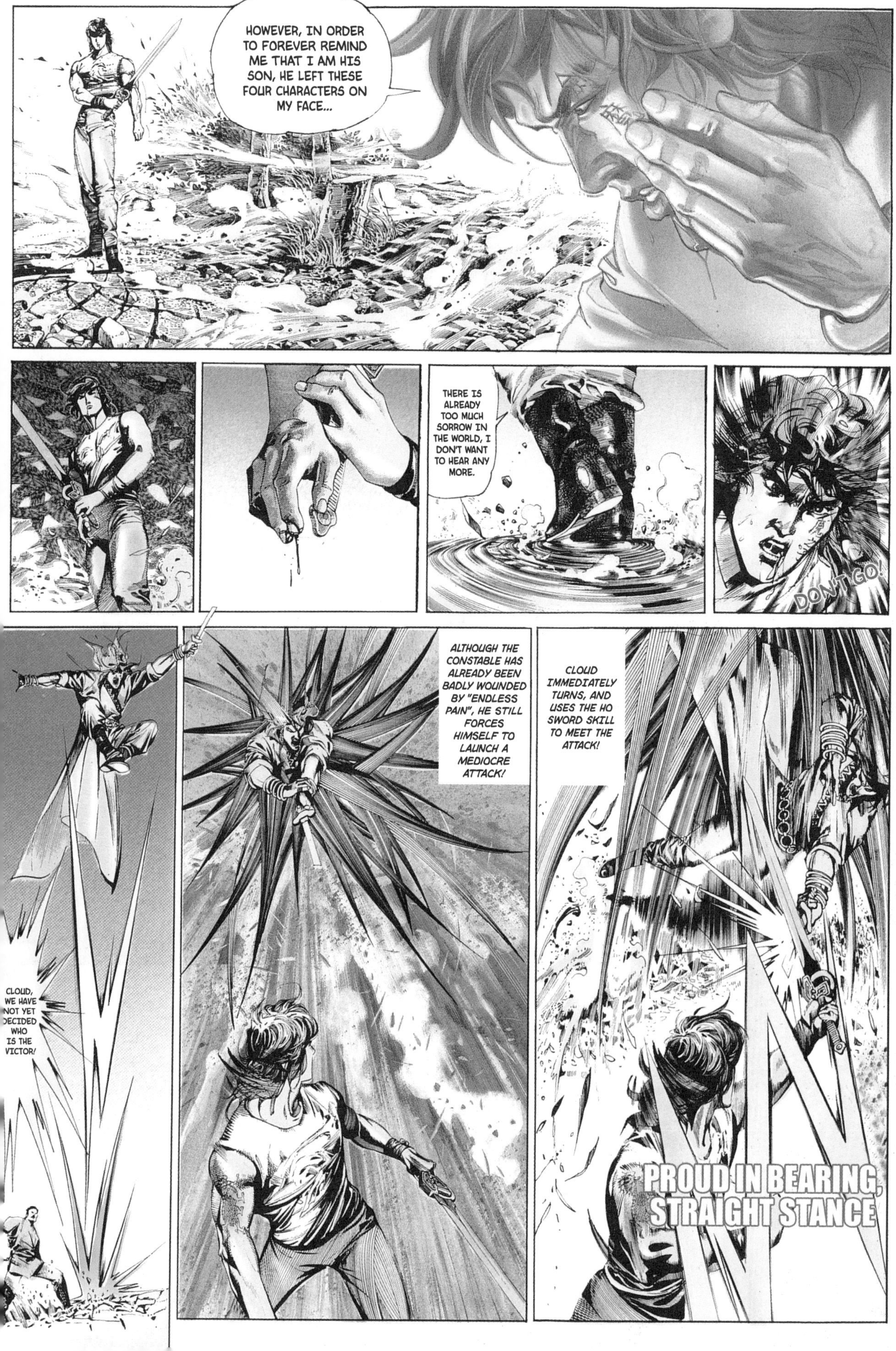

HOWEVER, IN ORDER TO FOREVER REMIND ME THAT I AM HIS SON, HE LEFT THESE FOUR CHARACTERS ON MY FACE...
THERE IS ALREADY TOO MUCH SORROW IN THE WORLD, I DON'T WANT TO HEAR ANY MORE.
DON'T GO!
CLOUD, WE HAVE NOT YET DECIDED WHO IS THE VICTOR!
ALTHOUGH THE CONSTABLE HAS ALREADY BEEN BADLY WOUNDED BY "ENDLESS PAIN", HE STILL FORCES HIMSELF TO LAUNCH A MEDIOCRE ATTACK!
CLOUD IMMEDIATELY TURNS, AND USES THE HO SWORD SKILL TO MEET THE ATTACK!
PROUD IN BEARING, STRAIGHT STANCE

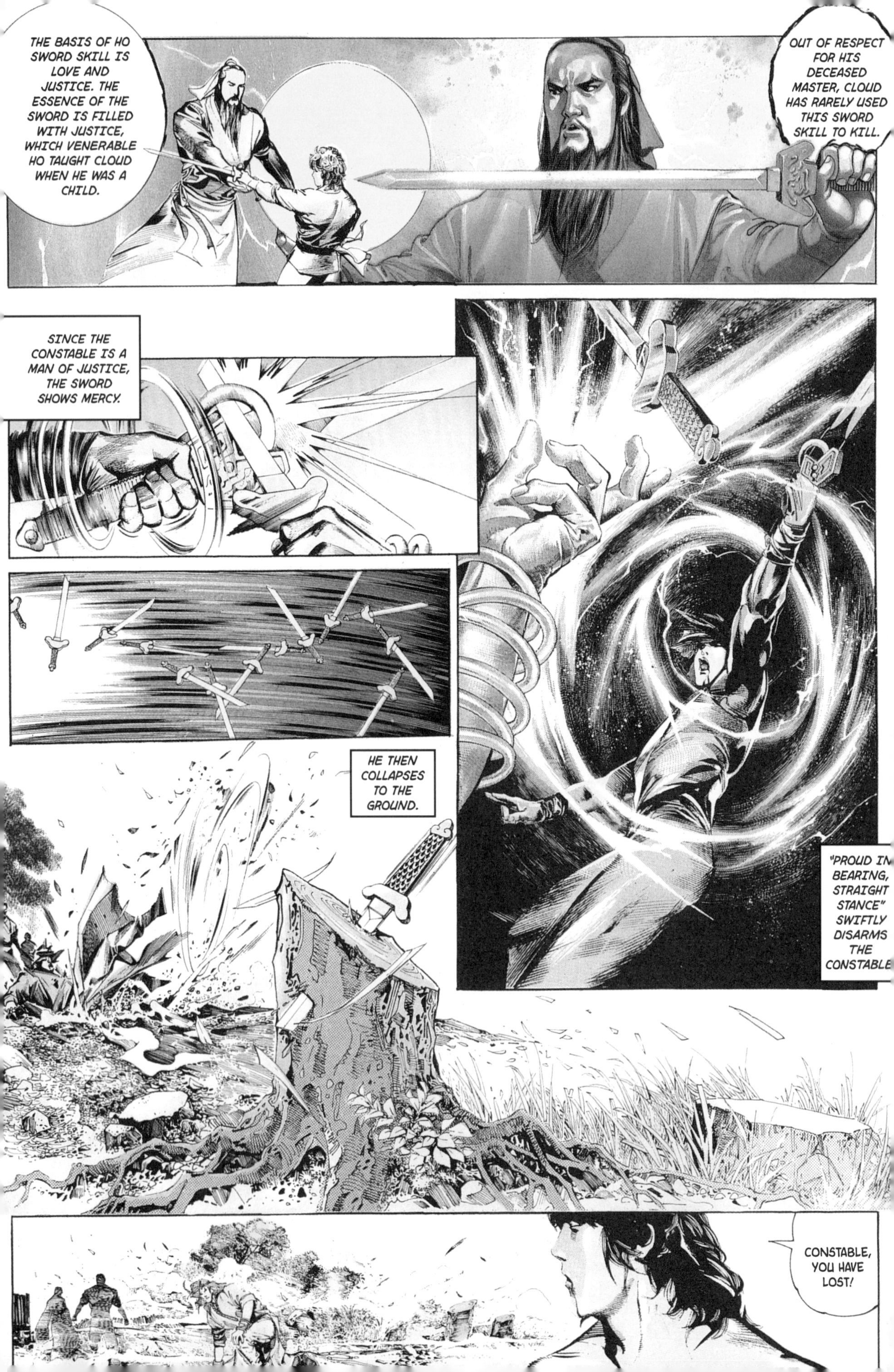
THE BASIS OF HO SWORD SKILL IS LOVE AND JUSTICE. THE ESSENCE OF THE SWORD IS FILLED WITH JUSTICE, WHICH VENERABLE HO TAUGHT CLOUD WHEN HE WAS A CHILD.
OUT OF RESPECT FOR HIS DECEASED MASTER, CLOUD HAS RARELY USED THIS SWORD SKILL TO KILL.
SINCE THE CONSTABLE IS A MAN OF JUSTICE, THE SWORD SHOWS MERCY.
"PROUD IN BEARING, STRAIGHT STANCE" SWIFTLY DISARMS THE CONSTABLE
HE THEN COLLAPSES TO THE GROUND.
CONSTABLE, YOU HAVE LOST!

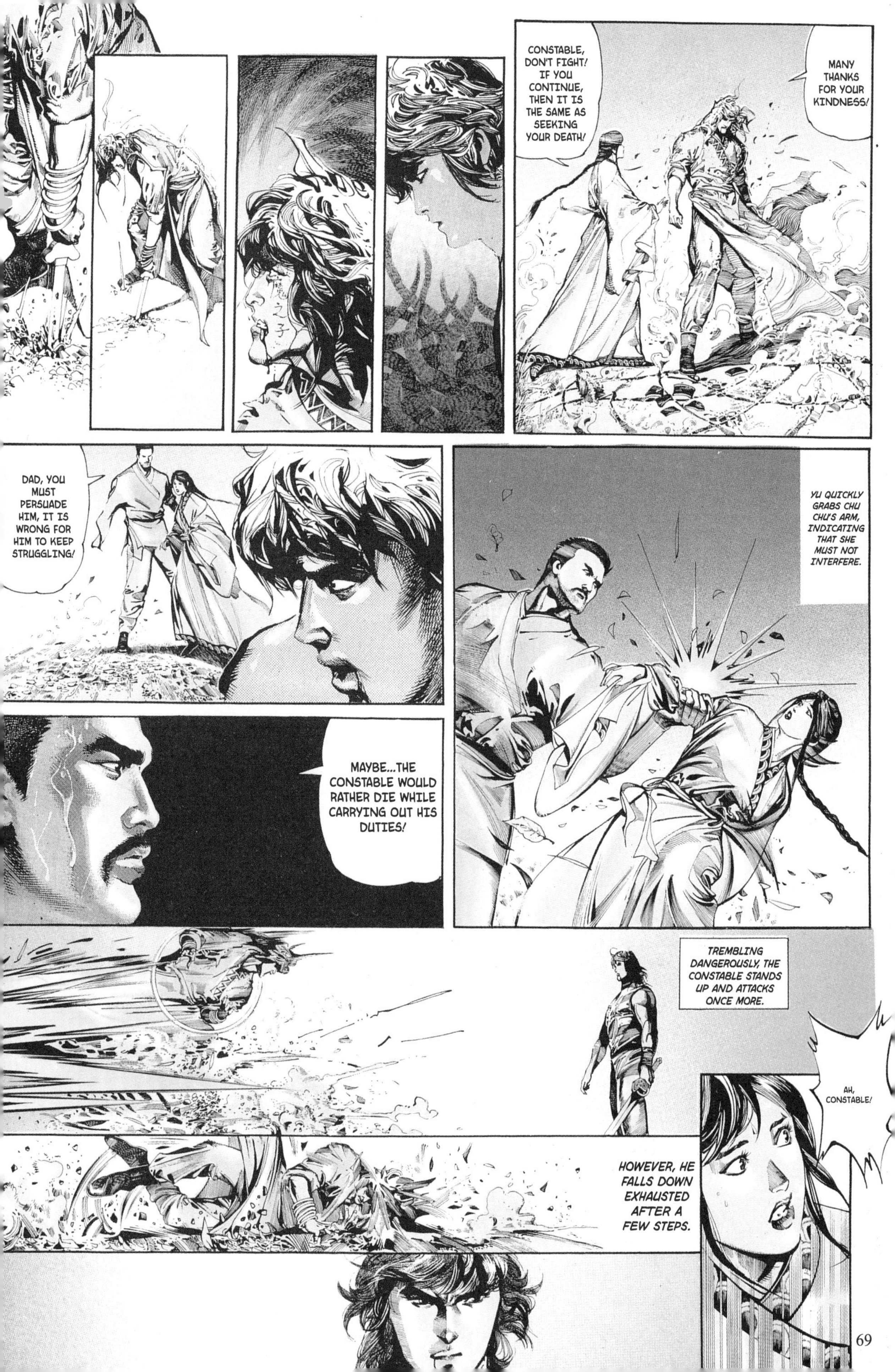
CONSTABLE, DON'T FIGHT! IF YOU CONTINUE, THEN IT IS THE SAME AS SEEKING YOUR DEATH!
MANY THANKS FOR YOUR KINDNESS!
DAD, YOU MUST PERSUADE HIM, IT IS WRONG FOR HIM TO KEEP STRUGGLING!
MAYBE...THE CONSTABLE WOULD RATHER DIE WHILE CARRYING OUT HIS DUTIES!
YU QUICKLY GRABS CHU CHU'S ARM, INDICATING THAT SHE MUST NOT INTERFERE.
TREMBLING DANGEROUSLY, THE CONSTABLE STANDS UP AND ATTACKS ONCE MORE.
HOWEVER, HE FALLS DOWN EXHAUSTED AFTER A FEW STEPS.
AH, CONSTABLE!

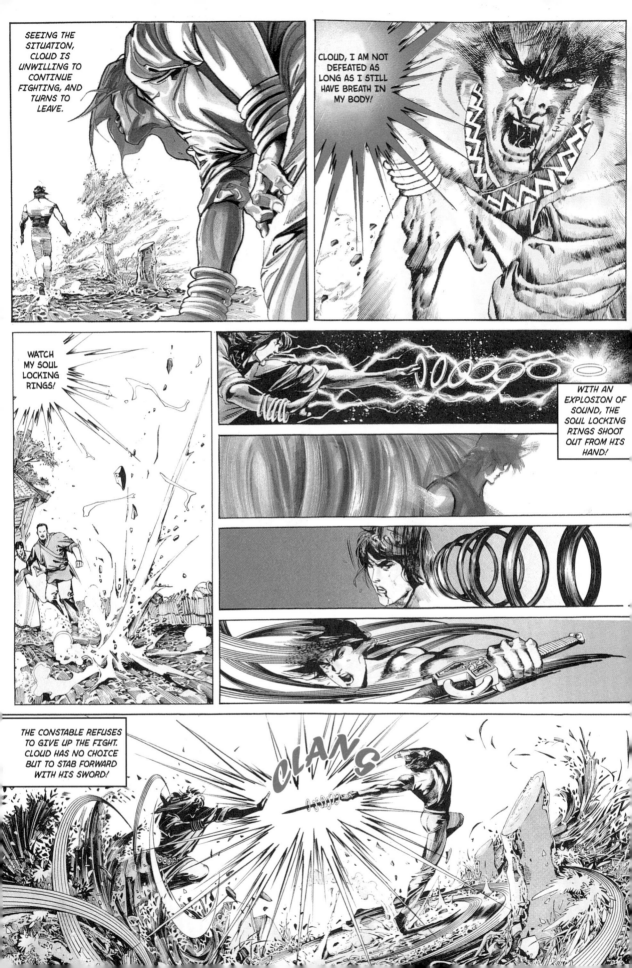

SEEING THE SITUATION, CLOUD IS UNWILLING TO CONTINUE FIGHTING, AND TURNS TO LEAVE.

CLOUD, I AM NOT DEFEATED AS LONG AS I STILL HAVE BREATH IN MY BODY!

WATCH MY SOUL LOCKING RINGS!

WITH AN EXPLOSION OF SOUND, THE SOUL LOCKING RINGS SHOOT OUT FROM HIS HAND!

THE CONSTABLE REFUSES TO GIVE UP THE FIGHT. CLOUD HAS NO CHOICE BUT TO STAB FORWARD WITH HIS SWORD!

CIANG

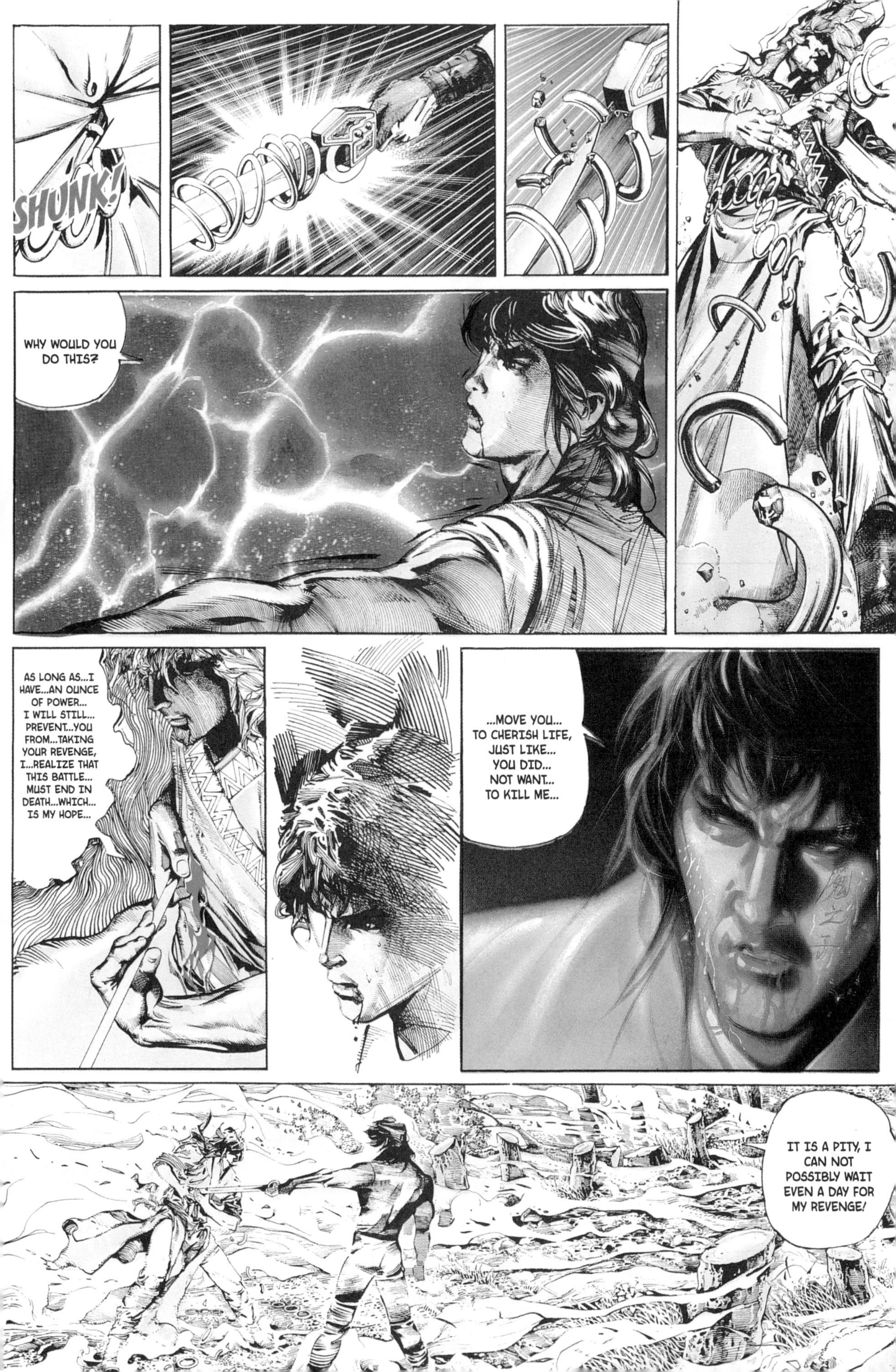
SHUNK!
WHY WOULD YOU DO THIS?
AS LONG AS...I HAVE...AN OUNCE OF POWER... I WILL STILL... PREVENT...YOU FROM...TAKING YOUR REVENGE, I...REALIZE THAT THIS BATTLE... MUST END IN DEATH...WHICH... IS MY HOPE...
...MOVE YOU... TO CHERISH LIFE, JUST LIKE... YOU DID... NOT WANT... TO KILL ME...
IT IS A PITY, I CAN NOT POSSIBLY WAIT EVEN A DAY FOR MY REVENGE!

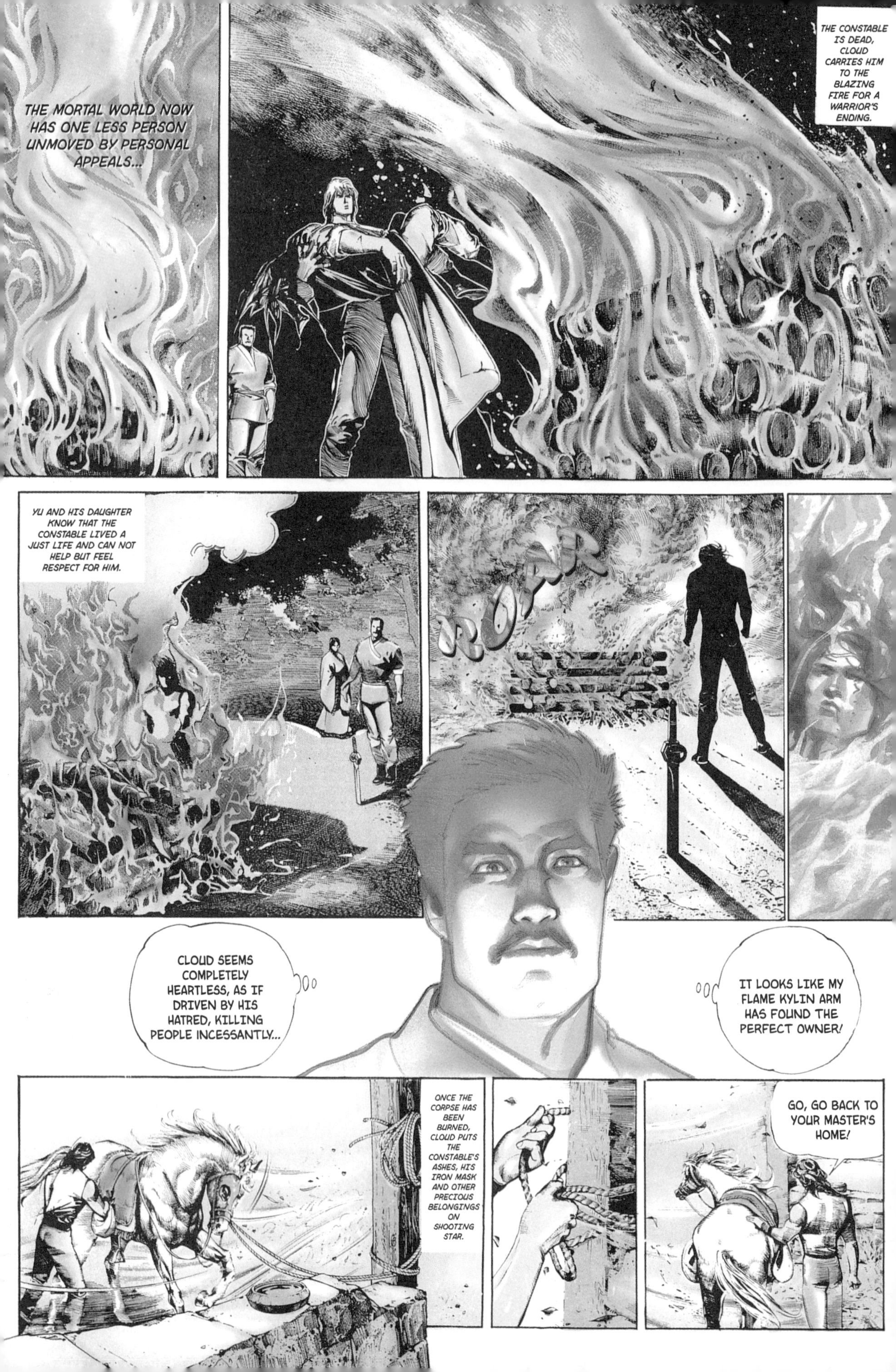
THE MORTAL WORLD NOW HAS ONE LESS PERSON UNMOVED BY PERSONAL APPEALS...
THE CONSTABLE IS DEAD, CLOUD CARRIES HIM TO THE BLAZING FIRE FOR A WARRIOR'S ENDING.
YU AND HIS DAUGHTER KNOW THAT THE CONSTABLE LIVED A JUST LIFE AND CAN NOT HELP BUT FEEL RESPECT FOR HIM.
ROAR
CLOUD SEEMS COMPLETELY HEARTLESS, AS IF DRIVEN BY HIS HATRED, KILLING PEOPLE INCESSANTLY...
IT LOOKS LIKE MY FLAME KYLIN ARM HAS FOUND THE PERFECT OWNER!
ONCE THE CORPSE HAS BEEN BURNED, CLOUD PUTS THE CONSTABLE'S ASHES, HIS IRON MASK AND OTHER PRECIOUS BELONGINGS ON SHOOTING STAR.
GO, GO BACK TO YOUR MASTER'S HOME!

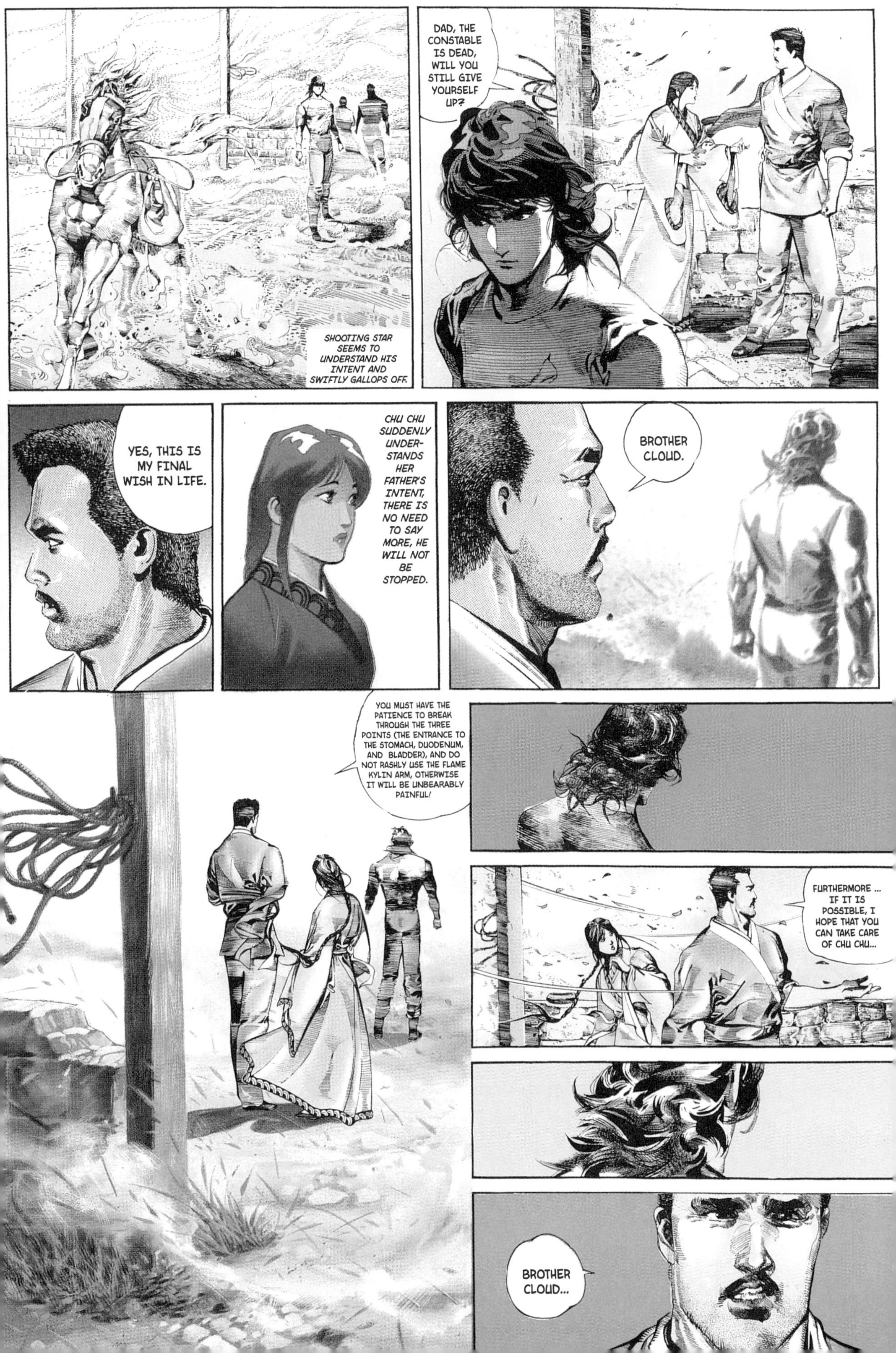
SHOOTING STAR SEEMS TO UNDERSTAND HIS INTENT AND SWIFTLY GALLOPS OFF.
DAD, THE CONSTABLE IS DEAD, WILL YOU STILL GIVE YOURSELF UP?
YES, THIS IS MY FINAL WISH IN LIFE.
CHU CHU SUDDENLY UNDER-STANDS HER FATHER'S INTENT, THERE IS NO NEED TO SAY MORE, HE WILL NOT BE STOPPED.
BROTHER CLOUD.
YOU MUST HAVE THE PATIENCE TO BREAK THROUGH THE THREE POINTS (THE ENTRANCE TO THE STOMACH, DUODENUM, AND BLADDER), AND DO NOT RASHLY USE THE FLAME KYLIN ARM, OTHERWISE IT WILL BE UNBEARABLY PAINFUL!
FURTHERMORE ... IF IT IS POSSIBLE, I HOPE THAT YOU CAN TAKE CARE OF CHU CHU...
BROTHER CLOUD...

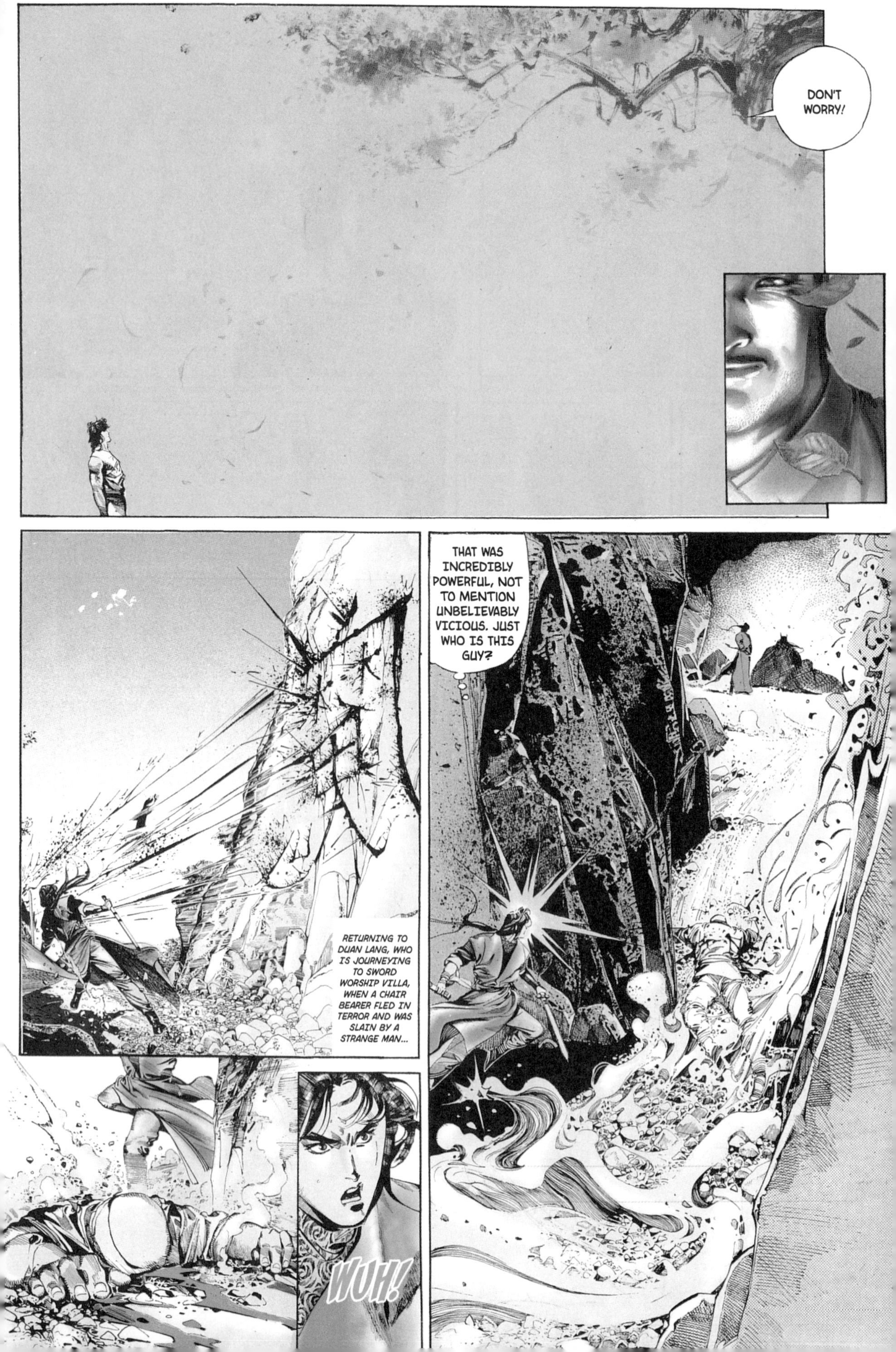
DON'T WORRY!
THAT WAS INCREDIBLY POWERFUL, NOT TO MENTION UNBELIEVABLY VICIOUS. JUST WHO IS THIS GUY?
RETURNING TO DUAN LANG, WHO IS JOURNEYING TO SWORD WORSHIP VILLA, WHEN A CHAIR BEARER FLED IN TERROR AND WAS SLAIN BY A STRANGE MAN...
WUH!

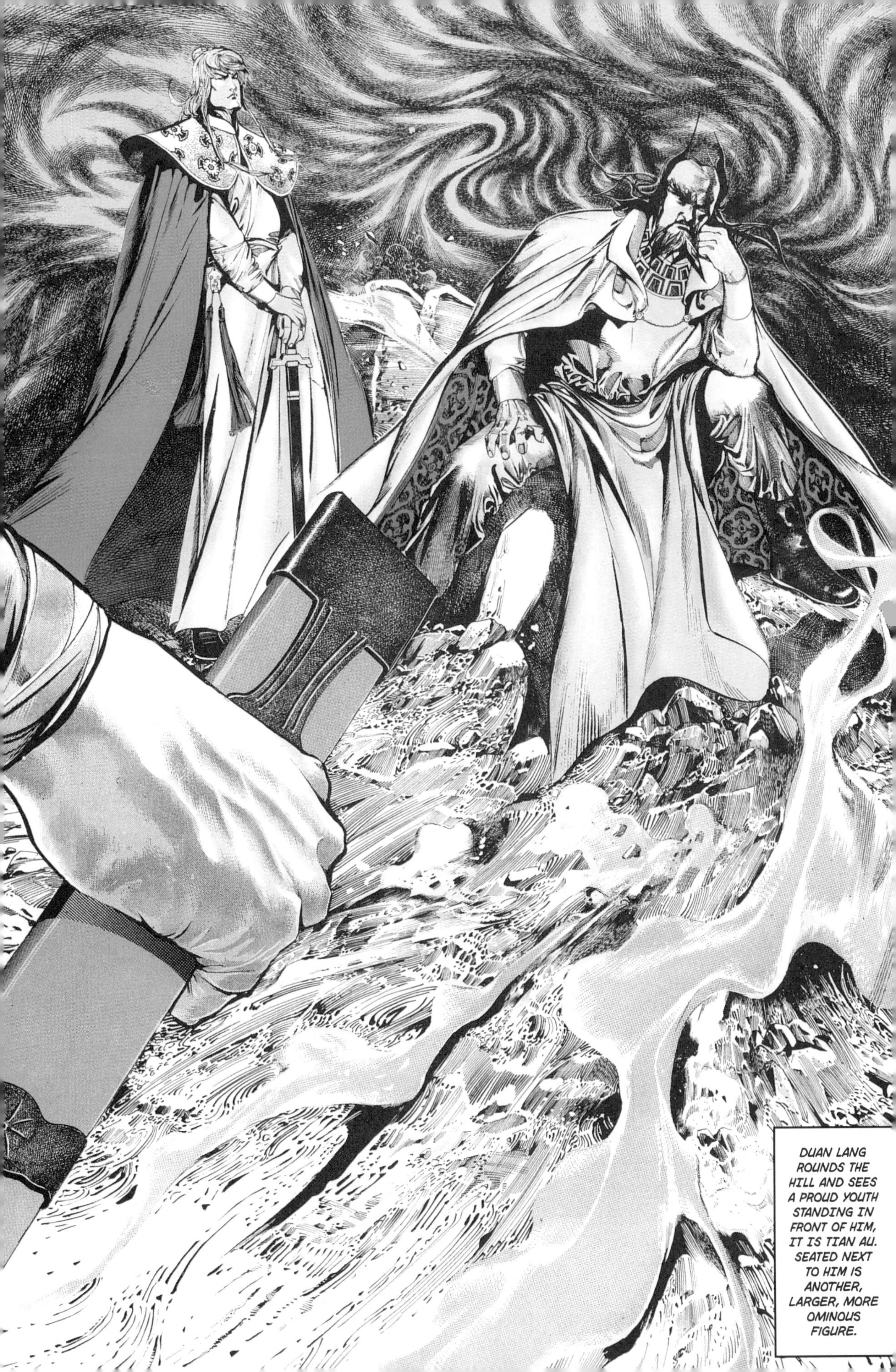
DUAN LANG ROUNDS THE HILL AND SEES A PROUD YOUTH STANDING IN FRONT OF HIM, IT IS TIAN AU. SEATED NEXT TO HIM IS ANOTHER, LARGER, MORE OMINOUS FIGURE.

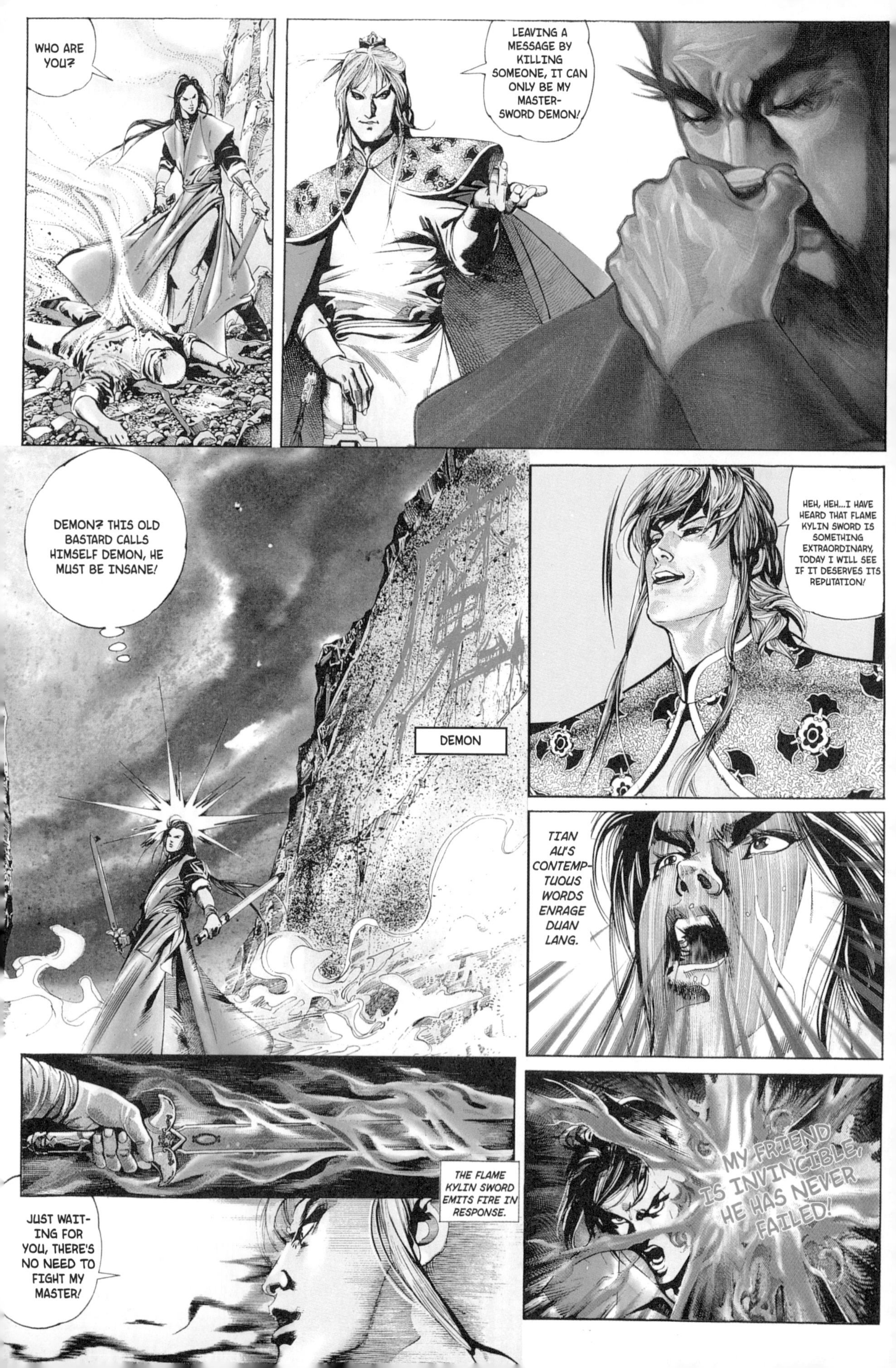
WHO ARE YOU?
LEAVING A MESSAGE BY KILLING SOMEONE, IT CAN ONLY BE MY MASTER-SWORD DEMON!
DEMON? THIS OLD BASTARD CALLS HIMSELF DEMON, HE MUST BE INSANE!
DEMON
HEH, HEH...I HAVE HEARD THAT FLAME KYLIN SWORD IS SOMETHING EXTRAORDINARY, TODAY I WILL SEE IF IT DESERVES ITS REPUTATION!
TIAN AU'S CONTEMPTUOUS WORDS ENRAGE DUAN LANG.
THE FLAME KYLIN SWORD EMITS FIRE IN RESPONSE.
JUST WAITING FOR YOU, THERE'S NO NEED TO FIGHT MY MASTER!
MY FRIEND IS INVINCIBLE, HE HAS NEVER FAILED!

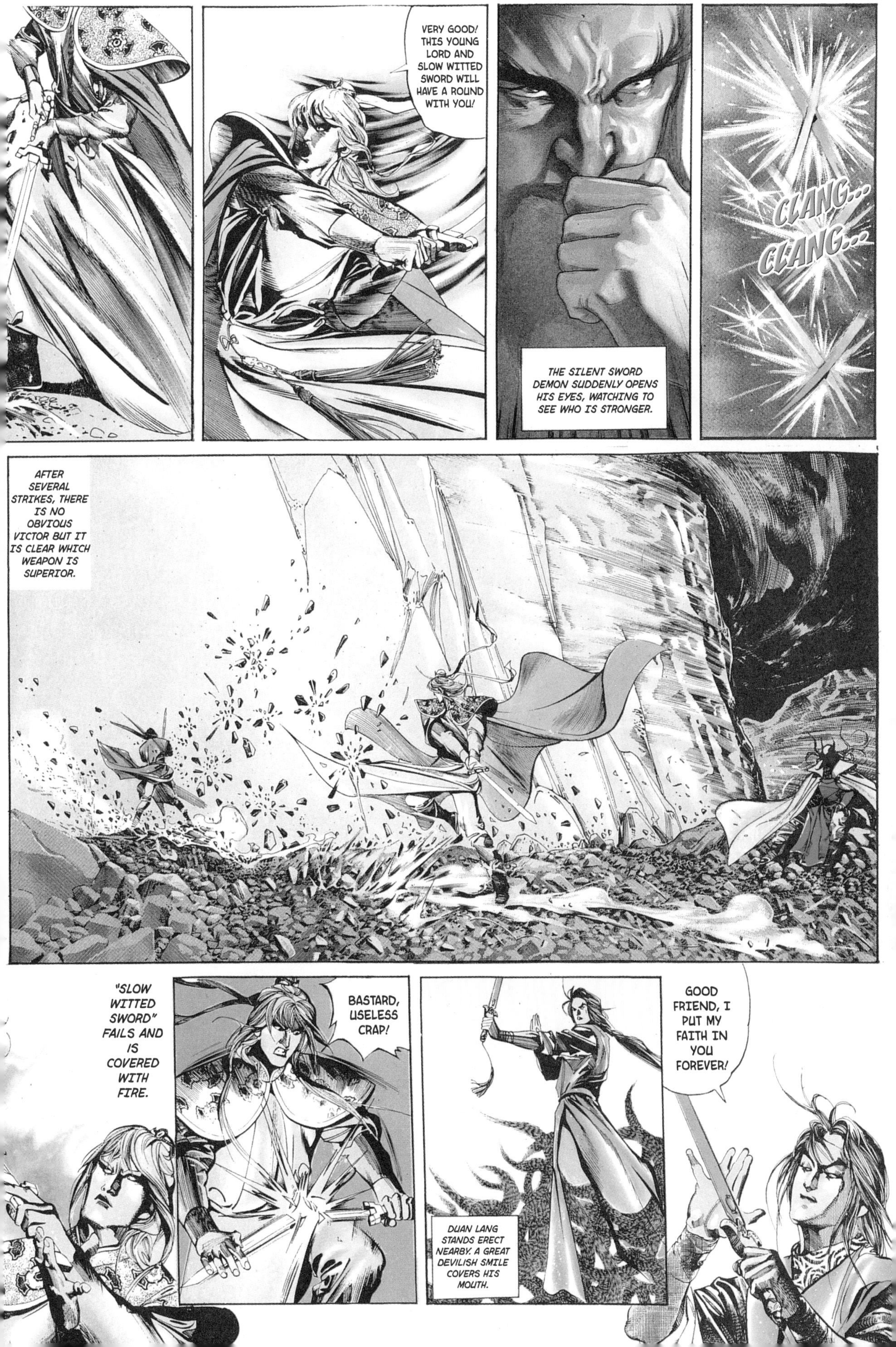
VERY GOOD! THIS YOUNG LORD AND SLOW WITTED SWORD WILL HAVE A ROUND WITH YOU!
THE SILENT SWORD DEMON SUDDENLY OPENS HIS EYES, WATCHING TO SEE WHO IS STRONGER.
CLANG...
CLANG...
AFTER SEVERAL STRIKES, THERE IS NO OBVIOUS VICTOR BUT IT IS CLEAR WHICH WEAPON IS SUPERIOR.
"SLOW WITTED SWORD" FAILS AND IS COVERED WITH FIRE.
BASTARD, USELESS CRAP!
DUAN LANG STANDS ERECT NEARBY. A GREAT DEVILISH SMILE COVERS HIS MOUTH.
GOOD FRIEND, I PUT MY FAITH IN YOU FOREVER!

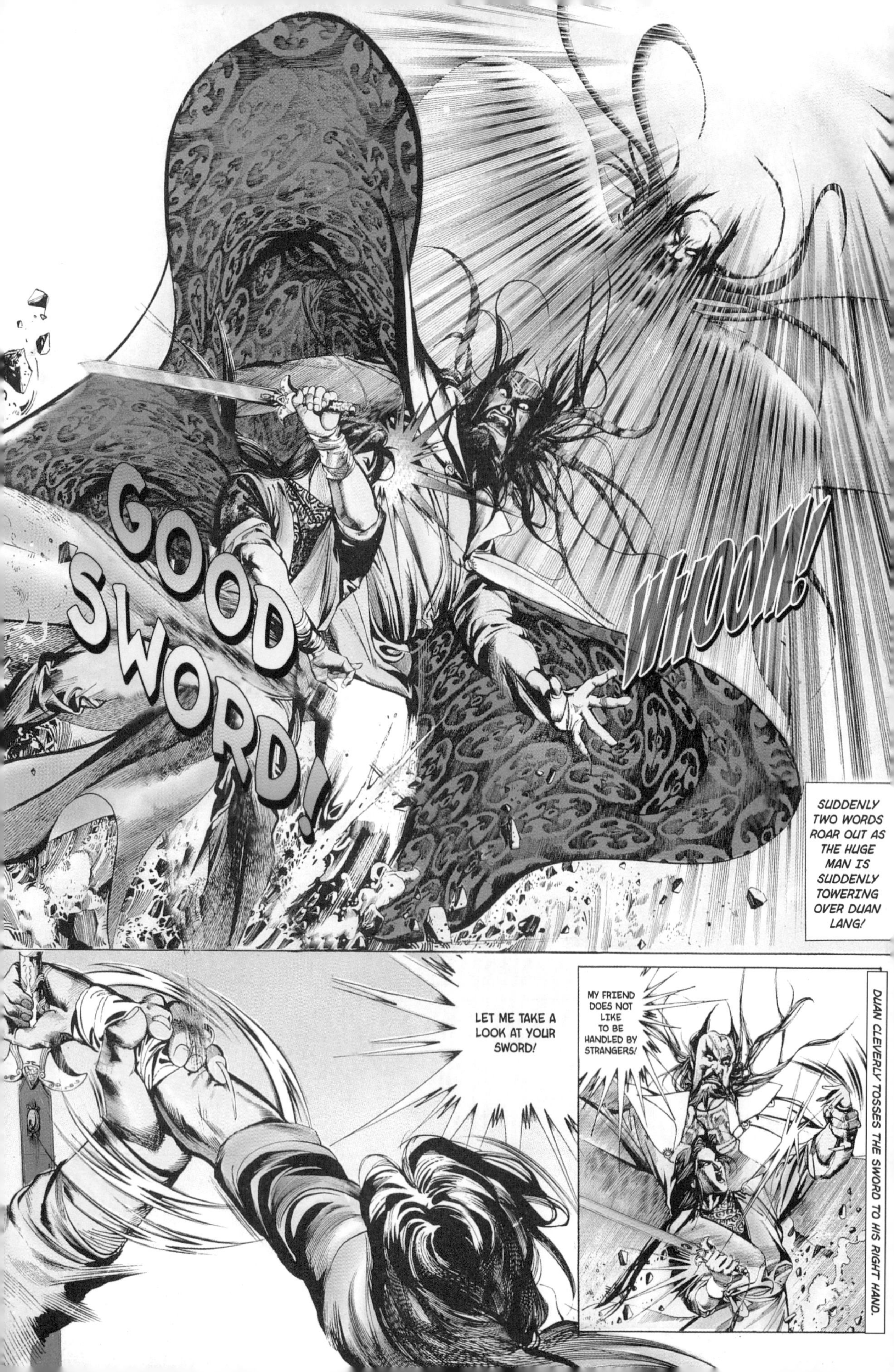
GOOD SWORD!!
WHOOM!
SUDDENLY TWO WORDS ROAR OUT AS THE HUGE MAN IS SUDDENLY TOWERING OVER DUAN LANG!
LET ME TAKE A LOOK AT YOUR SWORD!
MY FRIEND DOES NOT LIKE TO BE HANDLED BY STRANGERS!
DUAN CLEVERLY TOSSES THE SWORD TO HIS RIGHT HAND.

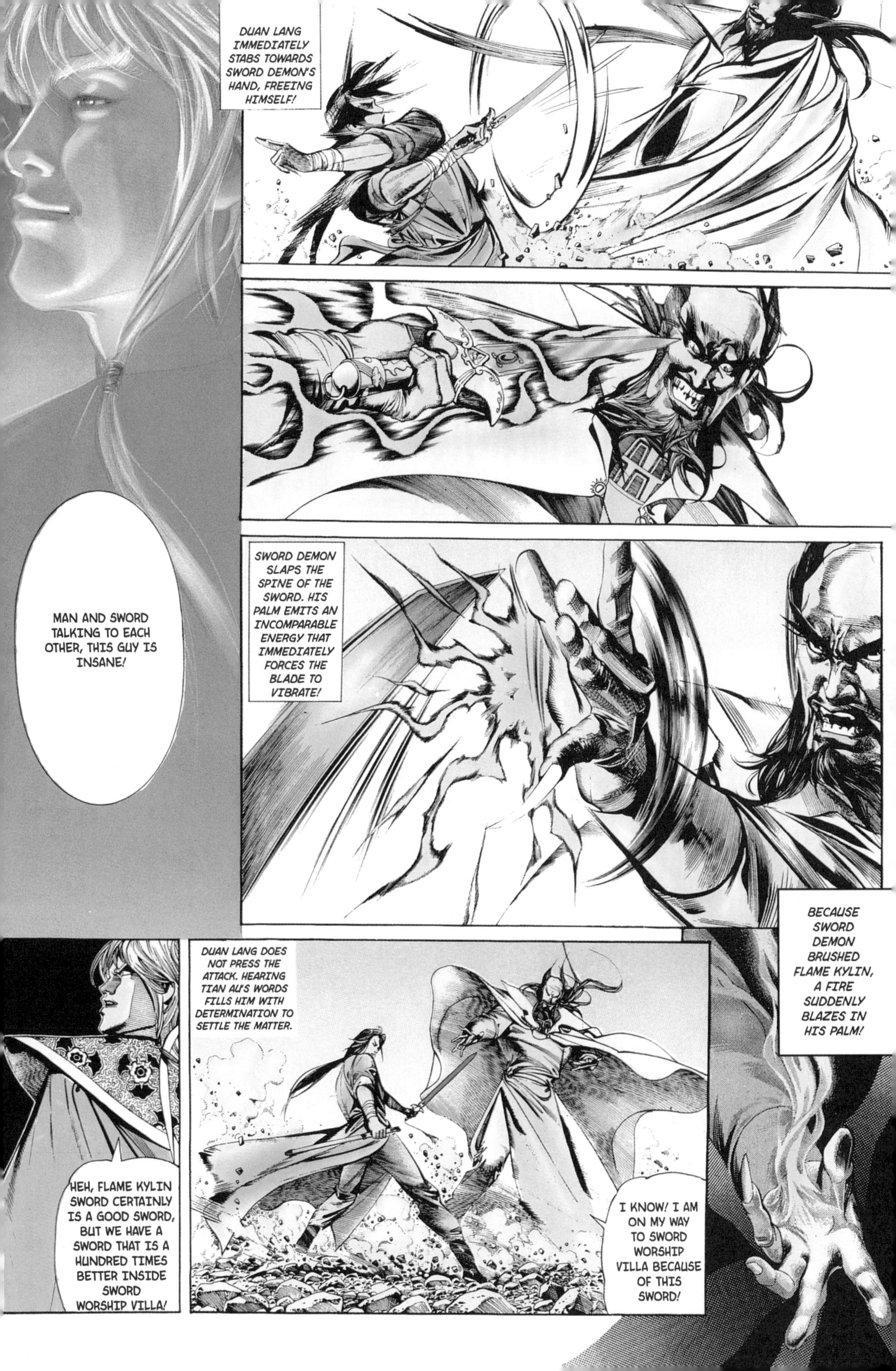
DUAN LANG IMMEDIATELY STABS TOWARDS SWORD DEMON'S HAND, FREEING HIMSELF!
MAN AND SWORD TALKING TO EACH OTHER, THIS GUY IS INSANE!
SWORD DEMON SLAPS THE SPINE OF THE SWORD. HIS PALM EMITS AN INCOMPARABLE ENERGY THAT IMMEDIATELY FORCES THE BLADE TO VIBRATE!
BECAUSE SWORD DEMON BRUSHED FLAME KYLIN, A FIRE SUDDENLY BLAZES IN HIS PALM!
DUAN LANG DOES NOT PRESS THE ATTACK. HEARING TIAN AU'S WORDS FILLS HIM WITH DETERMINATION TO SETTLE THE MATTER.
HEH, FLAME KYLIN SWORD CERTAINLY IS A GOOD SWORD, BUT WE HAVE A SWORD THAT IS A HUNDRED TIMES BETTER INSIDE SWORD WORSHIP VILLA!
I KNOW! I AM ON MY WAY TO SWORD WORSHIP VILLA BECAUSE OF THIS SWORD!

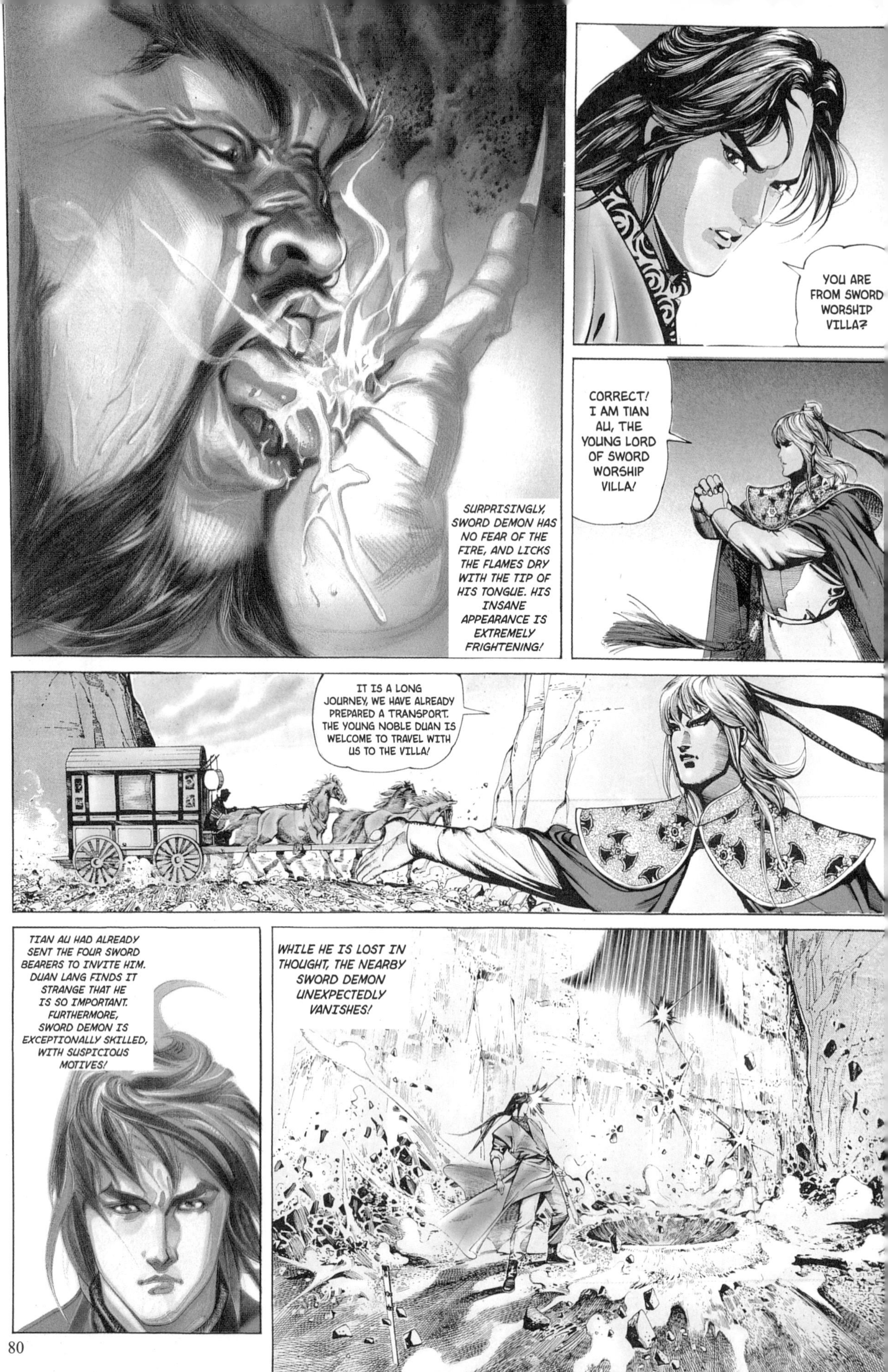
SURPRISINGLY, SWORD DEMON HAS NO FEAR OF THE FIRE, AND LICKS THE FLAMES DRY WITH THE TIP OF HIS TONGUE. HIS INSANE APPEARANCE IS EXTREMELY FRIGHTENING!
YOU ARE FROM SWORD WORSHIP VILLA?
CORRECT! I AM TIAN AU, THE YOUNG LORD OF SWORD WORSHIP VILLA!
IT IS A LONG JOURNEY, WE HAVE ALREADY PREPARED A TRANSPORT. THE YOUNG NOBLE DUAN IS WELCOME TO TRAVEL WITH US TO THE VILLA!
TIAN AU HAD ALREADY SENT THE FOUR SWORD BEARERS TO INVITE HIM. DUAN LANG FINDS IT STRANGE THAT HE IS SO IMPORTANT. FURTHERMORE, SWORD DEMON IS EXCEPTIONALLY SKILLED, WITH SUSPICIOUS MOTIVES!
WHILE HE IS LOST IN THOUGHT, THE NEARBY SWORD DEMON UNEXPECTEDLY VANISHES!

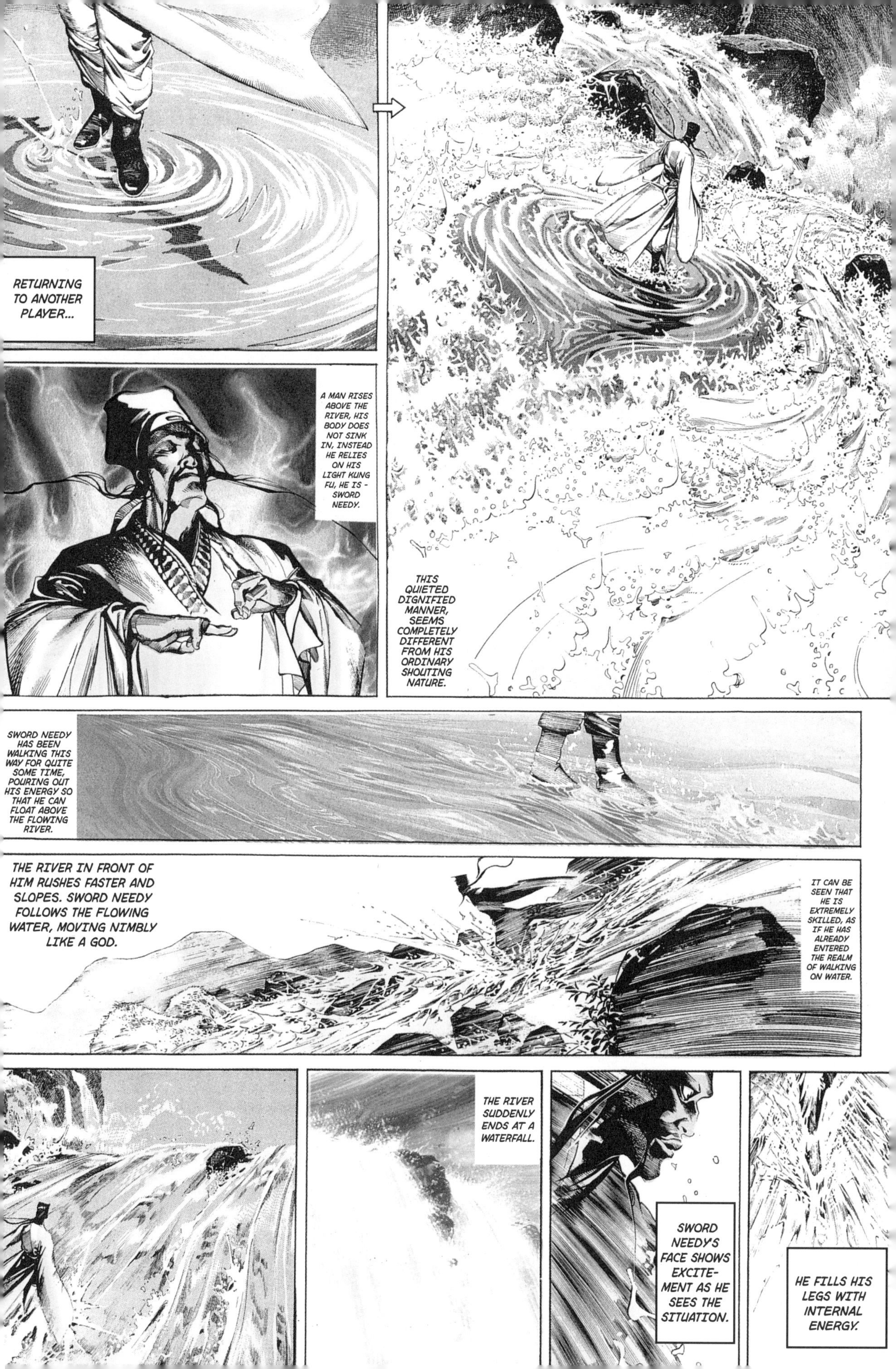
RETURNING TO ANOTHER PLAYER...
A MAN RISES ABOVE THE RIVER, HIS BODY DOES NOT SINK IN, INSTEAD HE RELIES ON HIS LIGHT KUNG FU, HE IS - SWORD NEEDY.
THIS QUIETED DIGNIFIED MANNER, SEEMS COMPLETELY DIFFERENT FROM HIS ORDINARY SHOUTING NATURE.
SWORD NEEDY HAS BEEN WALKING THIS WAY FOR QUITE SOME TIME, POURING OUT HIS ENERGY SO THAT HE CAN FLOAT ABOVE THE FLOWING RIVER.
THE RIVER IN FRONT OF HIM RUSHES FASTER AND SLOPES. SWORD NEEDY FOLLOWS THE FLOWING WATER, MOVING NIMBLY LIKE A GOD.
IT CAN BE SEEN THAT HE IS EXTREMELY SKILLED, AS IF HE HAS ALREADY ENTERED THE REALM OF WALKING ON WATER.
THE RIVER SUDDENLY ENDS AT A WATERFALL.
SWORD NEEDY'S FACE SHOWS EXCITE-MENT AS HE SEES THE SITUATION.
HE FILLS HIS LEGS WITH INTERNAL ENERGY.

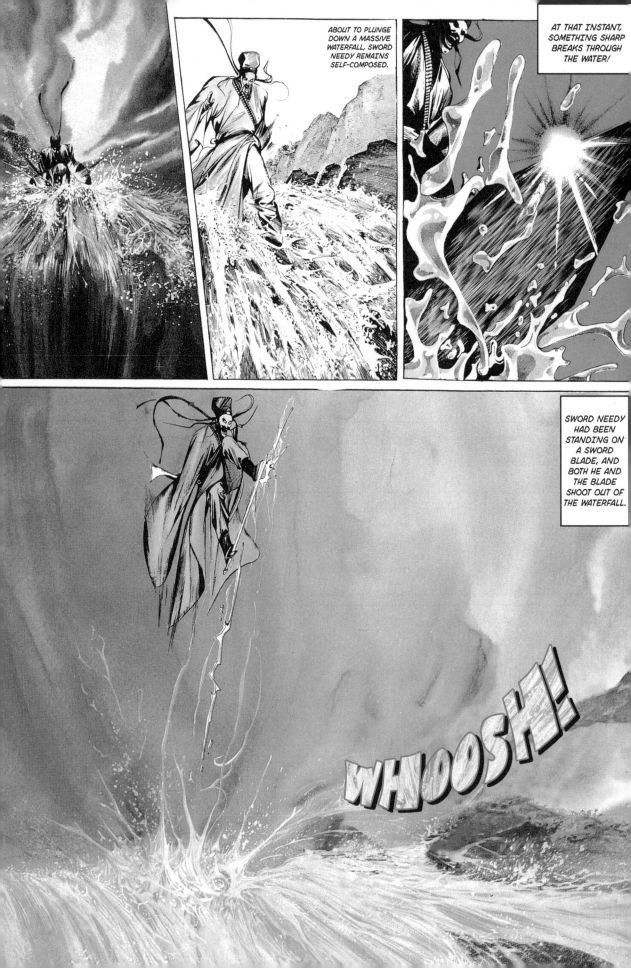

ABOUT TO PLUNGE DOWN A MASSIVE WATERFALL, SWORD NEEDY REMAINS SELF-COMPOSED.

AT THAT INSTANT, SOMETHING SHARP BREAKS THROUGH THE WATER!

SWORD NEEDY HAD BEEN STANDING ON A SWORD BLADE, AND BOTH HE AND THE BLADE SHOOT OUT OF THE WATERFALL.

WHOOSH!

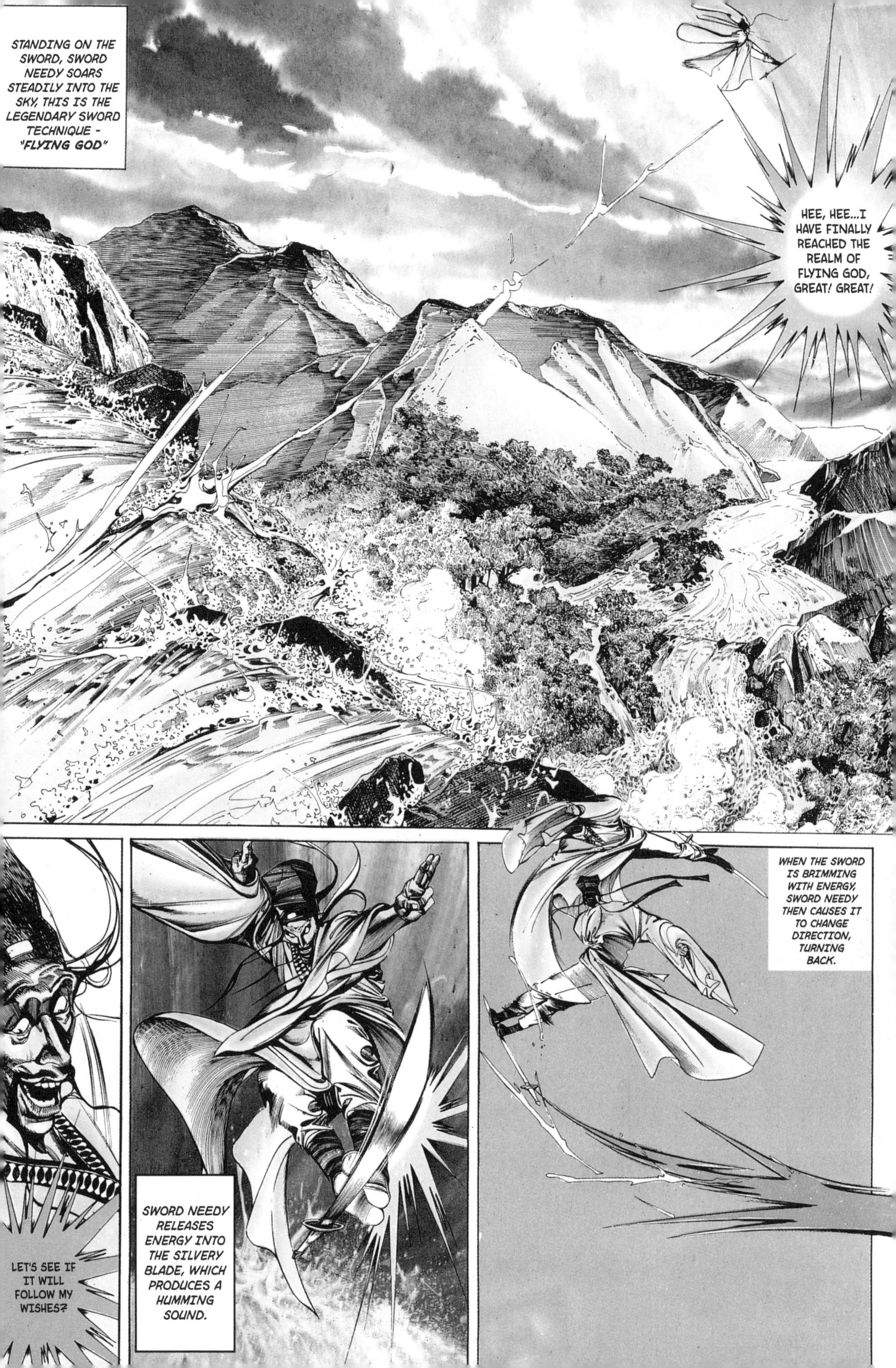
STANDING ON THE SWORD, SWORD NEEDY SOARS STEADILY INTO THE SKY, THIS IS THE LEGENDARY SWORD TECHNIQUE - "FLYING GOD"
HEE, HEE...I HAVE FINALLY REACHED THE REALM OF FLYING GOD, GREAT! GREAT!
LET'S SEE IF IT WILL FOLLOW MY WISHES?
SWORD NEEDY RELEASES ENERGY INTO THE SILVERY BLADE, WHICH PRODUCES A HUMMING SOUND.
WHEN THE SWORD IS BRIMMING WITH ENERGY, SWORD NEEDY THEN CAUSES IT TO CHANGE DIRECTION, TURNING BACK.

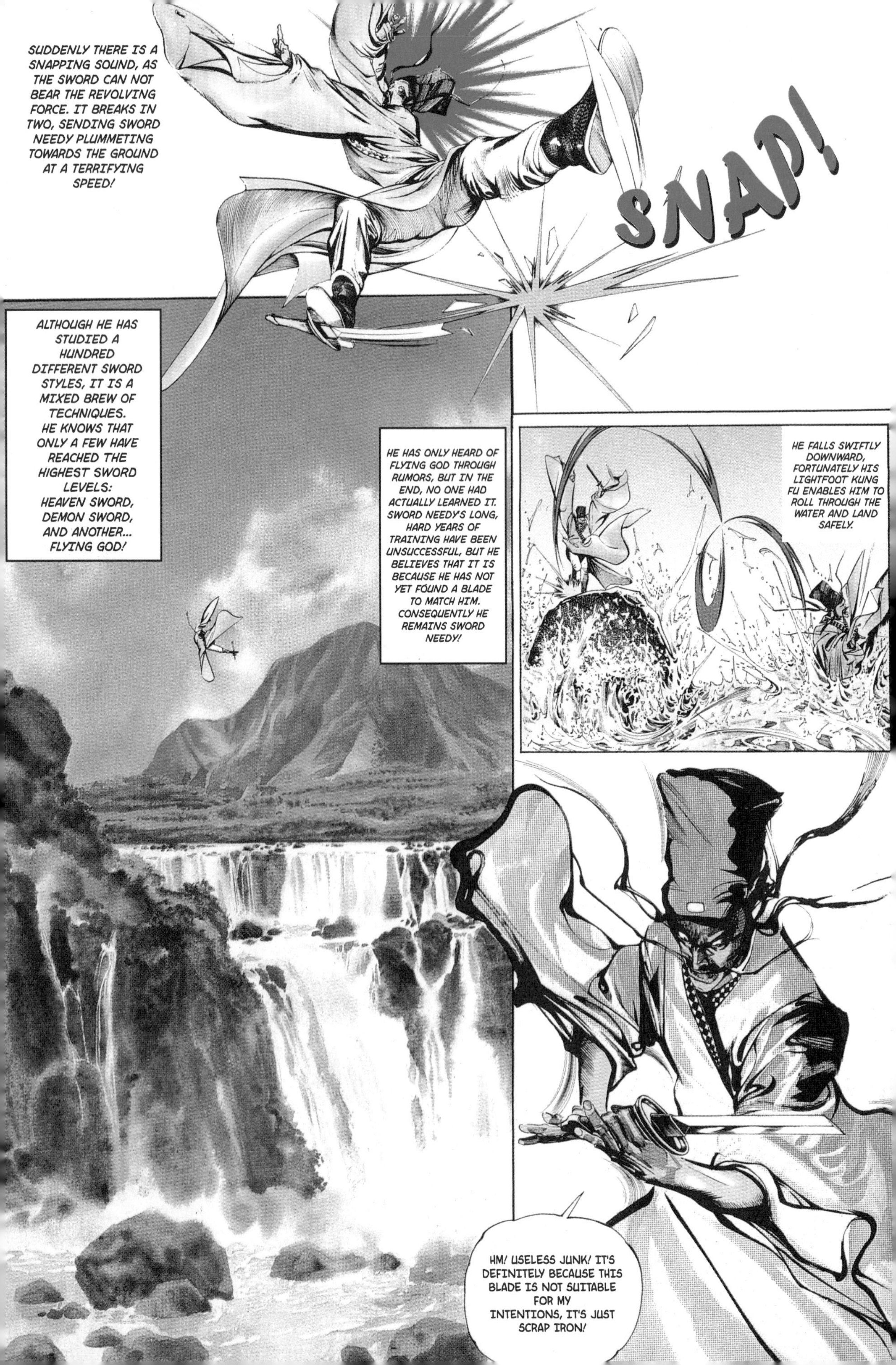
SUDDENLY THERE IS A SNAPPING SOUND, AS THE SWORD CAN NOT BEAR THE REVOLVING FORCE. IT BREAKS IN TWO, SENDING SWORD NEEDY PLUMMETING TOWARDS THE GROUND AT A TERRIFYING SPEED!
SNAP!
ALTHOUGH HE HAS STUDIED A HUNDRED DIFFERENT SWORD STYLES, IT IS A MIXED BREW OF TECHNIQUES. HE KNOWS THAT ONLY A FEW HAVE REACHED THE HIGHEST SWORD LEVELS: HEAVEN SWORD, DEMON SWORD, AND ANOTHER... FLYING GOD!
HE HAS ONLY HEARD OF FLYING GOD THROUGH RUMORS, BUT IN THE END, NO ONE HAD ACTUALLY LEARNED IT. SWORD NEEDY'S LONG, HARD YEARS OF TRAINING HAVE BEEN UNSUCCESSFUL, BUT HE BELIEVES THAT IT IS BECAUSE HE HAS NOT YET FOUND A BLADE TO MATCH HIM. CONSEQUENTLY HE REMAINS SWORD NEEDY!
HE FALLS SWIFTLY DOWNWARD, FORTUNATELY HIS LIGHTFOOT KUNG FU ENABLES HIM TO ROLL THROUGH THE WATER AND LAND SAFELY.
HM! USELESS JUNK! IT'S DEFINITELY BECAUSE THIS BLADE IS NOT SUITABLE FOR MY INTENTIONS, IT'S JUST SCRAP IRON!

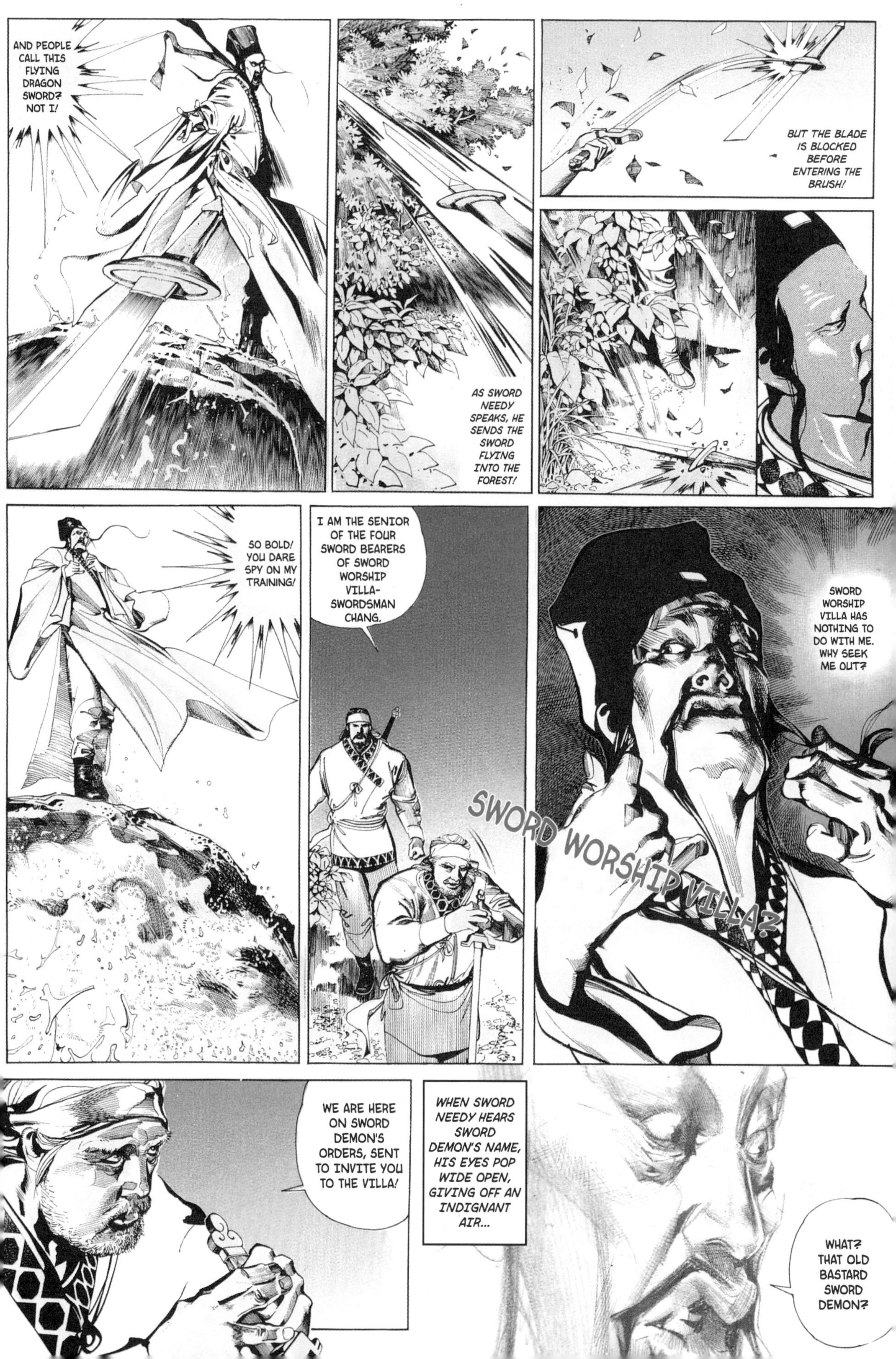
AND PEOPLE CALL THIS FLYING DRAGON SWORD? NOT I!
AS SWORD NEEDY SPEAKS, HE SENDS THE SWORD FLYING INTO THE FOREST!
BUT THE BLADE IS BLOCKED BEFORE ENTERING THE BRUSH!
SO BOLD! YOU DARE SPY ON MY TRAINING!
I AM THE SENIOR OF THE FOUR SWORD BEARERS OF SWORD WORSHIP VILLA- SWORDSMAN CHANG.
SWORD WORSHIP VILLA?
SWORD WORSHIP VILLA HAS NOTHING TO DO WITH ME. WHY SEEK ME OUT?
WE ARE HERE ON SWORD DEMON'S ORDERS, SENT TO INVITE YOU TO THE VILLA!
WHEN SWORD NEEDY HEARS SWORD DEMON'S NAME, HIS EYES POP WIDE OPEN, GIVING OFF AN INDIGNANT AIR...
WHAT? THAT OLD BASTARD SWORD DEMON?

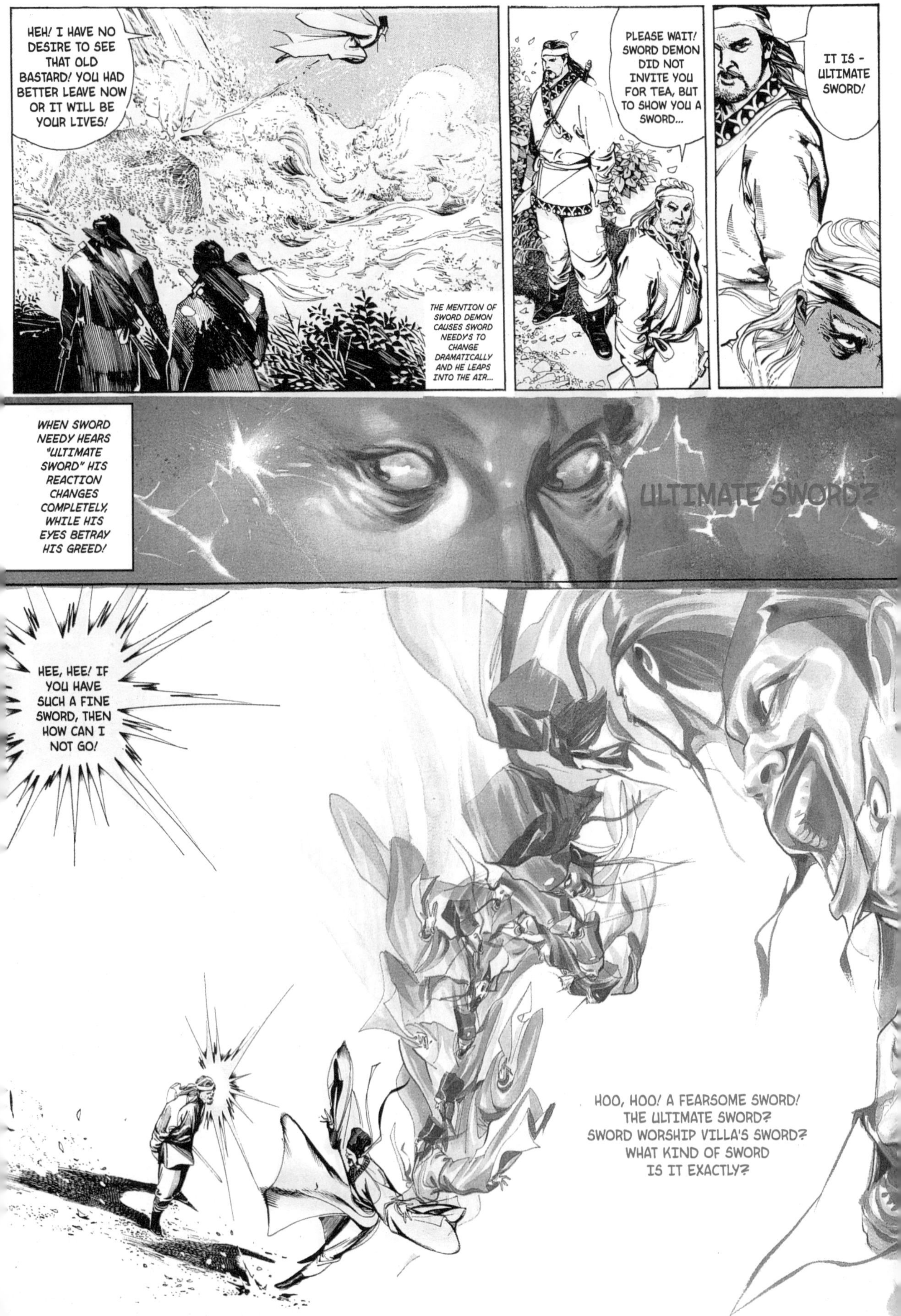

HEH! I HAVE NO DESIRE TO SEE THAT OLD BASTARD! YOU HAD BETTER LEAVE NOW OR IT WILL BE YOUR LIVES!
THE MENTION OF SWORD DEMON CAUSES SWORD NEEDY'S TO CHANGE DRAMATICALLY AND HE LEAPS INTO THE AIR...
PLEASE WAIT! SWORD DEMON DID NOT INVITE YOU FOR TEA, BUT TO SHOW YOU A SWORD...
IT IS - ULTIMATE SWORD!
WHEN SWORD NEEDY HEARS "ULTIMATE SWORD" HIS REACTION CHANGES COMPLETELY, WHILE HIS EYES BETRAY HIS GREED!
ULTIMATE SWORD?
HEE, HEE! IF YOU HAVE SUCH A FINE SWORD, THEN HOW CAN I NOT GO!
HOO, HOO! A FEARSOME SWORD! THE ULTIMATE SWORD? SWORD WORSHIP VILLA'S SWORD? WHAT KIND OF SWORD IS IT EXACTLY?

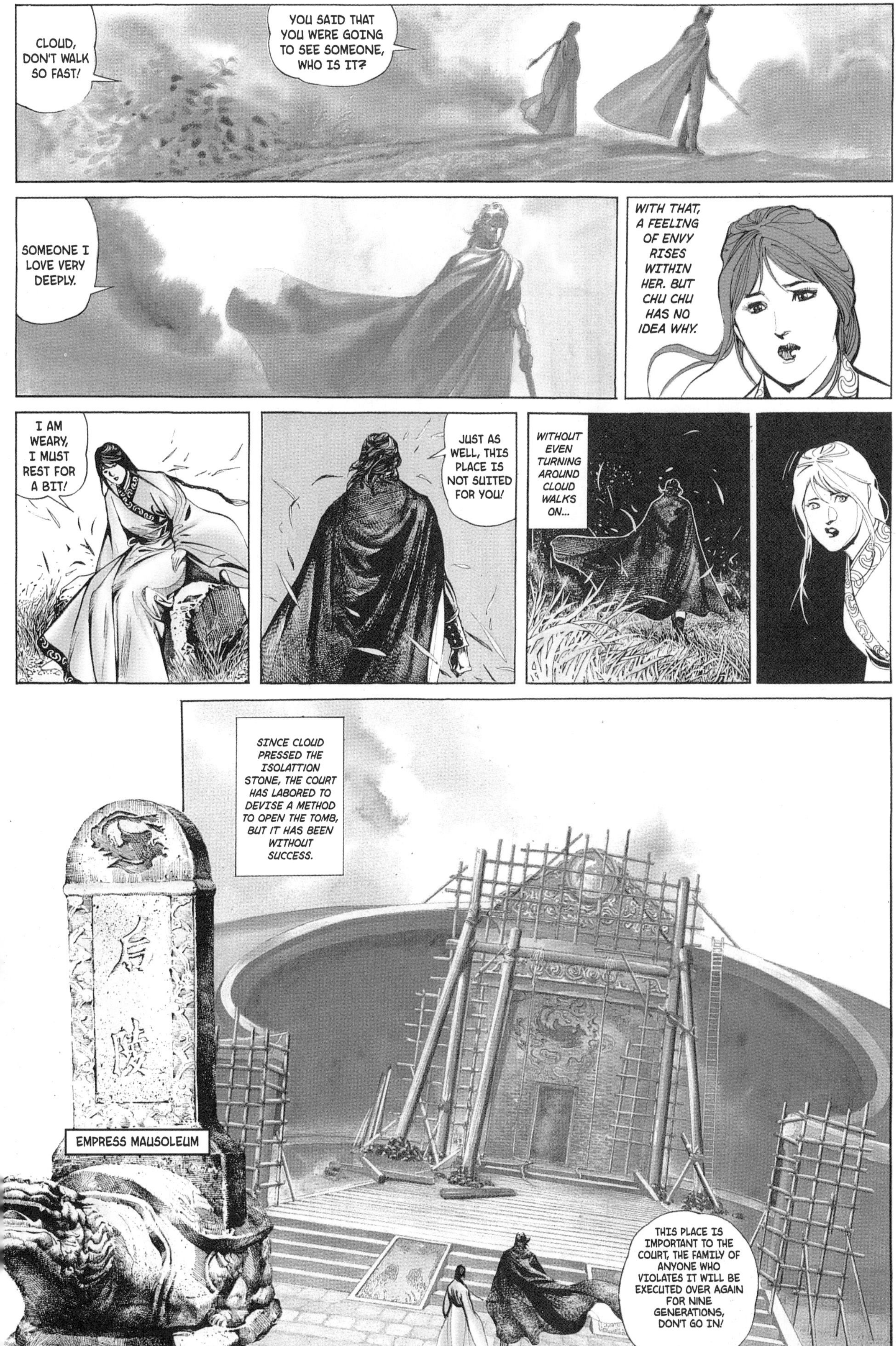

CLOUD, DON'T WALK SO FAST!
YOU SAID THAT YOU WERE GOING TO SEE SOMEONE, WHO IS IT?
SOMEONE I LOVE VERY DEEPLY.
WITH THAT, A FEELING OF ENVY RISES WITHIN HER. BUT CHU CHU HAS NO IDEA WHY.
I AM WEARY, I MUST REST FOR A BIT!
JUST AS WELL, THIS PLACE IS NOT SUITED FOR YOU!
WITHOUT EVEN TURNING AROUND CLOUD WALKS ON...
SINCE CLOUD PRESSED THE ISOLATTION STONE, THE COURT HAS LABORED TO DEVISE A METHOD TO OPEN THE TOMB, BUT IT HAS BEEN WITHOUT SUCCESS.
EMPRESS MAUSOLEUM
THIS PLACE IS IMPORTANT TO THE COURT, THE FAMILY OF ANYONE WHO VIOLATES IT WILL BE EXECUTED OVER AGAIN FOR NINE GENERATIONS, DON'T GO IN!

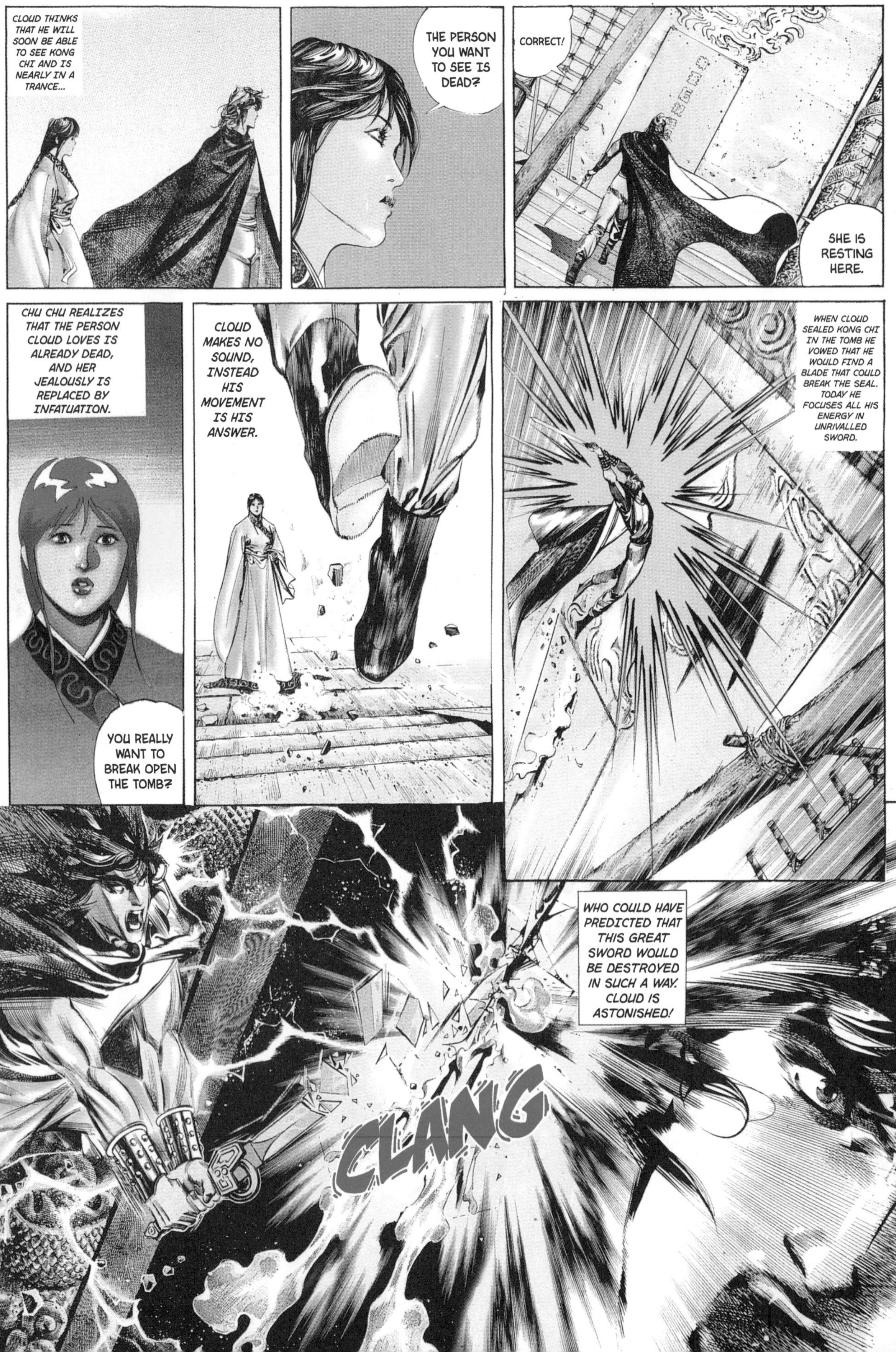

CLOUD THINKS THAT HE WILL SOON BE ABLE TO SEE KONG CHI AND IS NEARLY IN A TRANCE...
THE PERSON YOU WANT TO SEE IS DEAD?
CORRECT!
SHE IS RESTING HERE.
CHU CHU REALIZES THAT THE PERSON CLOUD LOVES IS ALREADY DEAD, AND HER JEALOUSLY IS REPLACED BY INFATUATION.
YOU REALLY WANT TO BREAK OPEN THE TOMB?
CLOUD MAKES NO SOUND, INSTEAD HIS MOVEMENT IS HIS ANSWER.
WHEN CLOUD SEALED KONG CHI IN THE TOMB HE VOWED THAT HE WOULD FIND A BLADE THAT COULD BREAK THE SEAL. TODAY HE FOCUSES ALL HIS ENERGY IN UNRIVALLED SWORD.
WHO COULD HAVE PREDICTED THAT THIS GREAT SWORD WOULD BE DESTROYED IN SUCH A WAY. CLOUD IS ASTONISHED!
CLANG

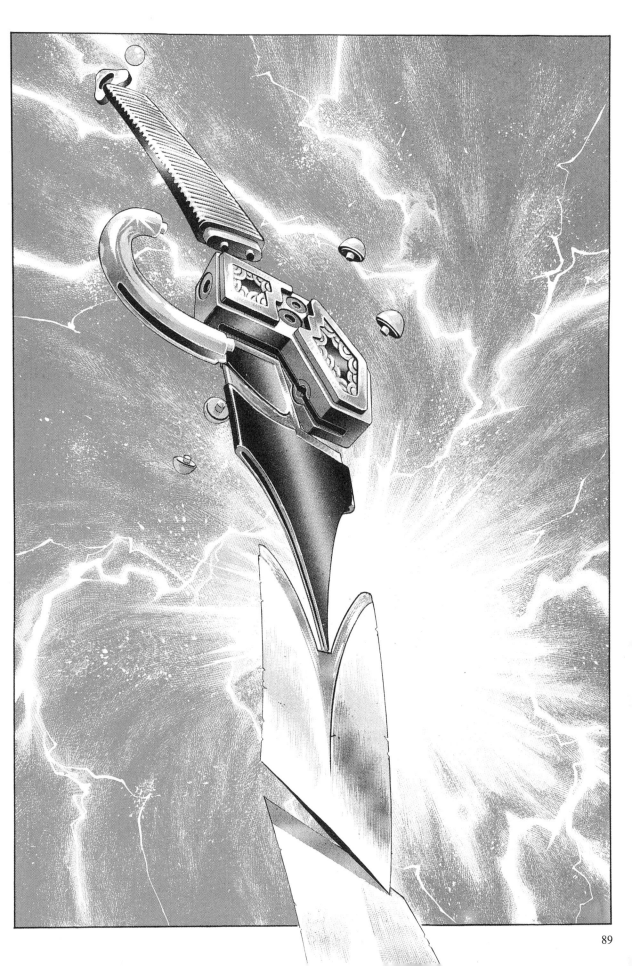

# CHAPTER 43: SWORD TEST

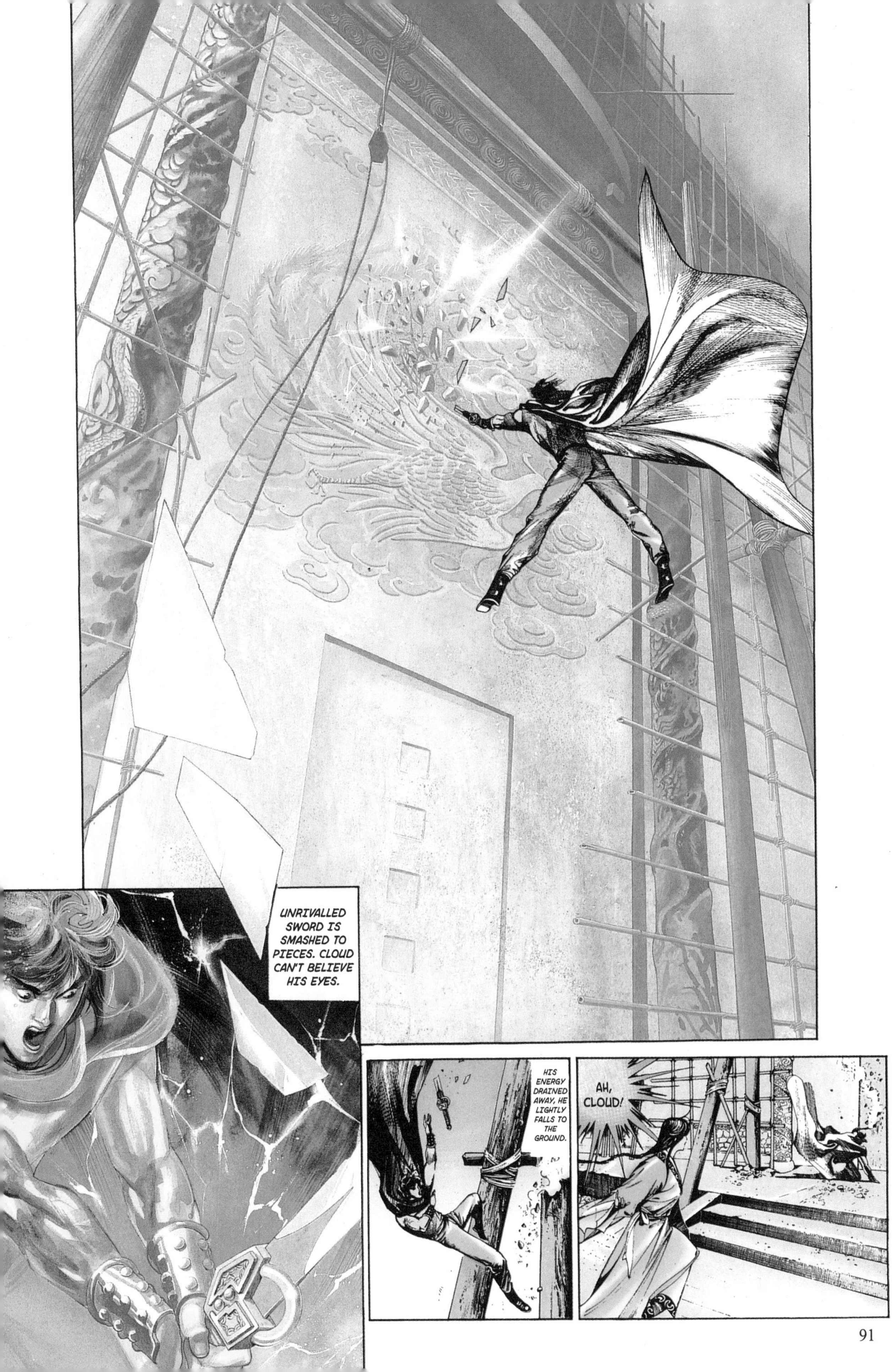
UNRIVALLED SWORD IS SMASHED TO PIECES. CLOUD CAN'T BELIEVE HIS EYES.
HIS ENERGY DRAINED AWAY, HE LIGHTLY FALLS TO THE GROUND.
AH, CLOUD!

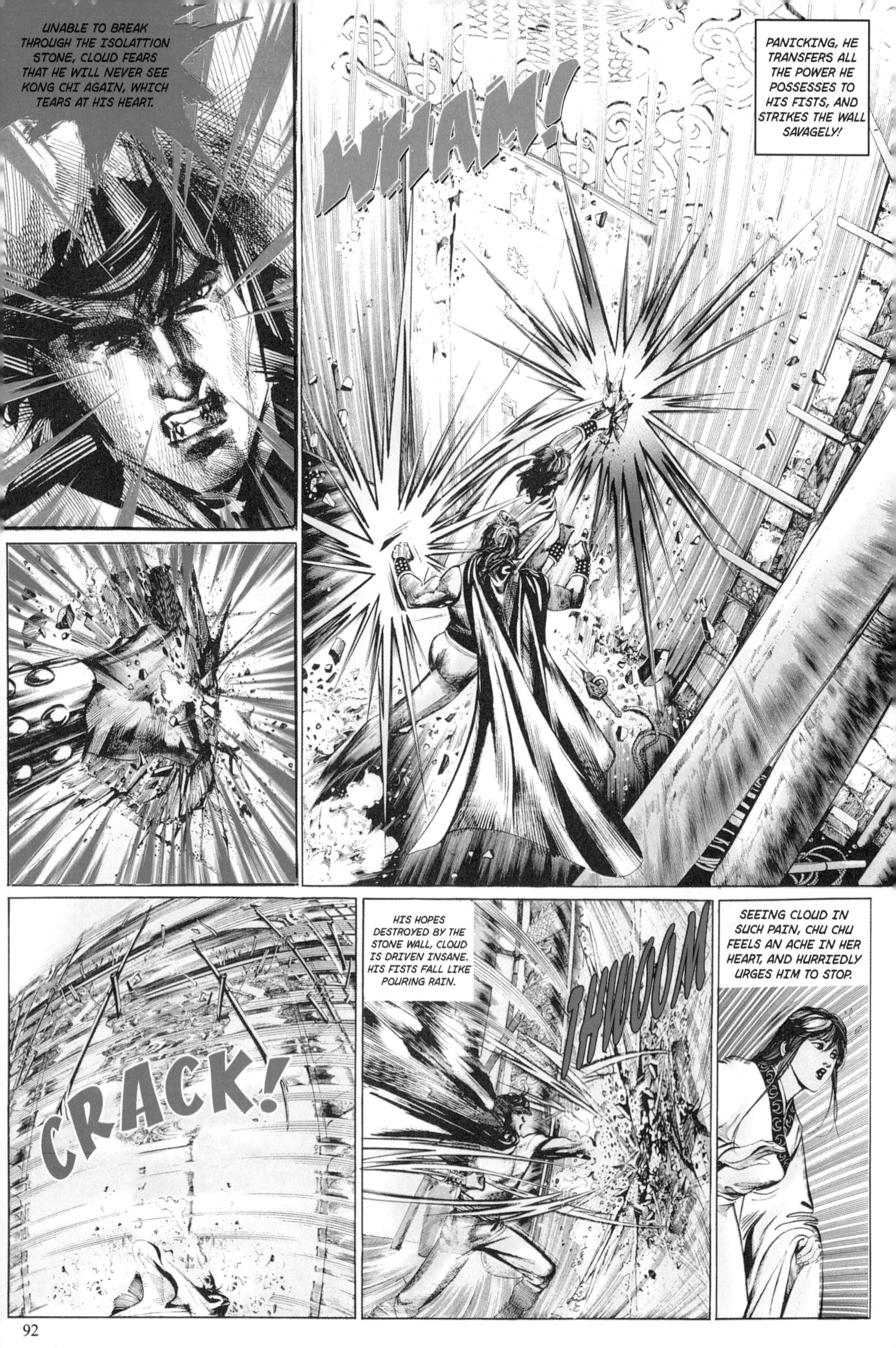
UNABLE TO BREAK THROUGH THE ISOLATTION STONE, CLOUD FEARS THAT HE WILL NEVER SEE KONG CHI AGAIN, WHICH TEARS AT HIS HEART.
PANICKING, HE TRANSFERS ALL THE POWER HE POSSESSES TO HIS FISTS, AND STRIKES THE WALL SAVAGELY!
WHAM!
CRACK!
HIS HOPES DESTROYED BY THE STONE WALL, CLOUD IS DRIVEN INSANE. HIS FISTS FALL LIKE POURING RAIN.
THWOOM
SEEING CLOUD IN SUCH PAIN, CHU CHU FEELS AN ACHE IN HER HEART, AND HURRIEDLY URGES HIM TO STOP.

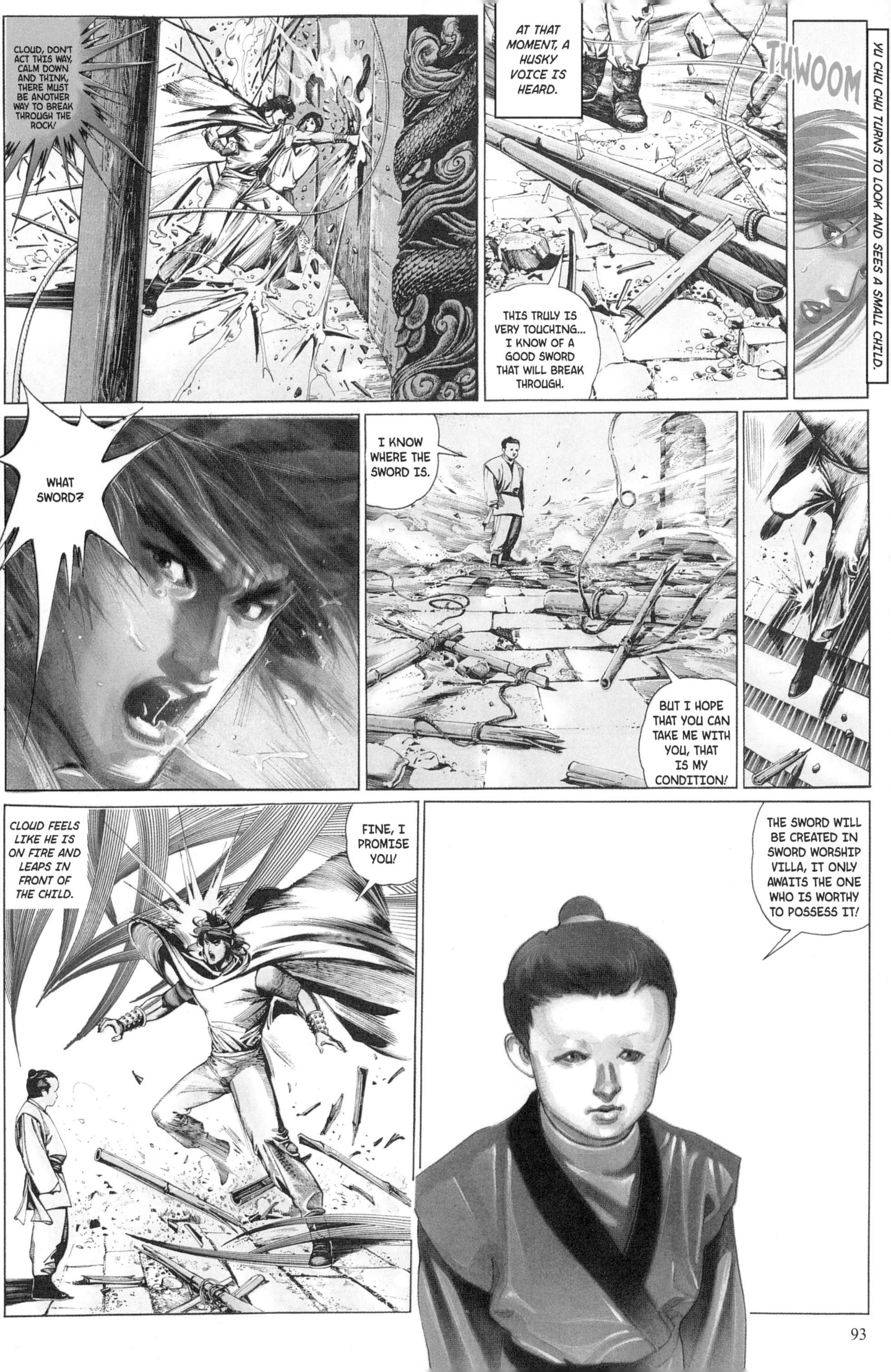
CLOUD, DON'T ACT THIS WAY, CALM DOWN AND THINK, THERE MUST BE ANOTHER WAY TO BREAK THROUGH THE ROCK!
AT THAT MOMENT, A HUSKY VOICE IS HEARD.
THIS TRULY IS VERY TOUCHING... I KNOW OF A GOOD SWORD THAT WILL BREAK THROUGH.
THWOOM
YU CHU CHU TURNS TO LOOK AND SEES A SMALL CHILD.
WHAT SWORD?
I KNOW WHERE THE SWORD IS.
BUT I HOPE THAT YOU CAN TAKE ME WITH YOU, THAT IS MY CONDITION!
CLOUD FEELS LIKE HE IS ON FIRE AND LEAPS IN FRONT OF THE CHILD.
FINE, I PROMISE YOU!
THE SWORD WILL BE CREATED IN SWORD WORSHIP VILLA, IT ONLY AWAITS THE ONE WHO IS WORTHY TO POSSESS IT!

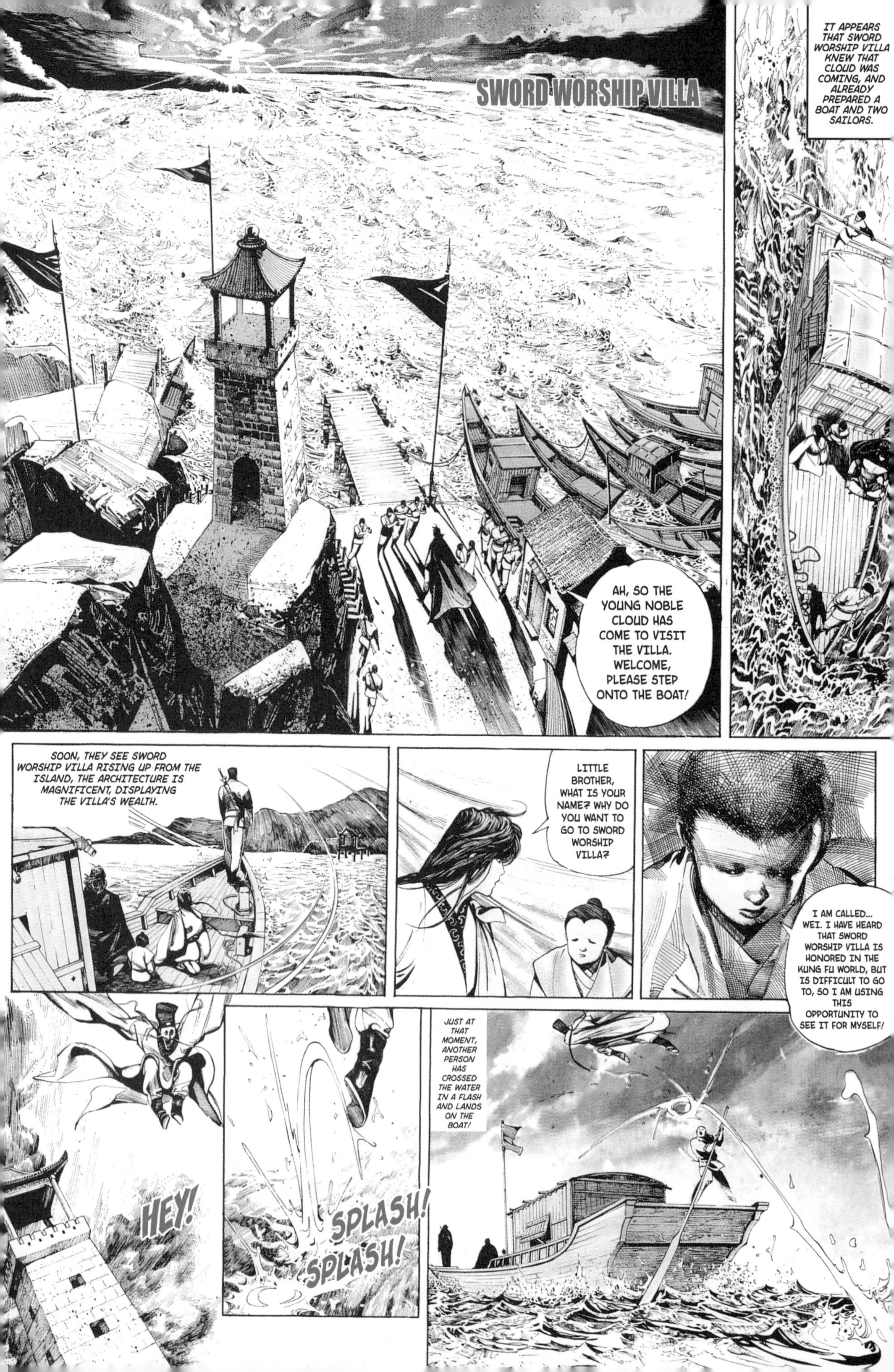
SWORD WORSHIP VILLA
IT APPEARS THAT SWORD WORSHIP VILLA KNEW THAT CLOUD WAS COMING, AND ALREADY PREPARED A BOAT AND TWO SAILORS.
AH, SO THE YOUNG NOBLE CLOUD HAS COME TO VISIT THE VILLA. WELCOME, PLEASE STEP ONTO THE BOAT!
SOON, THEY SEE SWORD WORSHIP VILLA RISING UP FROM THE ISLAND, THE ARCHITECTURE IS MAGNIFICENT, DISPLAYING THE VILLA'S WEALTH.
LITTLE BROTHER, WHAT IS YOUR NAME? WHY DO YOU WANT TO GO TO SWORD WORSHIP VILLA?
I AM CALLED... WEI. I HAVE HEARD THAT SWORD WORSHIP VILLA IS HONORED IN THE KUNG FU WORLD, BUT IS DIFFICULT TO GO TO, SO I AM USING THIS OPPORTUNITY TO SEE IT FOR MYSELF!
HEY!
SPLASH!
SPLASH!
JUST AT THAT MOMENT, ANOTHER PERSON HAS CROSSED THE WATER IN A FLASH AND LANDS ON THE BOAT!

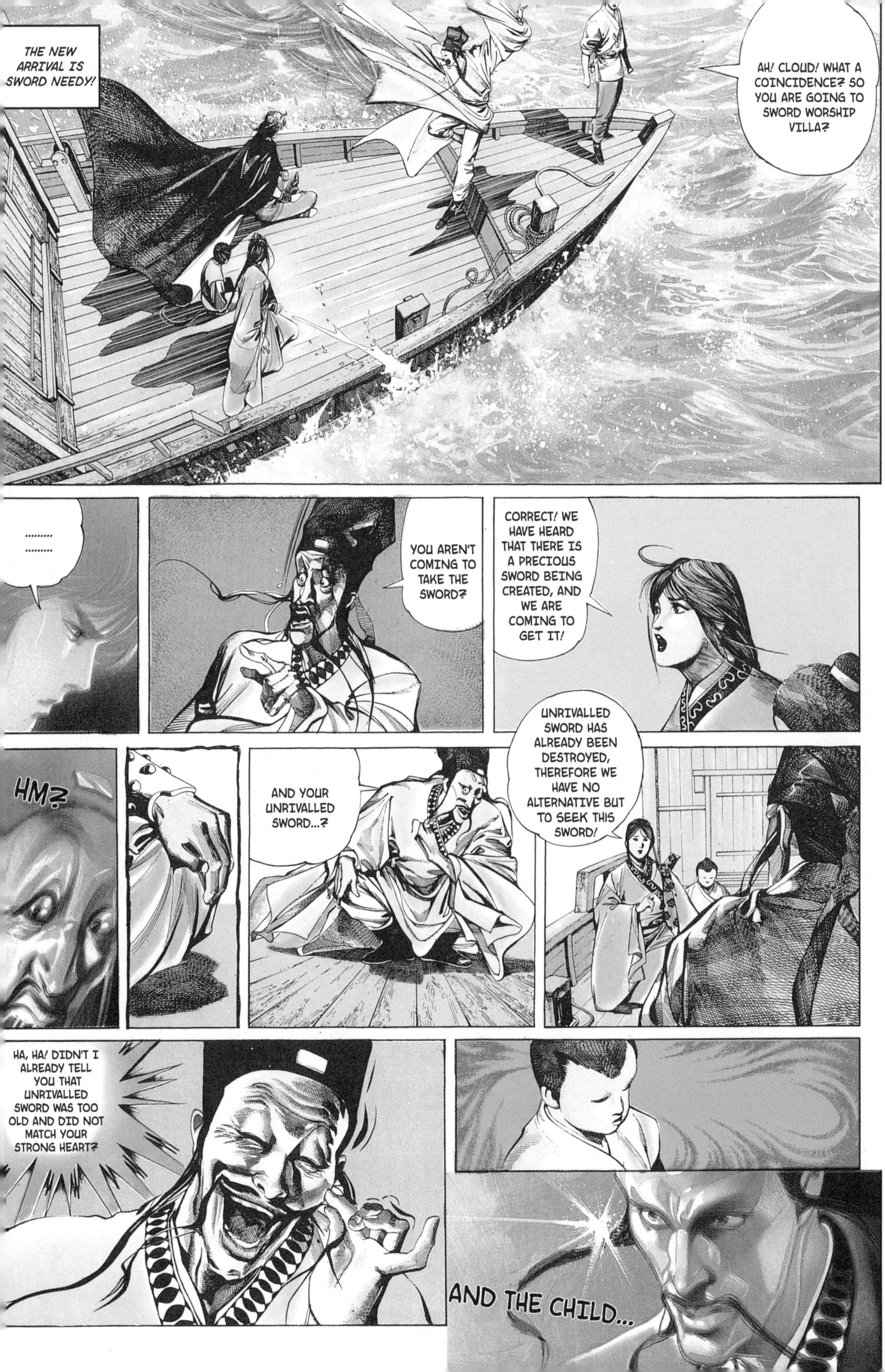
THE NEW ARRIVAL IS SWORD NEEDY!
AH! CLOUD! WHAT A COINCIDENCE? SO YOU ARE GOING TO SWORD WORSHIP VILLA?
.........
.........
YOU AREN'T COMING TO TAKE THE SWORD?
CORRECT! WE HAVE HEARD THAT THERE IS A PRECIOUS SWORD BEING CREATED, AND WE ARE COMING TO GET IT!
HM?
AND YOUR UNRIVALLED SWORD...?
UNRIVALLED SWORD HAS ALREADY BEEN DESTROYED, THEREFORE WE HAVE NO ALTERNATIVE BUT TO SEEK THIS SWORD!
HA, HA! DIDN'T I ALREADY TELL YOU THAT UNRIVALLED SWORD WAS TOO OLD AND DID NOT MATCH YOUR STRONG HEART?
AND THE CHILD...

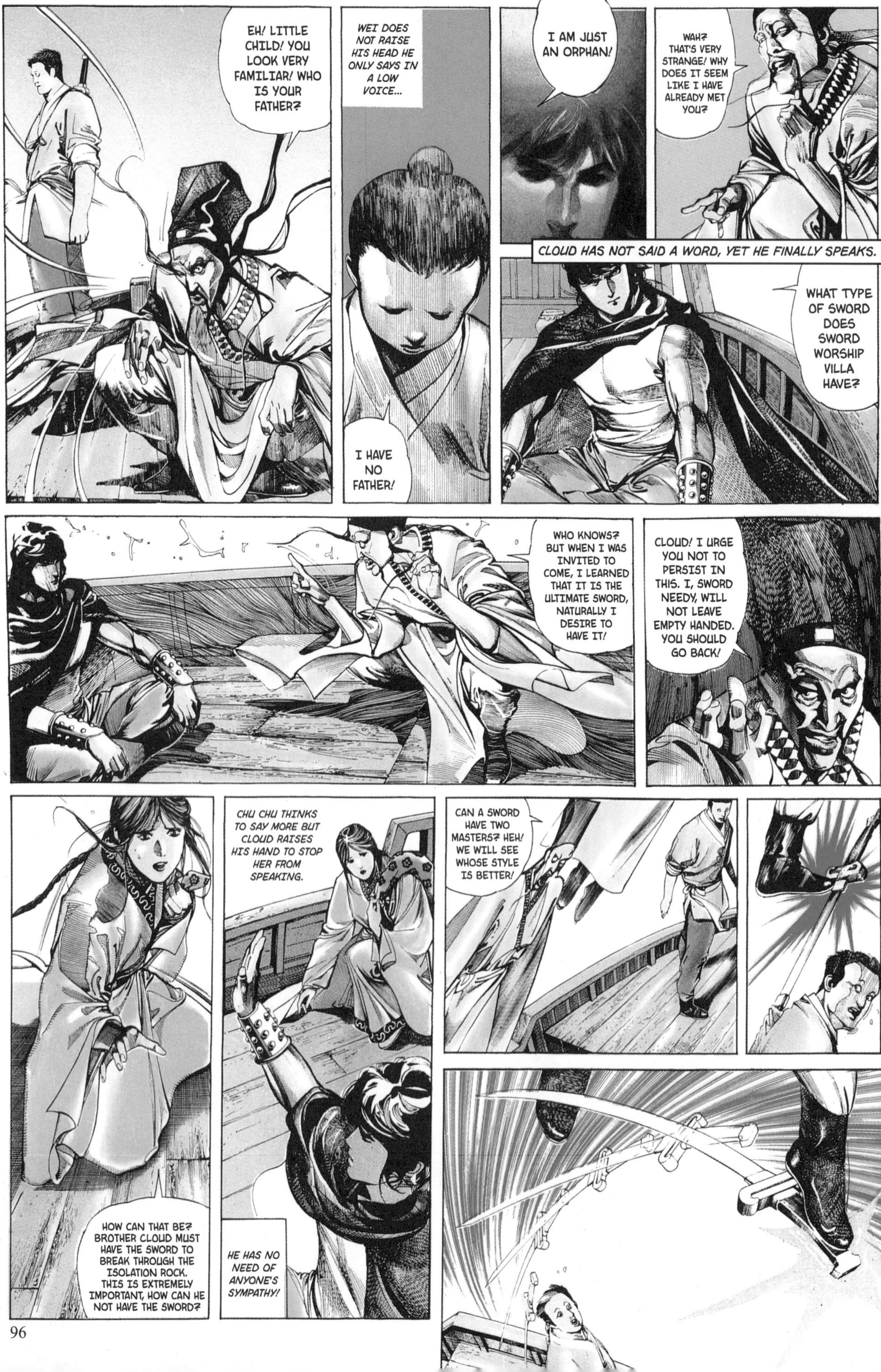
EH! LITTLE CHILD! YOU LOOK VERY FAMILIAR! WHO IS YOUR FATHER?
WEI DOES NOT RAISE HIS HEAD HE ONLY SAYS IN A LOW VOICE...
I HAVE NO FATHER!
I AM JUST AN ORPHAN!
WAH? THAT'S VERY STRANGE! WHY DOES IT SEEM LIKE I HAVE ALREADY MET YOU?
CLOUD HAS NOT SAID A WORD, YET HE FINALLY SPEAKS.
WHAT TYPE OF SWORD DOES SWORD WORSHIP VILLA HAVE?
WHO KNOWS? BUT WHEN I WAS INVITED TO COME, I LEARNED THAT IT IS THE ULTIMATE SWORD, NATURALLY I DESIRE TO HAVE IT!
CLOUD! I URGE YOU NOT TO PERSIST IN THIS. I, SWORD NEEDY, WILL NOT LEAVE EMPTY HANDED. YOU SHOULD GO BACK!
HOW CAN THAT BE? BROTHER CLOUD MUST HAVE THE SWORD TO BREAK THROUGH THE ISOLATION ROCK. THIS IS EXTREMELY IMPORTANT, HOW CAN HE NOT HAVE THE SWORD?
CHU CHU THINKS TO SAY MORE BUT CLOUD RAISES HIS HAND TO STOP HER FROM SPEAKING.
HE HAS NO NEED OF ANYONE'S SYMPATHY!
CAN A SWORD HAVE TWO MASTERS? HEH! WE WILL SEE WHOSE STYLE IS BETTER!

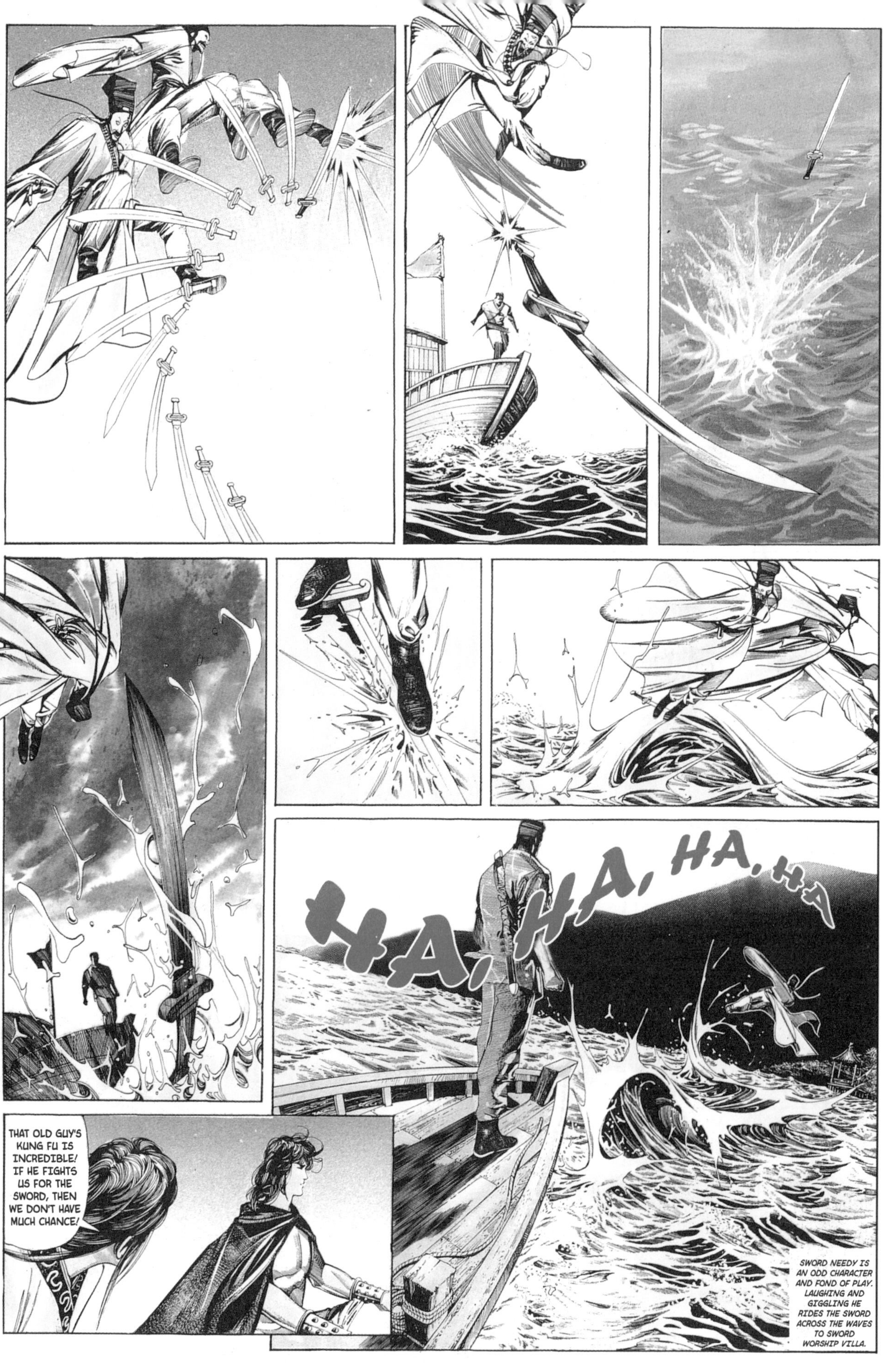
HA, HA, HA, HA, HA
THAT OLD GUY'S KUNG FU IS INCREDIBLE! IF HE FIGHTS US FOR THE SWORD, THEN WE DON'T HAVE MUCH CHANCE!
SWORD NEEDY IS AN ODD CHARACTER AND FOND OF PLAY. LAUGHING AND GIGGLING HE RIDES THE SWORD ACROSS THE WAVES TO SWORD WORSHIP VILLA.

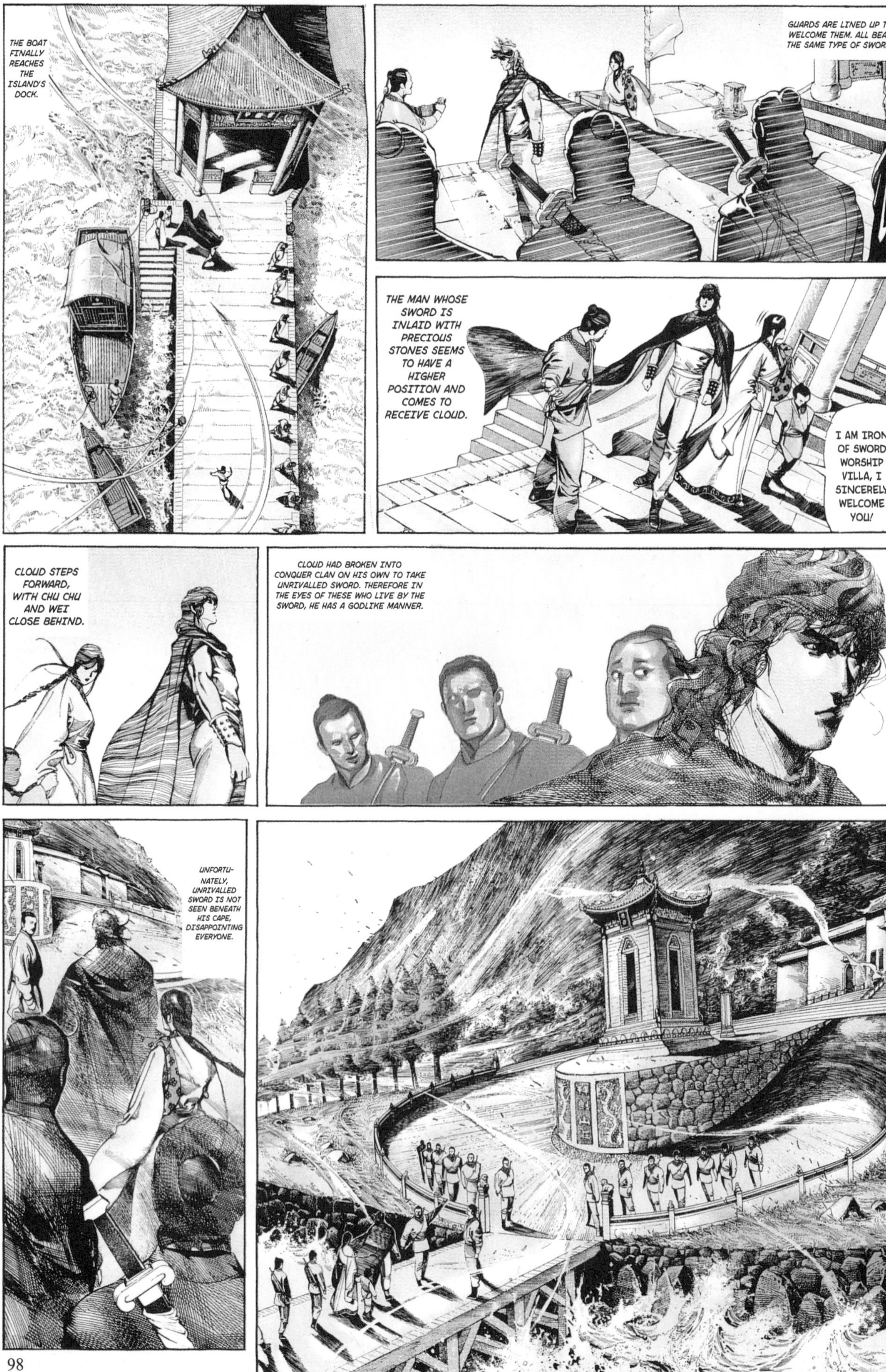
THE BOAT FINALLY REACHES THE ISLAND'S DOCK.
GUARDS ARE LINED UP TO WELCOME THEM. ALL BEAR THE SAME TYPE OF SWORD.
THE MAN WHOSE SWORD IS INLAID WITH PRECIOUS STONES SEEMS TO HAVE A HIGHER POSITION AND COMES TO RECEIVE CLOUD.
I AM IRON OF SWORD WORSHIP VILLA, I SINCERELY WELCOME YOU!
CLOUD STEPS FORWARD, WITH CHU CHU AND WEI CLOSE BEHIND.
CLOUD HAD BROKEN INTO CONQUER CLAN ON HIS OWN TO TAKE UNRIVALLED SWORD. THEREFORE IN THE EYES OF THESE WHO LIVE BY THE SWORD, HE HAS A GODLIKE MANNER.
UNFORTU-NATELY, UNRIVALLED SWORD IS NOT SEEN BENEATH HIS CAPE, DISAPPOINTING EVERYONE.

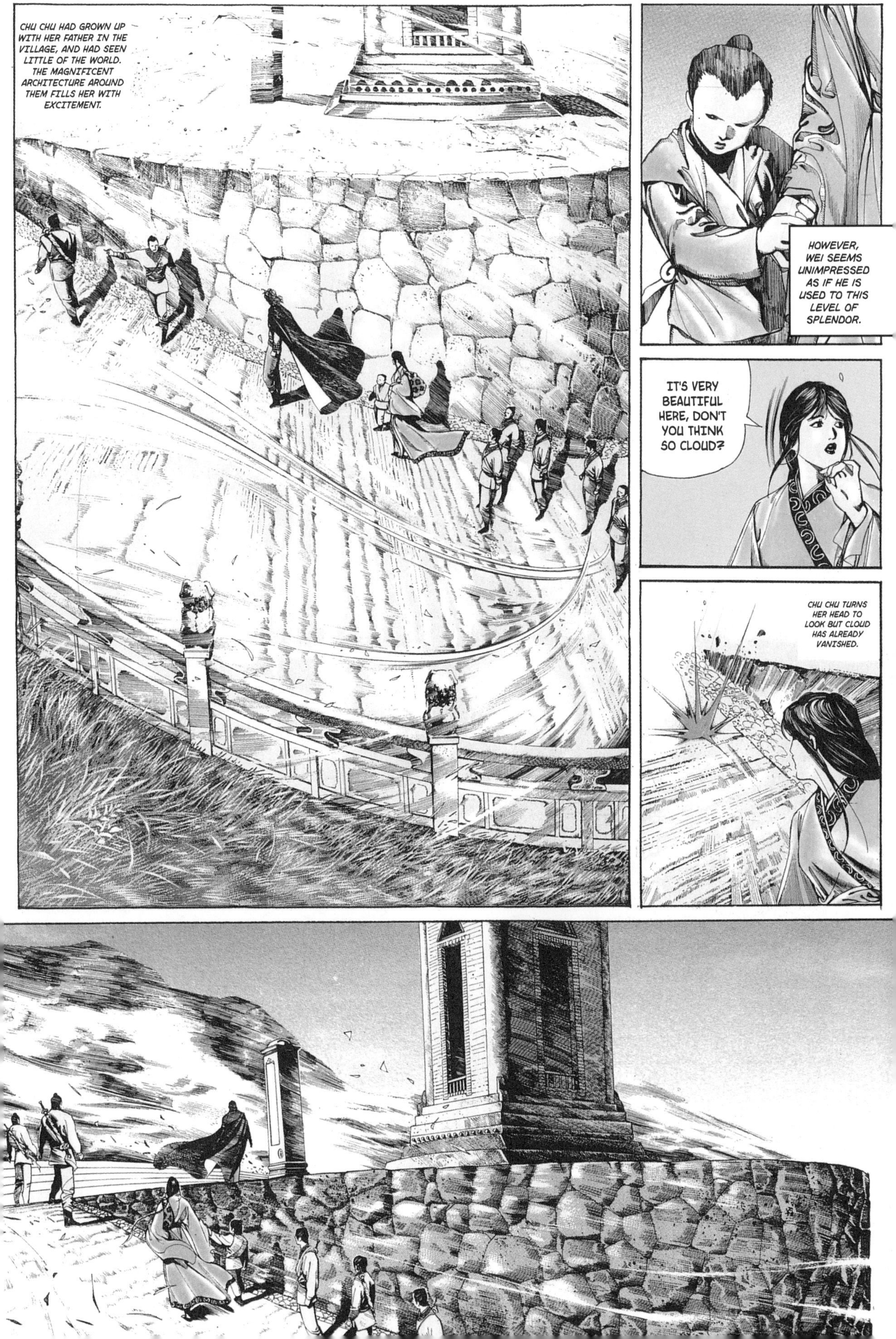
CHU CHU HAD GROWN UP WITH HER FATHER IN THE VILLAGE, AND HAD SEEN LITTLE OF THE WORLD. THE MAGNIFICENT ARCHITECTURE AROUND THEM FILLS HER WITH EXCITEMENT.
HOWEVER, WEI SEEMS UNIMPRESSED AS IF HE IS USED TO THIS LEVEL OF SPLENDOR.
IT'S VERY BEAUTIFUL HERE, DON'T YOU THINK SO CLOUD?
CHU CHU TURNS HER HEAD TO LOOK BUT CLOUD HAS ALREADY VANISHED.

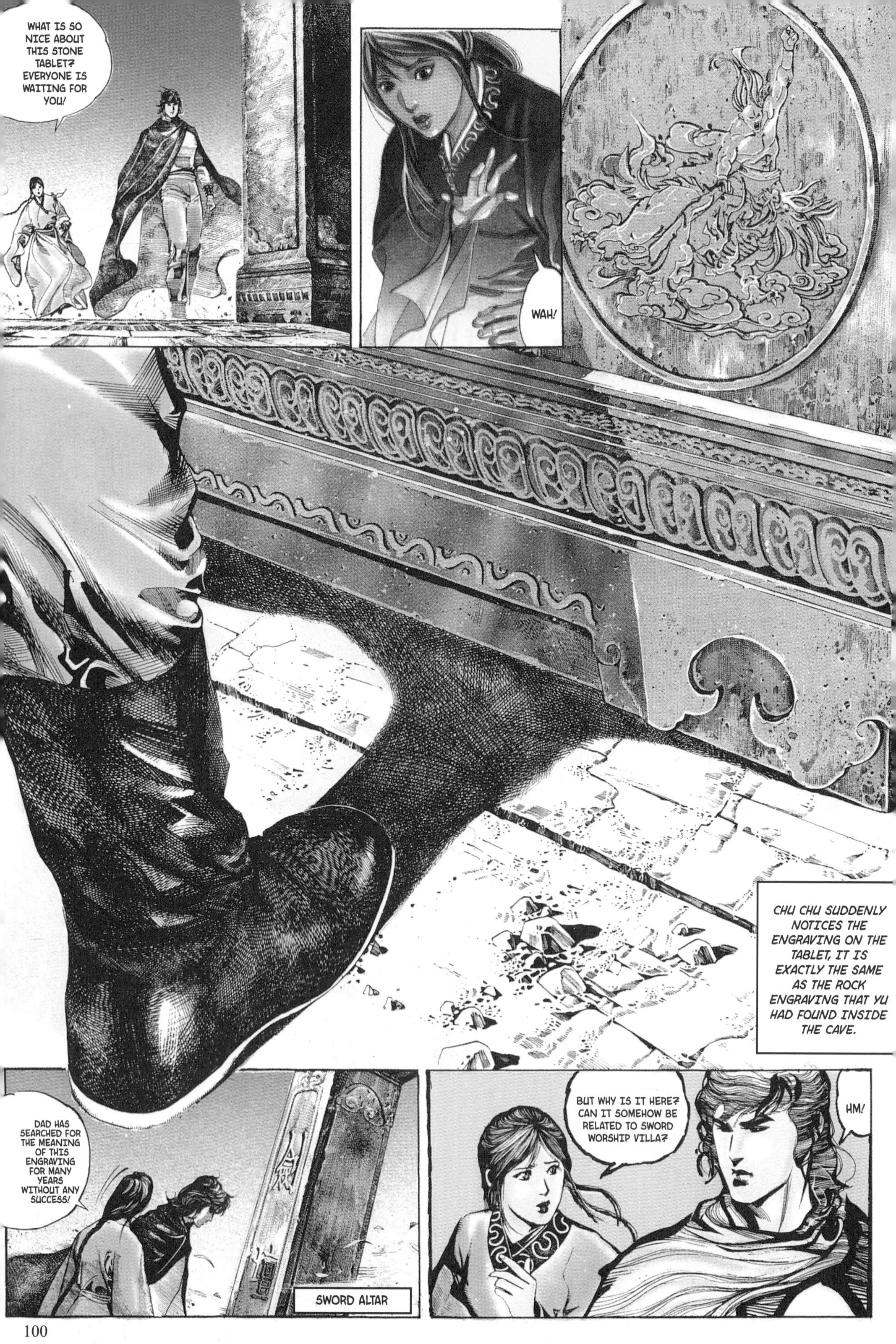
WHAT IS SO NICE ABOUT THIS STONE TABLET? EVERYONE IS WAITING FOR YOU!
WAH!
CHU CHU SUDDENLY NOTICES THE ENGRAVING ON THE TABLET, IT IS EXACTLY THE SAME AS THE ROCK ENGRAVING THAT YU HAD FOUND INSIDE THE CAVE.
DAD HAS SEARCHED FOR THE MEANING OF THIS ENGRAVING FOR MANY YEARS WITHOUT ANY SUCCESS!
SWORD ALTAR
BUT WHY IS IT HERE? CAN IT SOMEHOW BE RELATED TO SWORD WORSHIP VILLA?
HM!

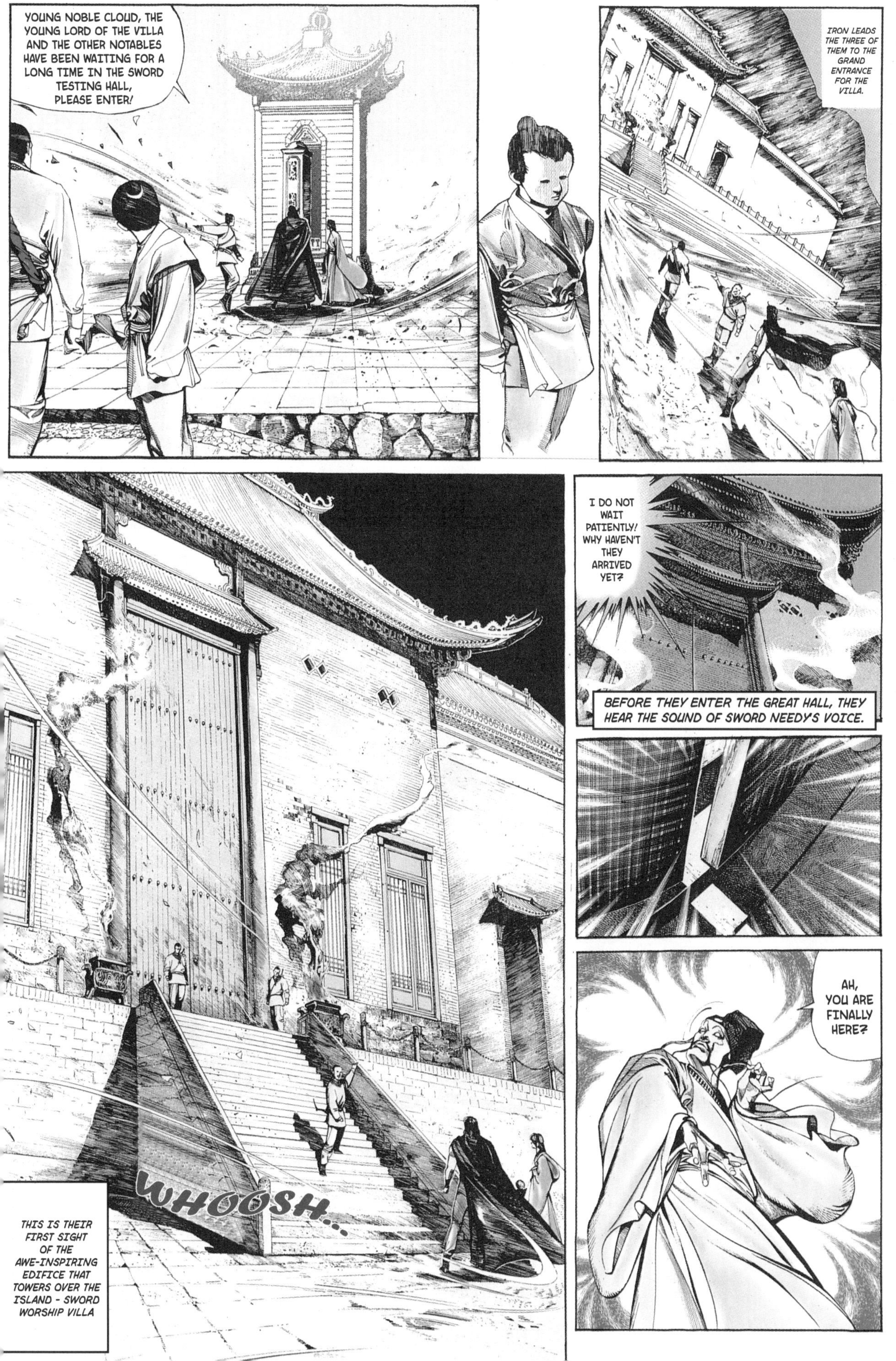
YOUNG NOBLE CLOUD, THE YOUNG LORD OF THE VILLA AND THE OTHER NOTABLES HAVE BEEN WAITING FOR A LONG TIME IN THE SWORD TESTING HALL, PLEASE ENTER!
IRON LEADS THE THREE OF THEM TO THE GRAND ENTRANCE FOR THE VILLA.
WHOOSH...
THIS IS THEIR FIRST SIGHT OF THE AWE-INSPIRING EDIFICE THAT TOWERS OVER THE ISLAND - SWORD WORSHIP VILLA
I DO NOT WAIT PATIENTLY! WHY HAVEN'T THEY ARRIVED YET?
BEFORE THEY ENTER THE GREAT HALL, THEY HEAR THE SOUND OF SWORD NEEDY'S VOICE.
AH, YOU ARE FINALLY HERE?

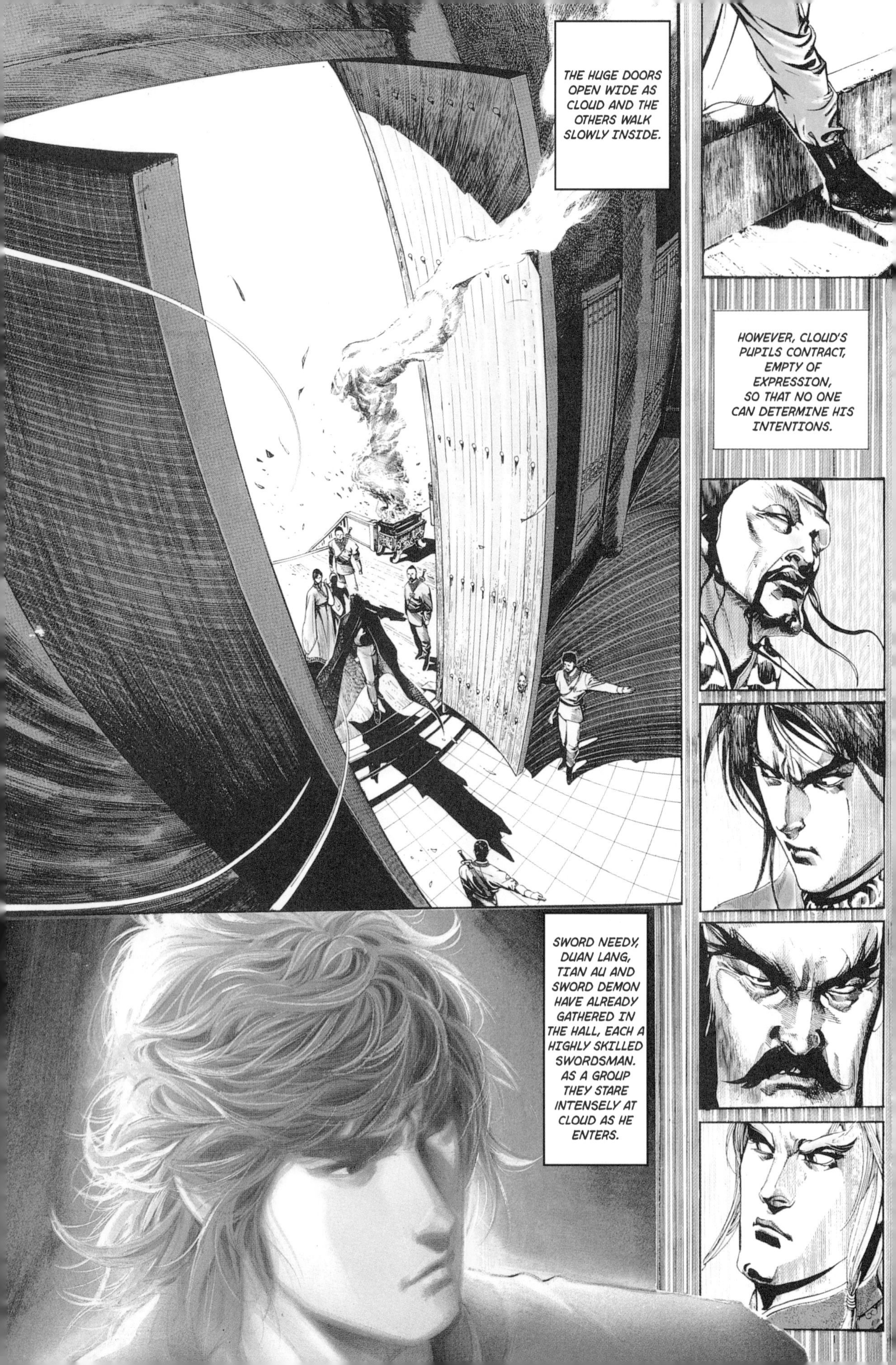
THE HUGE DOORS OPEN WIDE AS CLOUD AND THE OTHERS WALK SLOWLY INSIDE.
HOWEVER, CLOUD'S PUPILS CONTRACT, EMPTY OF EXPRESSION, SO THAT NO ONE CAN DETERMINE HIS INTENTIONS.
SWORD NEEDY, DUAN LANG, TIAN AU AND SWORD DEMON HAVE ALREADY GATHERED IN THE HALL, EACH A HIGHLY SKILLED SWORDSMAN. AS A GROUP THEY STARE INTENSELY AT CLOUD AS HE ENTERS.

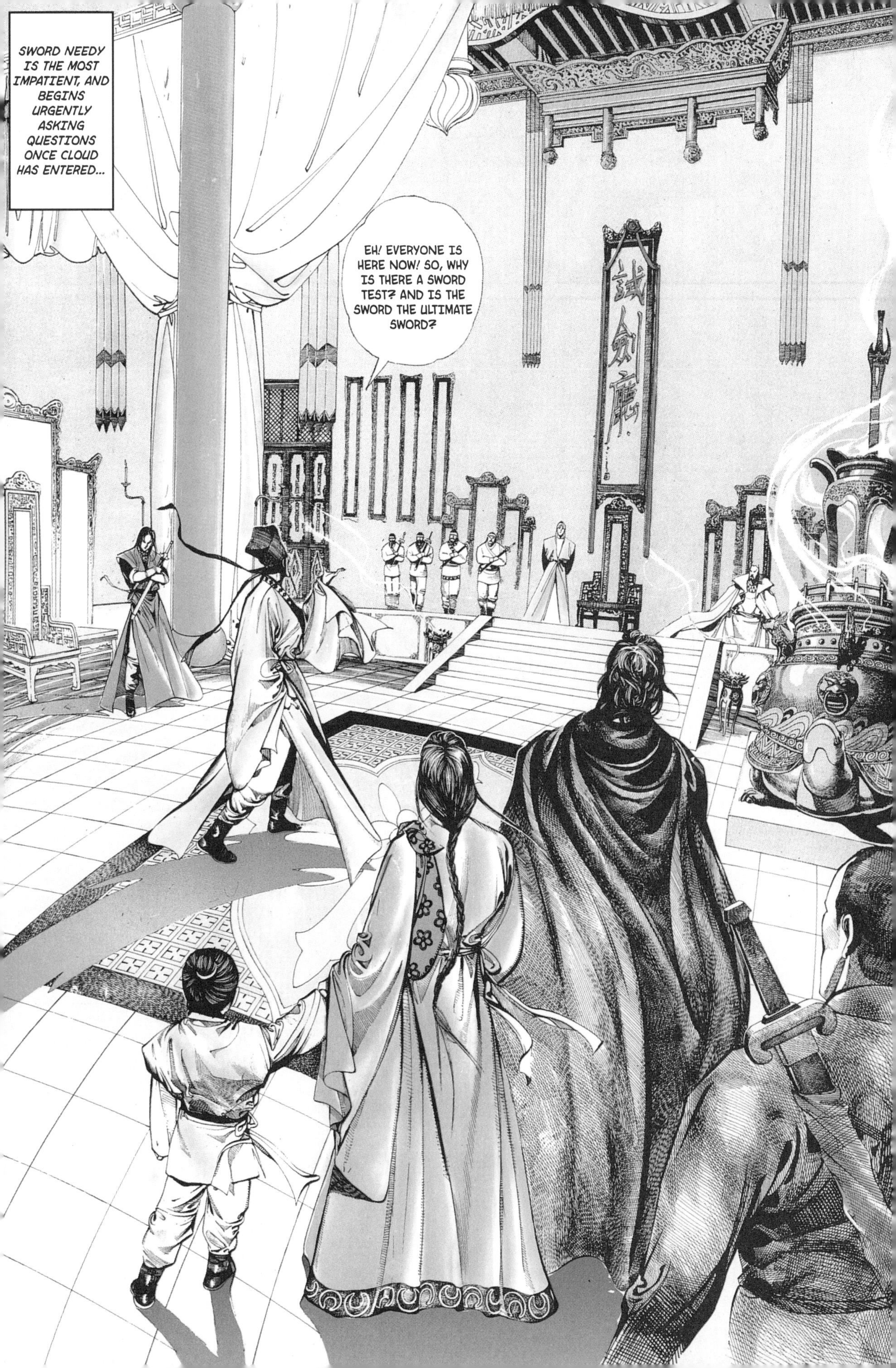
SWORD NEEDY IS THE MOST IMPATIENT, AND BEGINS URGENTLY ASKING QUESTIONS ONCE CLOUD HAS ENTERED...
EH! EVERYONE IS HERE NOW! SO, WHY IS THERE A SWORD TEST? AND IS THE SWORD THE ULTIMATE SWORD?
試劍廳

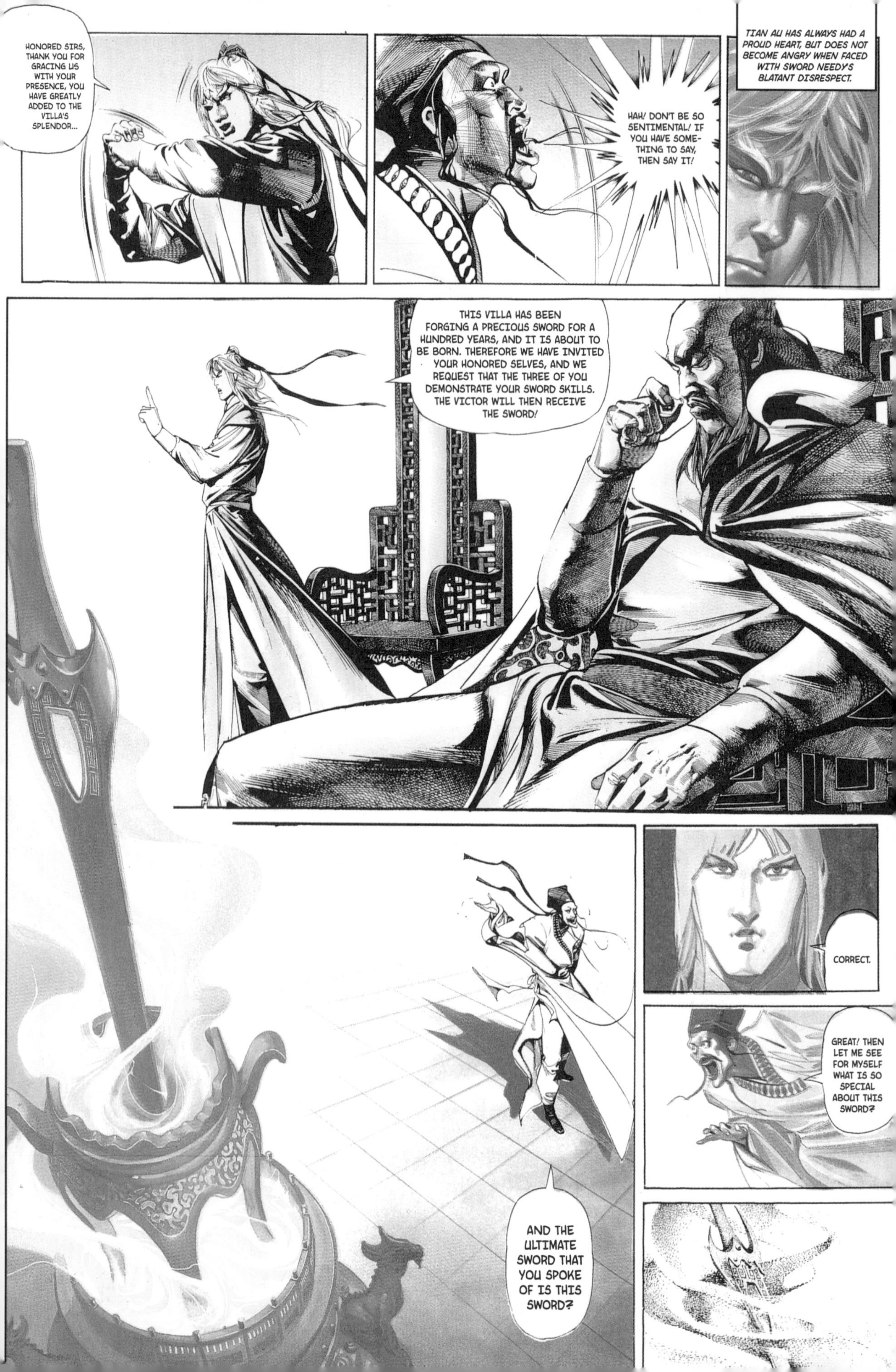
HONORED SIRS, THANK YOU FOR GRACING US WITH YOUR PRESENCE, YOU HAVE GREATLY ADDED TO THE VILLA'S SPLENDOR...
HAH! DON'T BE SO SENTIMENTAL! IF YOU HAVE SOME-THING TO SAY, THEN SAY IT!
TIAN AU HAS ALWAYS HAD A PROUD HEART, BUT DOES NOT BECOME ANGRY WHEN FACED WITH SWORD NEEDY'S BLATANT DISRESPECT.
THIS VILLA HAS BEEN FORGING A PRECIOUS SWORD FOR A HUNDRED YEARS, AND IT IS ABOUT TO BE BORN. THEREFORE WE HAVE INVITED YOUR HONORED SELVES, AND WE REQUEST THAT THE THREE OF YOU DEMONSTRATE YOUR SWORD SKILLS. THE VICTOR WILL THEN RECEIVE THE SWORD!
AND THE ULTIMATE SWORD THAT YOU SPOKE OF IS THIS SWORD?
CORRECT.
GREAT! THEN LET ME SEE FOR MYSELF WHAT IS SO SPECIAL ABOUT THIS SWORD?

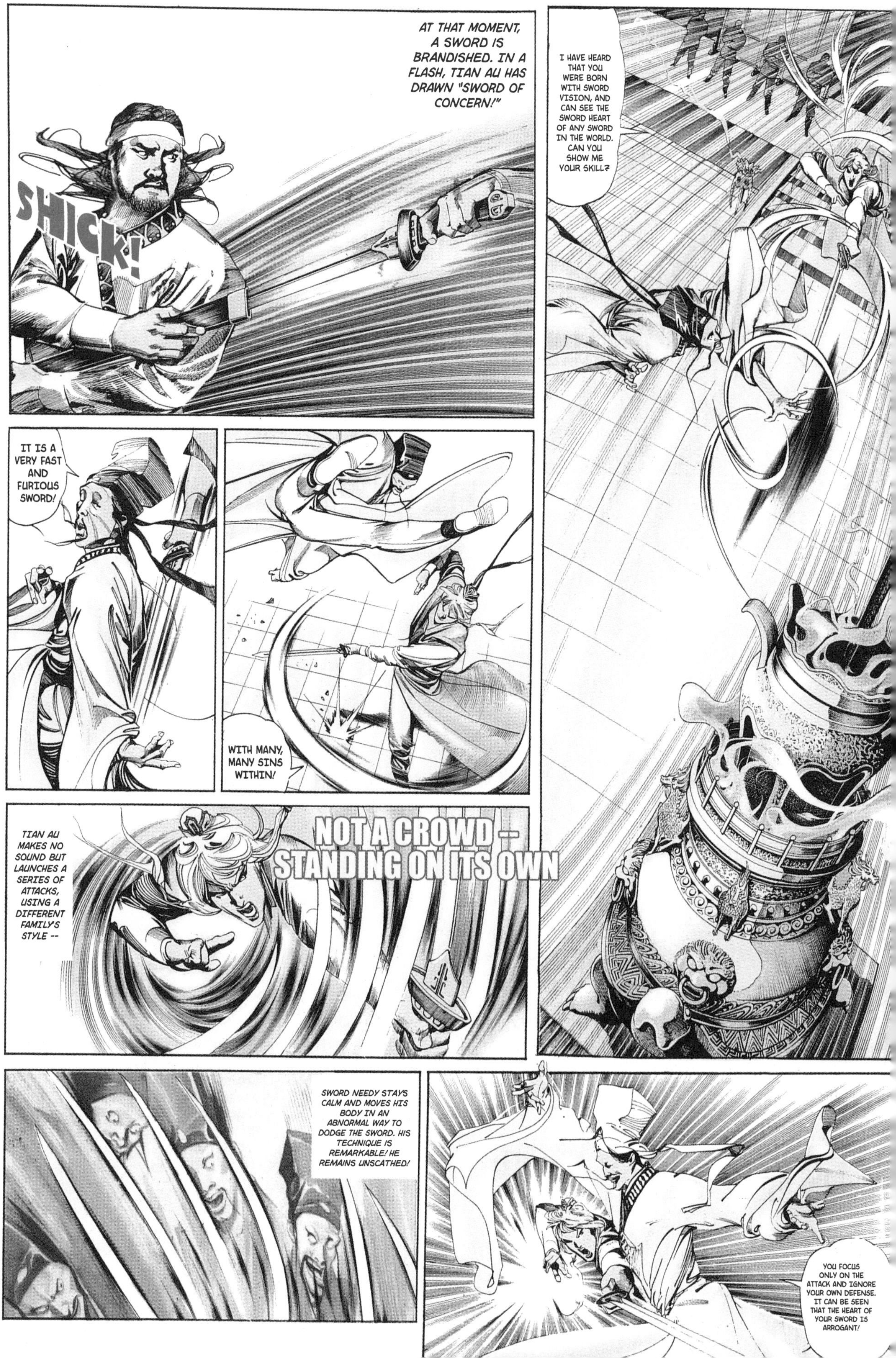
AT THAT MOMENT, A SWORD IS BRANDISHED. IN A FLASH, TIAN AU HAS DRAWN "SWORD OF CONCERN!"
SHICK!
I HAVE HEARD THAT YOU WERE BORN WITH SWORD VISION, AND CAN SEE THE SWORD HEART OF ANY SWORD IN THE WORLD. CAN YOU SHOW ME YOUR SKILL?
IT IS A VERY FAST AND FURIOUS SWORD!
WITH MANY, MANY SINS WITHIN!
TIAN AU MAKES NO SOUND BUT LAUNCHES A SERIES OF ATTACKS, USING A DIFFERENT FAMILY'S STYLE --
NOT A CROWD -- STANDING ON ITS OWN
SWORD NEEDY STAYS CALM AND MOVES HIS BODY IN AN ABNORMAL WAY TO DODGE THE SWORD. HIS TECHNIQUE IS REMARKABLE! HE REMAINS UNSCATHED!
YOU FOCUS ONLY ON THE ATTACK AND IGNORE YOUR OWN DEFENSE. IT CAN BE SEEN THAT THE HEART OF YOUR SWORD IS ARROGANT!

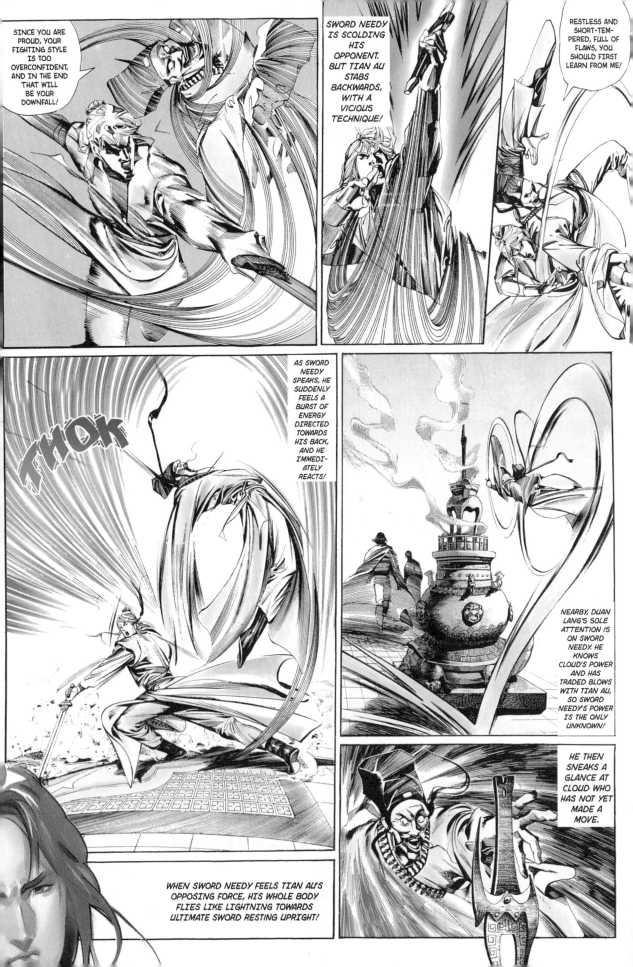

SINCE YOU ARE PROUD, YOUR FIGHTING STYLE IS TOO OVERCONFIDENT, AND IN THE END THAT WILL BE YOUR DOWNFALL!

SWORD NEEDY IS SCOLDING HIS OPPONENT. BUT TIAN AU STABS BACKWARDS, WITH A VICIOUS TECHNIQUE!

RESTLESS AND SHORT-TEMPERED, FULL OF FLAWS, YOU SHOULD FIRST LEARN FROM ME!

THOK

AS SWORD NEEDY SPEAKS, HE SUDDENLY FEELS A BURST OF ENERGY DIRECTED TOWARDS HIS BACK, AND HE IMMEDIATELY REACTS!

NEARBY, DUAN LANG'S SOLE ATTENTION IS ON SWORD NEEDY. HE KNOWS CLOUD'S POWER AND HAS TRADED BLOWS WITH TIAN AU, SO SWORD NEEDY'S POWER IS THE ONLY UNKNOWN!

HE THEN SNEAKS A GLANCE AT CLOUD WHO HAS NOT YET MADE A MOVE.

WHEN SWORD NEEDY FEELS TIAN AU'S OPPOSING FORCE, HIS WHOLE BODY FLIES LIKE LIGHTNING TOWARDS ULTIMATE SWORD RESTING UPRIGHT!

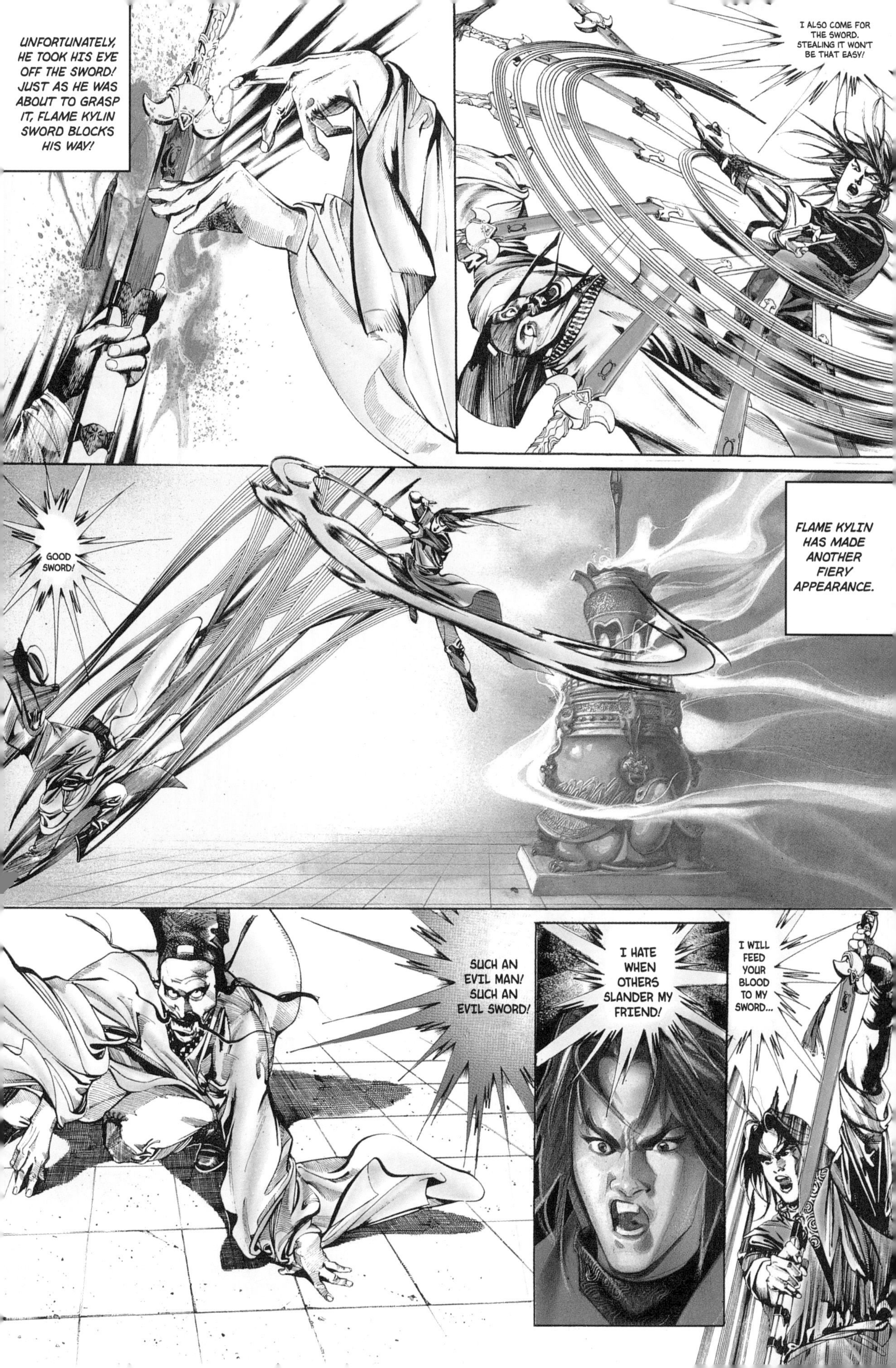
UNFORTUNATELY, HE TOOK HIS EYE OFF THE SWORD! JUST AS HE WAS ABOUT TO GRASP IT, FLAME KYLIN SWORD BLOCKS HIS WAY!
I ALSO COME FOR THE SWORD. STEALING IT WON'T BE THAT EASY!
GOOD SWORD!
FLAME KYLIN HAS MADE ANOTHER FIERY APPEARANCE.
SUCH AN EVIL MAN! SUCH AN EVIL SWORD!
I HATE WHEN OTHERS SLANDER MY FRIEND!
I WILL FEED YOUR BLOOD TO MY SWORD...

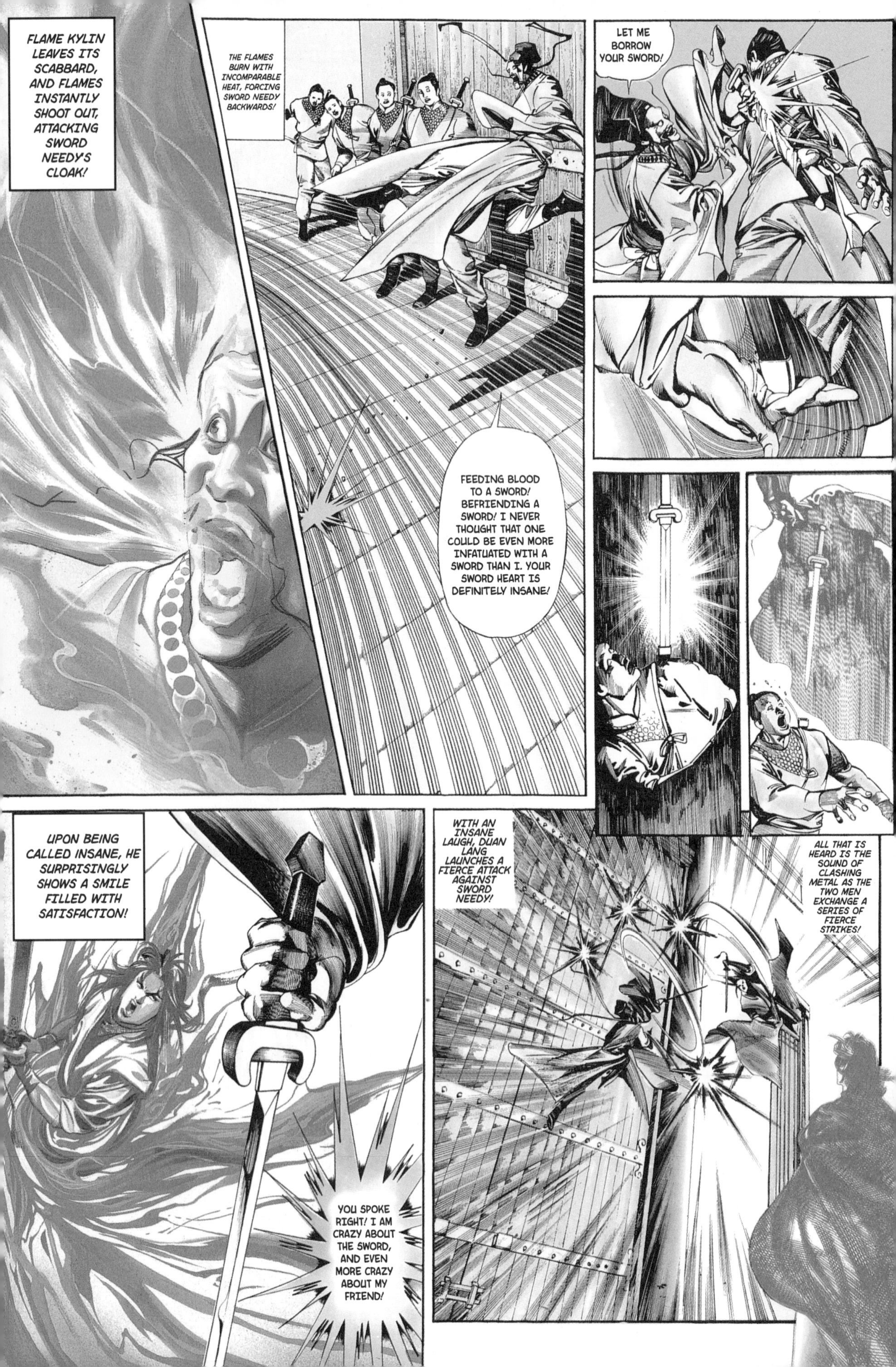
FLAME KYLIN LEAVES ITS SCABBARD, AND FLAMES INSTANTLY SHOOT OUT, ATTACKING SWORD NEEDY'S CLOAK!
THE FLAMES BURN WITH INCOMPARABLE HEAT, FORCING SWORD NEEDY BACKWARDS!
LET ME BORROW YOUR SWORD!
FEEDING BLOOD TO A SWORD! BEFRIENDING A SWORD! I NEVER THOUGHT THAT ONE COULD BE EVEN MORE INFATUATED WITH A SWORD THAN I. YOUR SWORD HEART IS DEFINITELY INSANE!
UPON BEING CALLED INSANE, HE SURPRISINGLY SHOWS A SMILE FILLED WITH SATISFACTION!
YOU SPOKE RIGHT! I AM CRAZY ABOUT THE SWORD, AND EVEN MORE CRAZY ABOUT MY FRIEND!
WITH AN INSANE LAUGH, DUAN LANG LAUNCHES A FIERCE ATTACK AGAINST SWORD NEEDY!
ALL THAT IS HEARD IS THE SOUND OF CLASHING METAL AS THE TWO MEN EXCHANGE A SERIES OF FIERCE STRIKES!

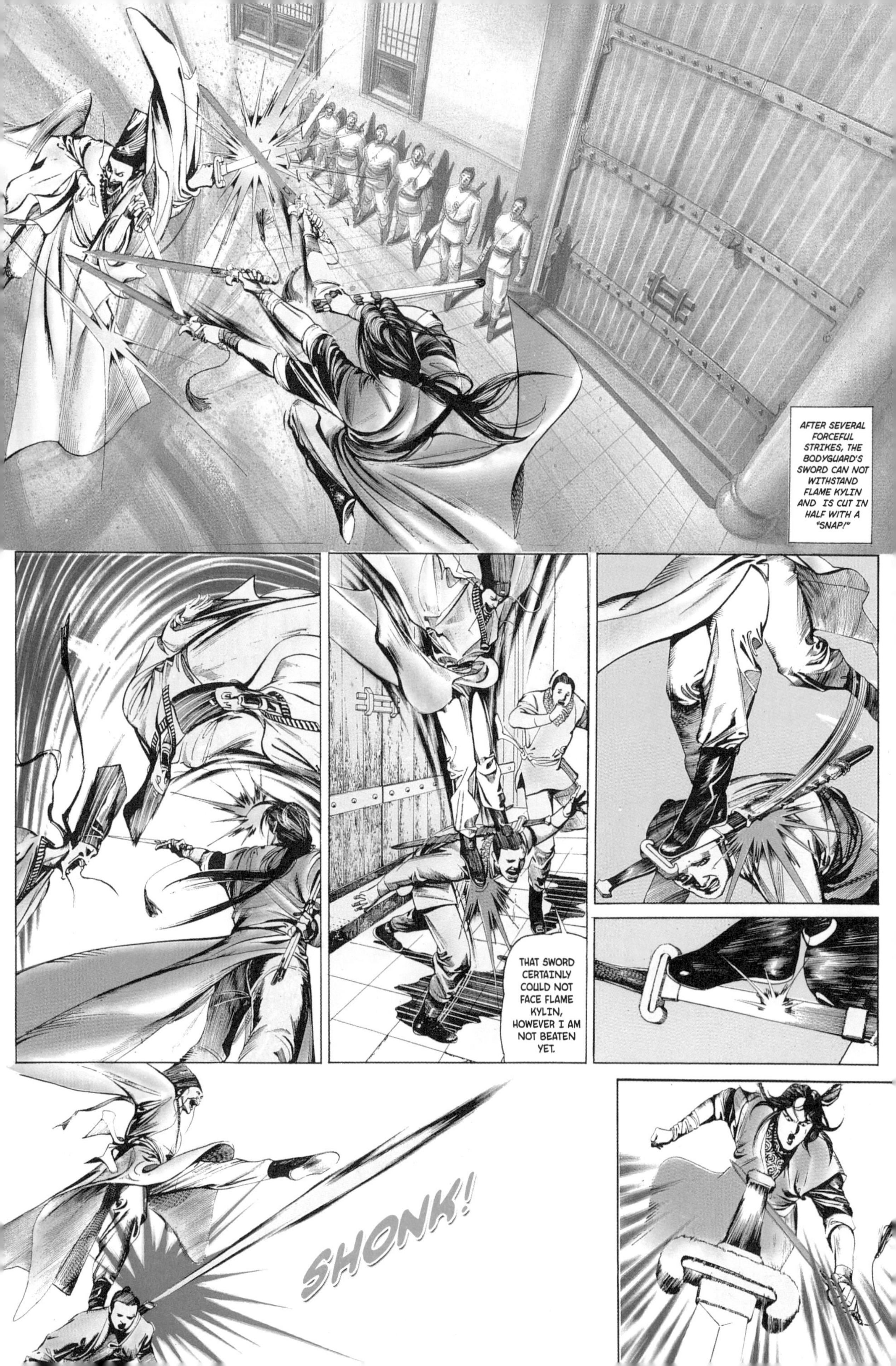

AFTER SEVERAL FORCEFUL STRIKES, THE BODYGUARD'S SWORD CAN NOT WITHSTAND FLAME KYLIN AND IS CUT IN HALF WITH A "SNAP!"
THAT SWORD CERTAINLY COULD NOT FACE FLAME KYLIN, HOWEVER I AM NOT BEATEN YET.
SHONK!

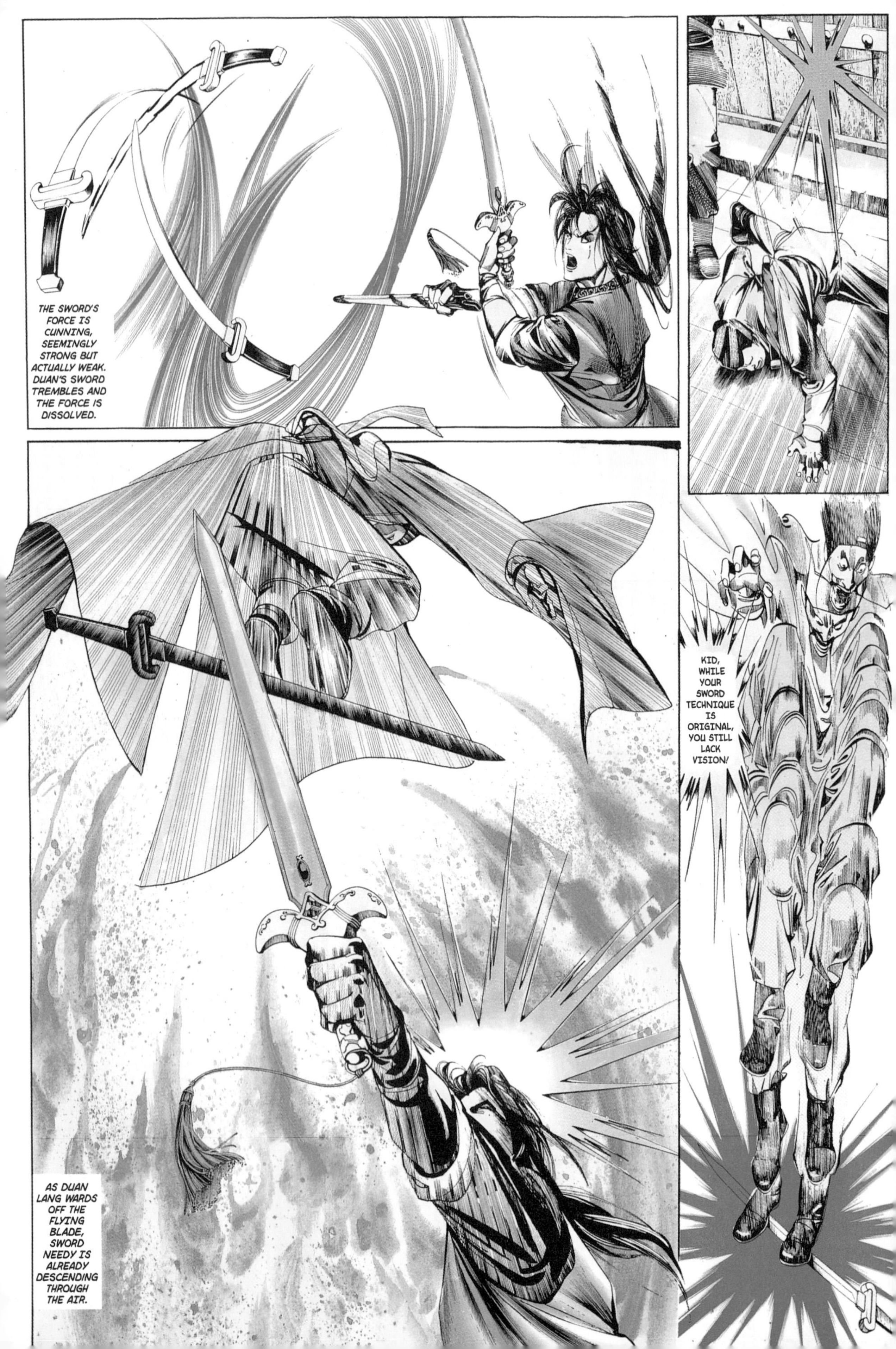
THE SWORD'S FORCE IS CUNNING, SEEMINGLY STRONG BUT ACTUALLY WEAK. DUAN'S SWORD TREMBLES AND THE FORCE IS DISSOLVED.
KID, WHILE YOUR SWORD TECHNIQUE IS ORIGINAL, YOU STILL LACK VISION!
AS DUAN LANG WARDS OFF THE FLYING BLADE, SWORD NEEDY IS ALREADY DESCENDING THROUGH THE AIR.

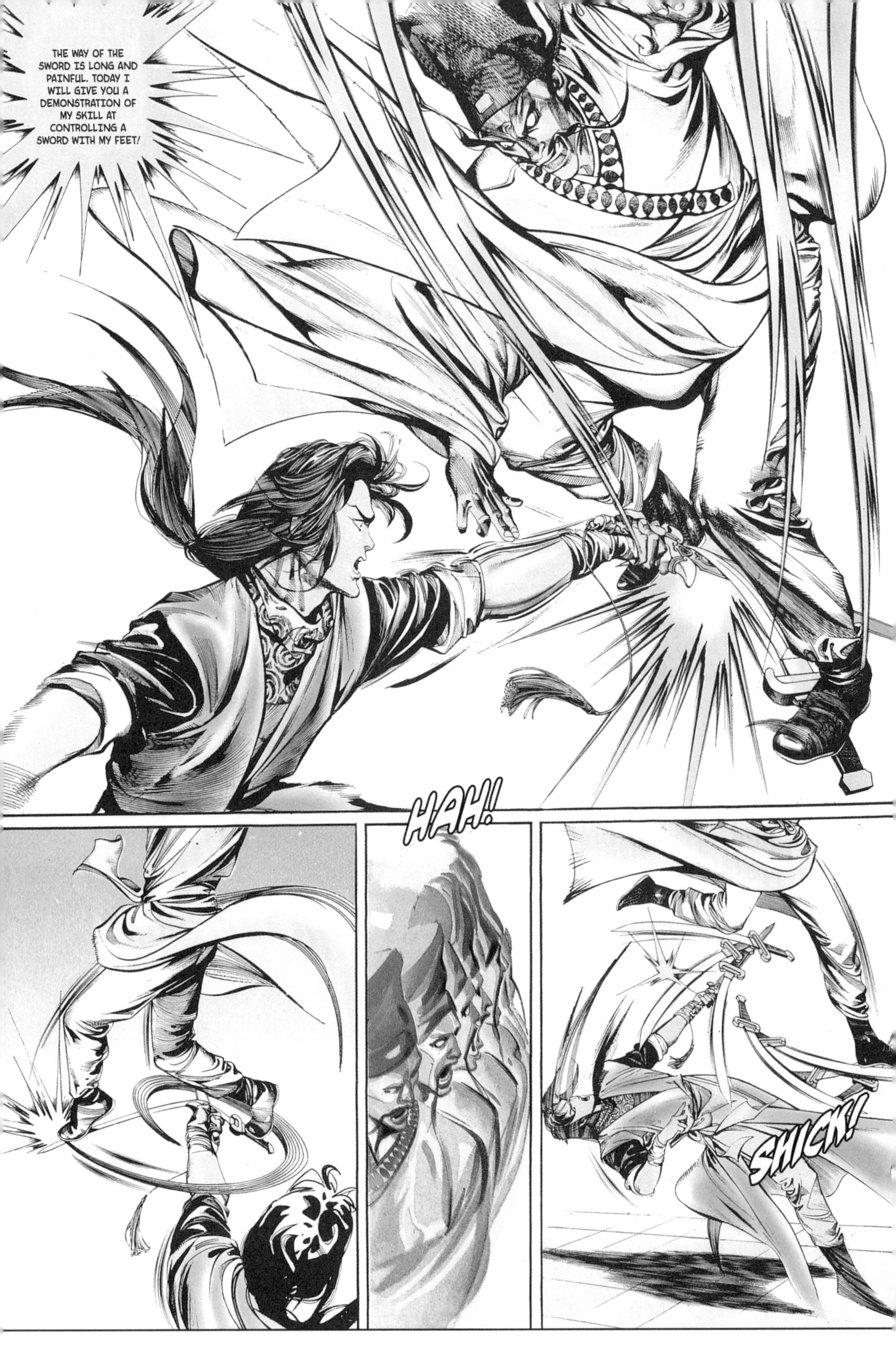
THE WAY OF THE SWORD IS LONG AND PAINFUL. TODAY I WILL GIVE YOU A DEMONSTRATION OF MY SKILL AT CONTROLLING A SWORD WITH MY FEET!
HAH!
SHICK!

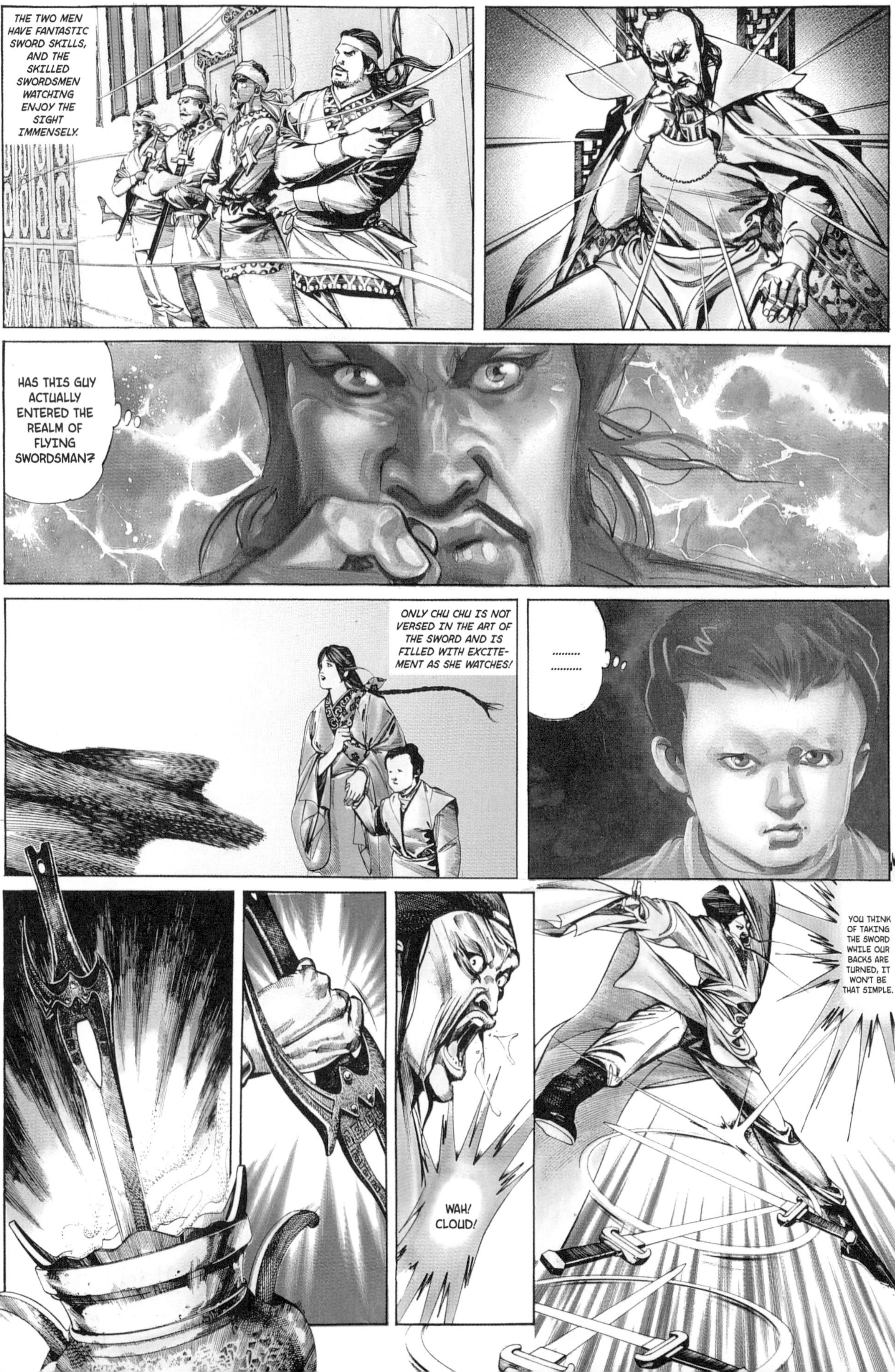
THE TWO MEN HAVE FANTASTIC SWORD SKILLS, AND THE SKILLED SWORDSMEN WATCHING ENJOY THE SIGHT IMMENSELY.
HAS THIS GUY ACTUALLY ENTERED THE REALM OF FLYING SWORDSMAN?
ONLY CHU CHU IS NOT VERSED IN THE ART OF THE SWORD AND IS FILLED WITH EXCITEMENT AS SHE WATCHES!
.........
..........
WAH! CLOUD!
YOU THINK OF TAKING THE SWORD WHILE OUR BACKS ARE TURNED, IT WON'T BE THAT SIMPLE.

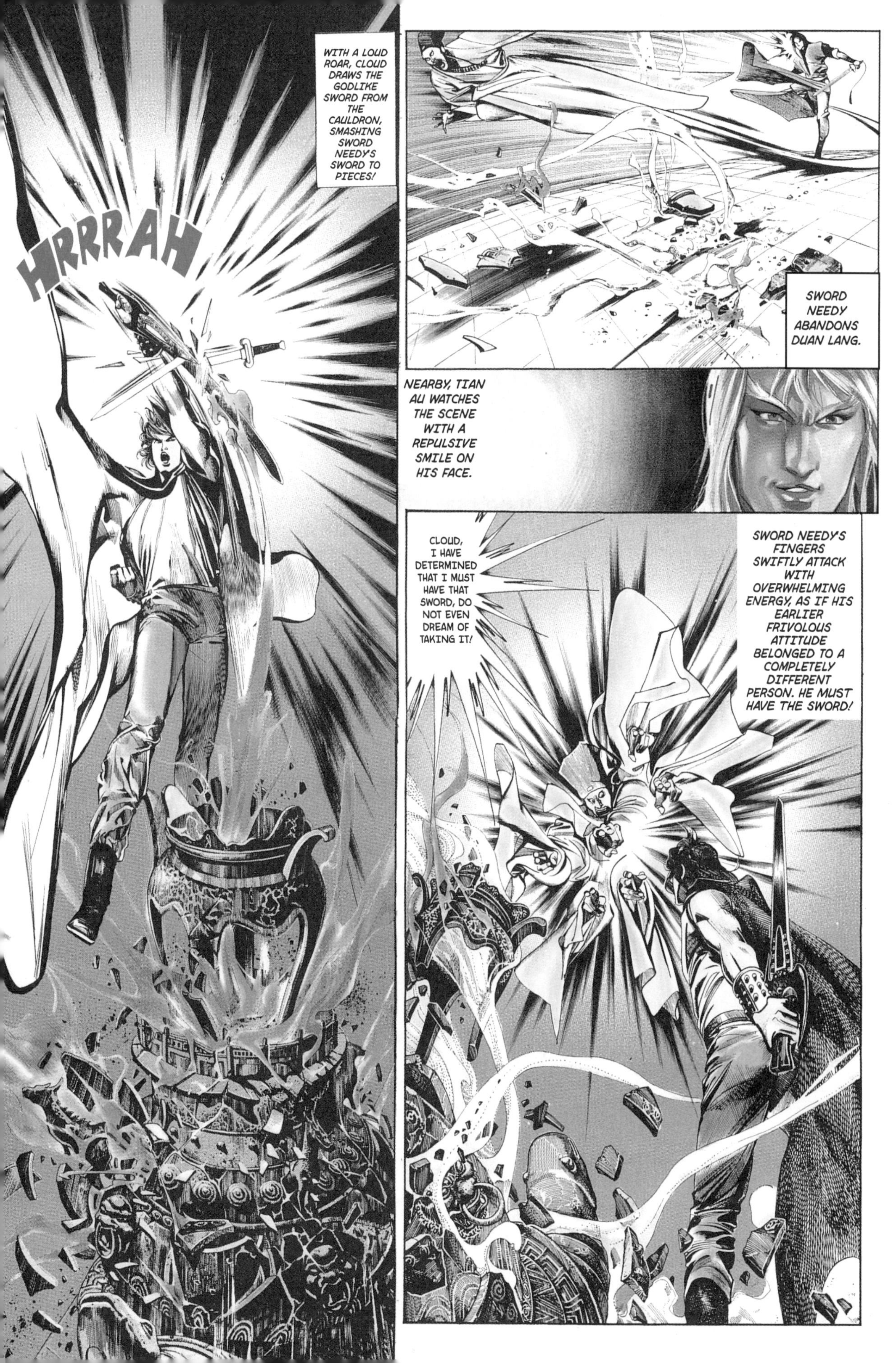
WITH A LOUD ROAR, CLOUD DRAWS THE GODLIKE SWORD FROM THE CAULDRON, SMASHING SWORD NEEDY'S SWORD TO PIECES!
HRRRAH
SWORD NEEDY ABANDONS DUAN LANG.
NEARBY, TIAN AU WATCHES THE SCENE WITH A REPULSIVE SMILE ON HIS FACE.
SWORD NEEDY'S FINGERS SWIFTLY ATTACK WITH OVERWHELMING ENERGY, AS IF HIS EARLIER FRIVOLOUS ATTITUDE BELONGED TO A COMPLETELY DIFFERENT PERSON. HE MUST HAVE THE SWORD!
CLOUD, I HAVE DETERMINED THAT I MUST HAVE THAT SWORD, DO NOT EVEN DREAM OF TAKING IT!

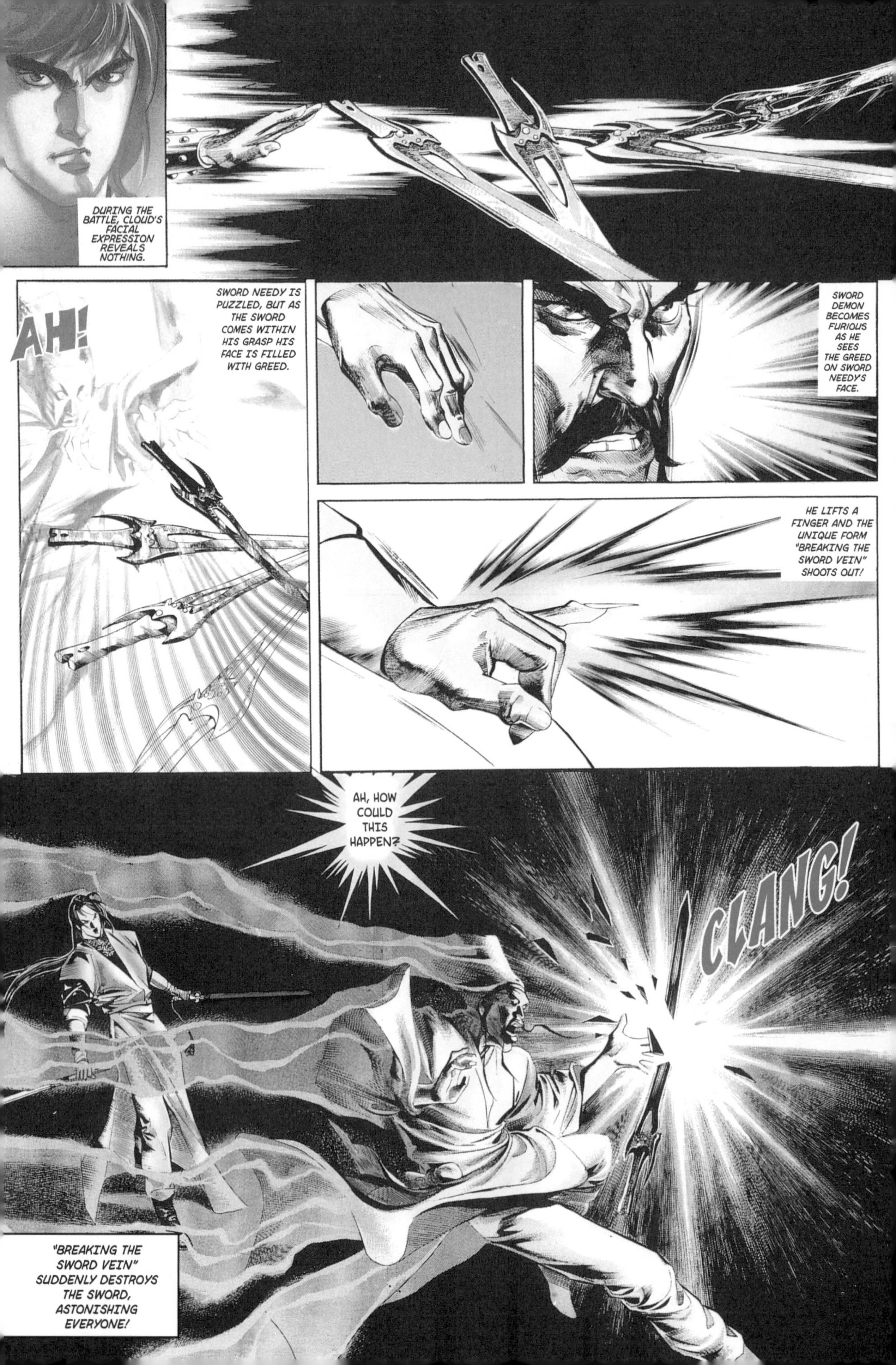
DURING THE BATTLE, CLOUD'S FACIAL EXPRESSION REVEALS NOTHING.
SWORD NEEDY IS PUZZLED, BUT AS THE SWORD COMES WITHIN HIS GRASP HIS FACE IS FILLED WITH GREED.
AH!
SWORD DEMON BECOMES FURIOUS AS HE SEES THE GREED ON SWORD NEEDY'S FACE.
HE LIFTS A FINGER AND THE UNIQUE FORM "BREAKING THE SWORD VEIN" SHOOTS OUT!
AH, HOW COULD THIS HAPPEN?
CLANG!
"BREAKING THE SWORD VEIN" SUDDENLY DESTROYS THE SWORD, ASTONISHING EVERYONE!

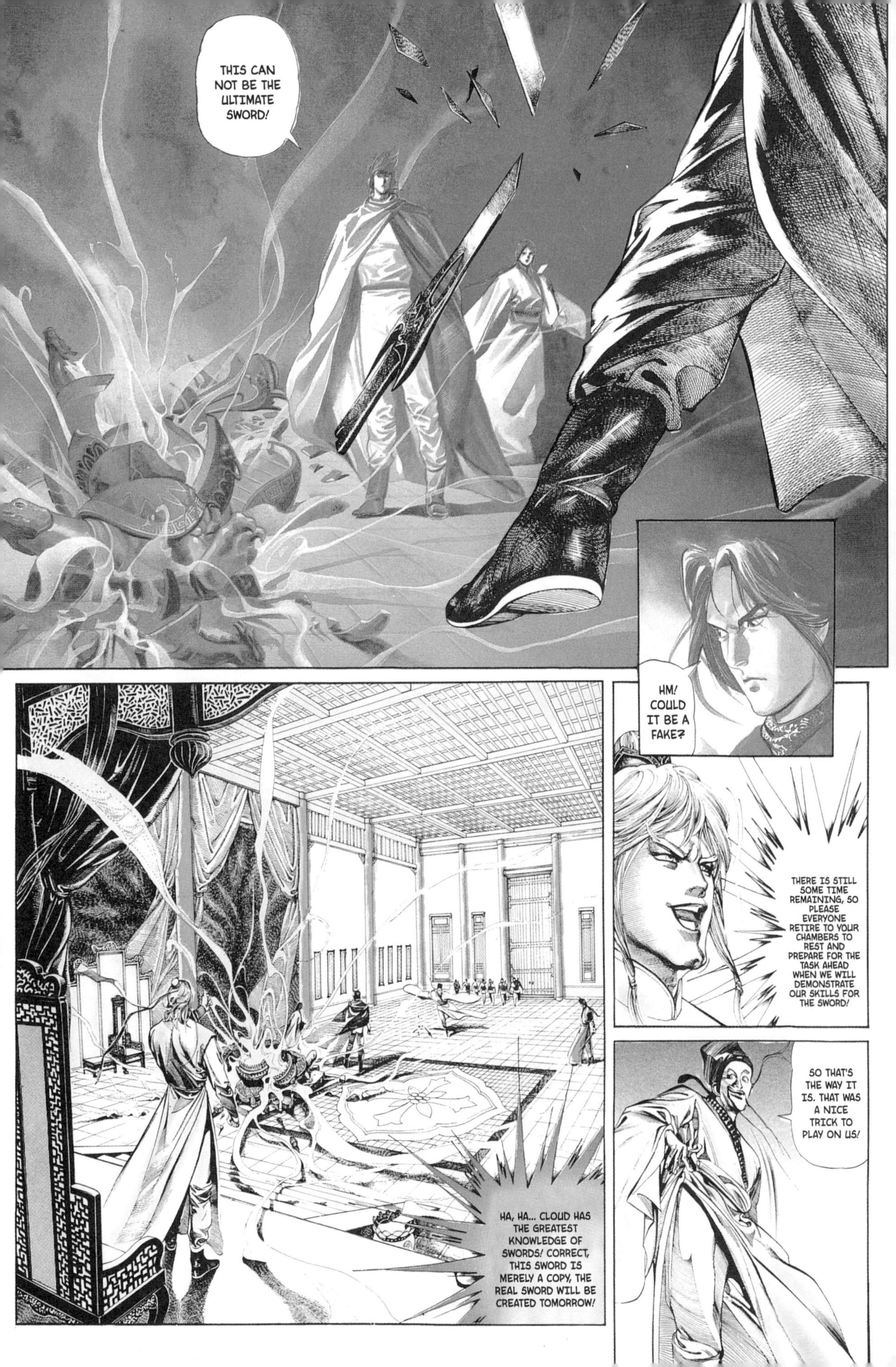
THIS CAN NOT BE THE ULTIMATE SWORD!
HM! COULD IT BE A FAKE?
THERE IS STILL SOME TIME REMAINING, SO PLEASE EVERYONE RETIRE TO YOUR CHAMBERS TO REST AND PREPARE FOR THE TASK AHEAD WHEN WE WILL DEMONSTRATE OUR SKILLS FOR THE SWORD!
HA, HA... CLOUD HAS THE GREATEST KNOWLEDGE OF SWORDS! CORRECT, THIS SWORD IS MERELY A COPY, THE REAL SWORD WILL BE CREATED TOMORROW!
SO THAT'S THE WAY IT IS. THAT WAS A NICE TRICK TO PLAY ON US!

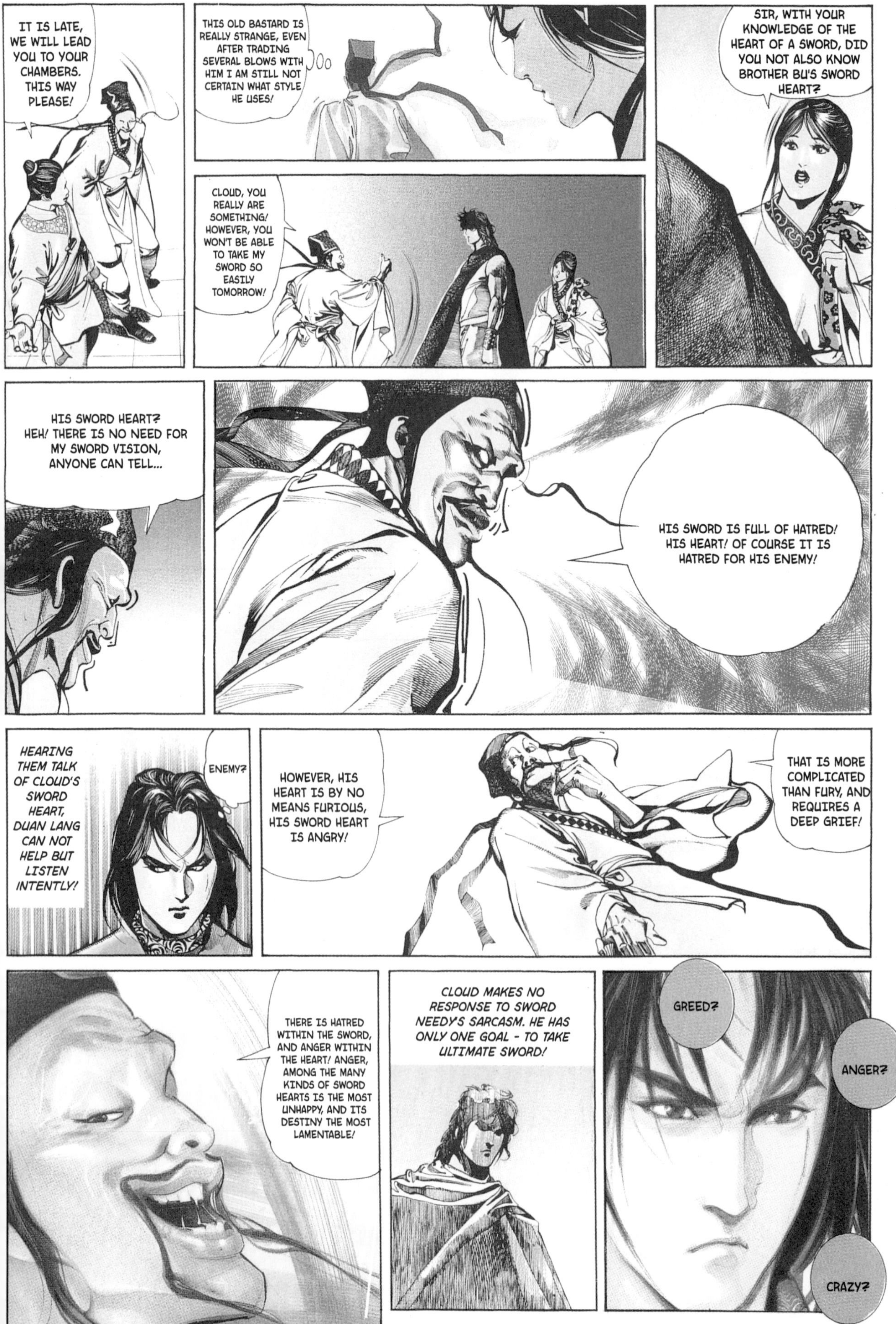
IT IS LATE, WE WILL LEAD YOU TO YOUR CHAMBERS. THIS WAY PLEASE!
THIS OLD BASTARD IS REALLY STRANGE, EVEN AFTER TRADING SEVERAL BLOWS WITH HIM I AM STILL NOT CERTAIN WHAT STYLE HE USES!
CLOUD, YOU REALLY ARE SOMETHING! HOWEVER, YOU WON'T BE ABLE TO TAKE MY SWORD SO EASILY TOMORROW!
SIR, WITH YOUR KNOWLEDGE OF THE HEART OF A SWORD, DID YOU NOT ALSO KNOW BROTHER BU'S SWORD HEART?
HIS SWORD HEART? HEH! THERE IS NO NEED FOR MY SWORD VISION, ANYONE CAN TELL...
HIS SWORD IS FULL OF HATRED! HIS HEART! OF COURSE IT IS HATRED FOR HIS ENEMY!
HEARING THEM TALK OF CLOUD'S SWORD HEART, DUAN LANG CAN NOT HELP BUT LISTEN INTENTLY!
ENEMY?
HOWEVER, HIS HEART IS BY NO MEANS FURIOUS, HIS SWORD HEART IS ANGRY!
THAT IS MORE COMPLICATED THAN FURY, AND REQUIRES A DEEP GRIEF!
THERE IS HATRED WITHIN THE SWORD, AND ANGER WITHIN THE HEART! ANGER, AMONG THE MANY KINDS OF SWORD HEARTS IS THE MOST UNHAPPY, AND ITS DESTINY THE MOST LAMENTABLE!
CLOUD MAKES NO RESPONSE TO SWORD NEEDY'S SARCASM. HE HAS ONLY ONE GOAL - TO TAKE ULTIMATE SWORD!
GREED?
ANGER?
CRAZY?

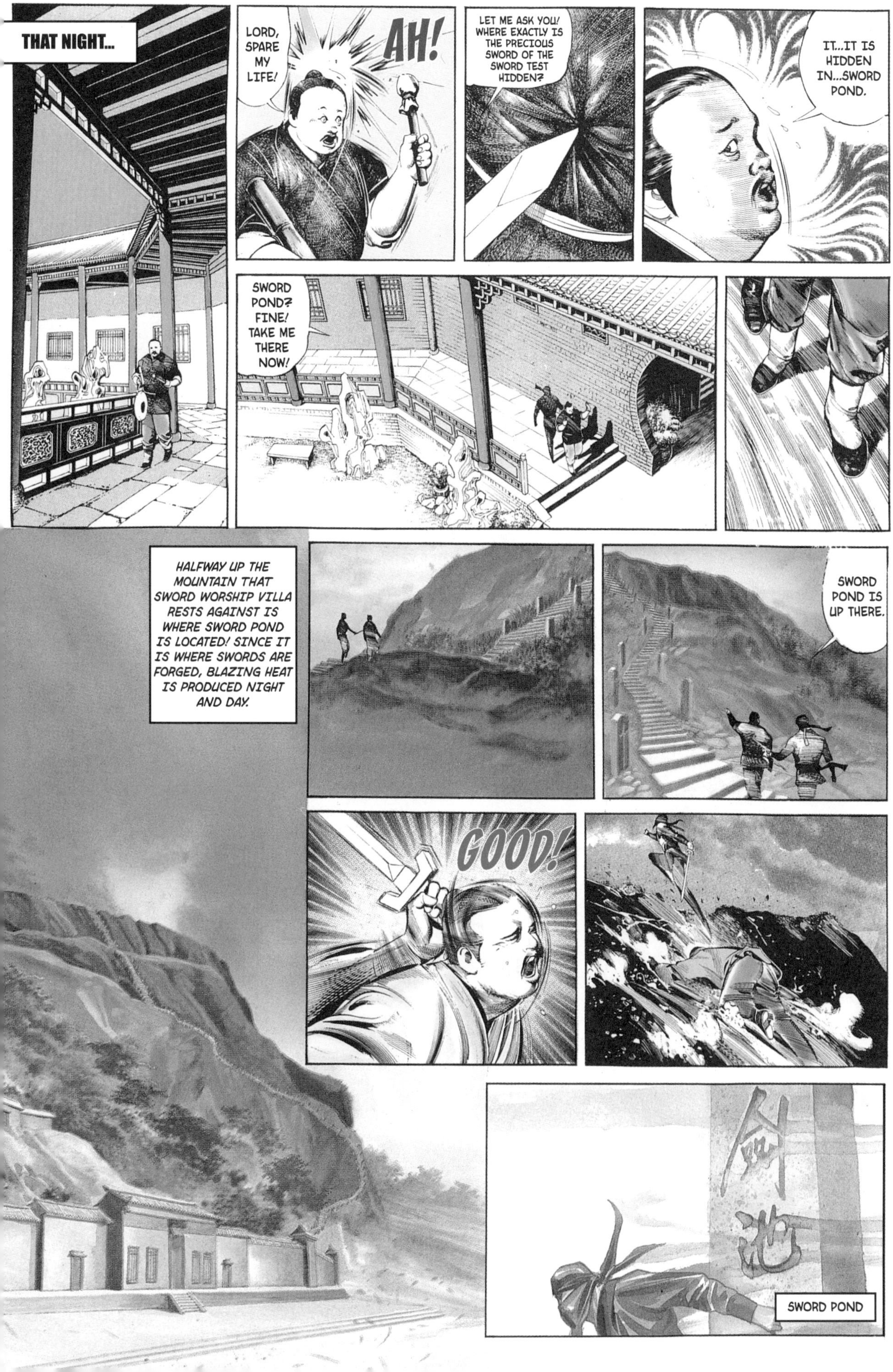
THAT NIGHT...
LORD, SPARE MY LIFE!
AH!
LET ME ASK YOU! WHERE EXACTLY IS THE PRECIOUS SWORD OF THE SWORD TEST HIDDEN?
IT...IT IS HIDDEN IN...SWORD POND.
SWORD POND? FINE! TAKE ME THERE NOW!
HALFWAY UP THE MOUNTAIN THAT SWORD WORSHIP VILLA RESTS AGAINST IS WHERE SWORD POND IS LOCATED! SINCE IT IS WHERE SWORDS ARE FORGED, BLAZING HEAT IS PRODUCED NIGHT AND DAY.
SWORD POND IS UP THERE.
GOOD!
SWORD POND

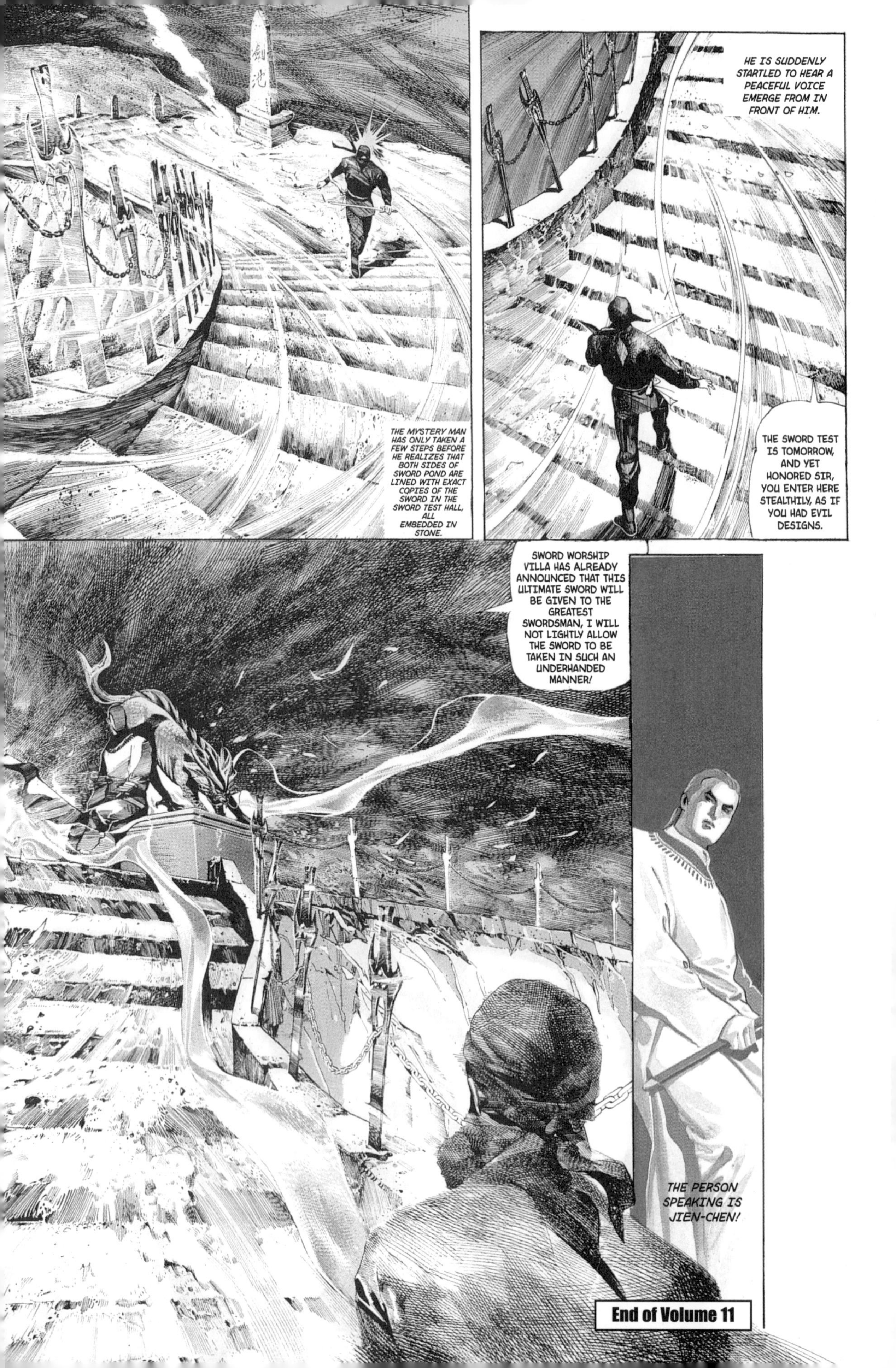
THE MYSTERY MAN HAS ONLY TAKEN A FEW STEPS BEFORE HE REALIZES THAT BOTH SIDES OF SWORD POND ARE LINED WITH EXACT COPIES OF THE SWORD IN THE SWORD TEST HALL, ALL EMBEDDED IN STONE.
HE IS SUDDENLY STARTLED TO HEAR A PEACEFUL VOICE EMERGE FROM IN FRONT OF HIM.
THE SWORD TEST IS TOMORROW, AND YET HONORED SIR, YOU ENTER HERE STEALTHILY, AS IF YOU HAD EVIL DESIGNS.
SWORD WORSHIP VILLA HAS ALREADY ANNOUNCED THAT THIS ULTIMATE SWORD WILL BE GIVEN TO THE GREATEST SWORDSMAN, I WILL NOT LIGHTLY ALLOW THE SWORD TO BE TAKEN IN SUCH AN UNDERHANDED MANNER!
THE PERSON SPEAKING IS JIEN-CHEN!
End of Volume 11

# Author's Notes

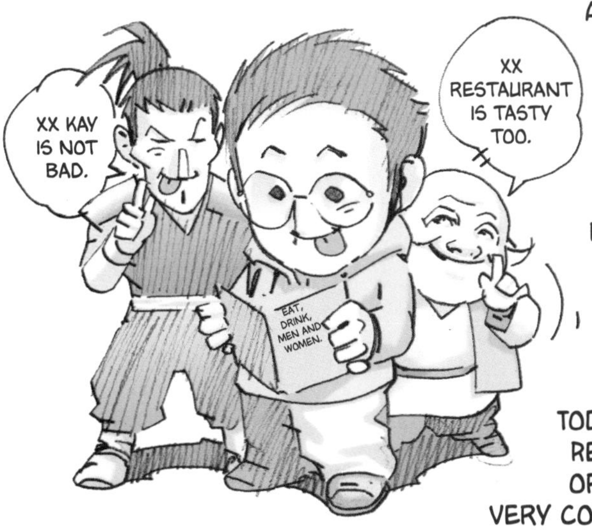
XX KAY IS NOT BAD.
XX RESTAURANT IS TASTY TOO.
EAT, DRINK, MEN AND WOMEN.

ALTHOUGH I'VE BEEN MARRIED FOR QUITE A LONG TIME, I STILL DINE OUT QUITE OFTEN. THE MAIN REASON IS THAT I ALWAYS WORK OVER-TIME FOR DRAWING AND CAN'T MATCH WITH MY FAMILY'S DINING HABITS.

I'M NOT USED TO EATING AT ONE SPECIFIC RESTAURANT. MOST OF THE TIME I WOULD TRY NEW PLACES BECAUSE OF WORD-OF-MOUTH OR FRIENDS' RECOMMENDATIONS. BUT THEN I WOULD EAT AT SOME REGULAR RESTAURANTS THAT I'M PARTICULARLY FOND OF.

TODAY, I'M GOING TO RECOMMEND YOU THE "FU YIU RESTAURANT" THAT IS SITUATED AT AUSTIN ROAD OF TSIMSHATSU. IT RUNS LATE AT NIGHT, WHICH IS VERY CONVENIENT FOR NIGHT SHIFTERS SUCH AS WE PAINTERS. ONE OF MY FRIENDS TAKES IT AS HIS CANTEEN, WHICH MEANS HE EATS THERE ALMOST THREE MEALS A DAY. IT'S HE WHO TOOK ME TO IT FIRST AND SINCE THEN, I'VE BEEN VISITING THIS PLACE FOR THE PAST FEW YEARS, JUST TO ENJOY THEIR DELICIOUS CUISINES.

THE DECORATION THERE IS ORDINARY, NOT THAT FANCY TYPE. BUT THE BEST THING IS GOOD SERVICE. ALL THE WAITERS ARE EXPERIENCED AND SOPHISTICATED. THEY KNOW THE TASTES OF THEIR GUESTS AND ALWAYS RECOMMEND SUPERB DISHES OF THE SEASONS. I HAVE A FEW FAVORITE DISHES THOUGH. THE FIRST ONE IS FRIED SHRIMP WITH SPRING ONION. WHAT I LIKE IS NOT THE SHRIMP BUT THE INGREDIENT, SPRING ONION. I CAN'T TELL WHY, BUT THEY CAN BRING OUT THE SPECIAL FRAGRANCE OF THE SPRING ONION THERE. I EVEN ATE A BOWL OF RICE ONLY WITH THE SPRING ONION!

THE SECOND DISH IS SOY SAUCE GOOSE BOWEL. THE BOWEL IS NOT HEAVY OR OILY, BUT CRISPY AND TASTY. COINCIDENTLY, IT IS NOT MY FAVORITE TOO. WHAT I LIKE IS THE SAUCE, ONE IS THE CHILLI SOY SAUCE AND THE SECOND IS THE OYSTER SAUCE. THE FORMER USES SPICY AND FRESH PEPPER AS MAIN INGREDIENT WHILE THE LATTER IS FRESH BUT NOT SALTY. EATING THE BOWELS WITH THESE TWO SAUCES IS A HEAVENLY ENJOYMENT.

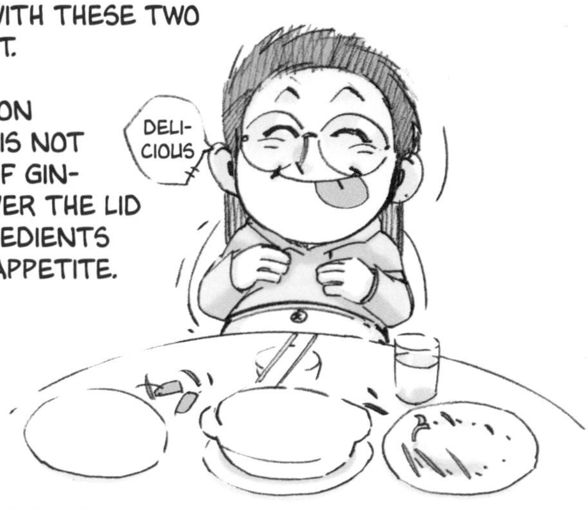
DELI-CIOUS

THE THIRD ONE IS GINGER AND SPRING ONION ABALONE POT. STRANGELY ENOUGH, ABALONE IS NOT MY FAVORITE, BUT AGAIN, THE INGREDIENTS OF GIN-GER AND SPRING ONION... WHENEVER I UNCOVER THE LID OF THE POT, THE RICH SMELL OF THESE INGREDIENTS RUSHES INTO MY NOSTRILS AND AROUSES MY APPETITE.

FROM THE ABOVE THREE DISHES, YOU CAN TELL THAT I HAVE A SPECIAL FONDNESS ON THEIR INGREDIENTS. THIS REFLECTS THAT THEIR CHEFS ARE HIGHLY SKILLFUL IN SHOW-ING THEIR EXPERTISE QUALITY THROUGH SOME ORDINARY FOODS AND INGREDIENTS. ANOTHER INSTANCE IS: ALMOND JUICE WITH EGG WHITE. IT HAS A LIGHT AND SWEET TASTE, BUT NOT TOO THICK. IT'S THE BEST CHOICE FOR DESSERT AFTER MEALS OR FOR A NIGHT SNACK.